What People Are Saying About
America's Democracy Betrayed

This One Will Challenge Your Beliefs
Jack M. Bourla, DC

If you are a status quo type person, you may want to stay away from Dr. Martingano's book, *America's Democracy Betrayed: Solutions to Fight Back.* Dr. Martingano has looked at the history of the United States and its current state of affairs and provided thought-provoking ideas on where we may have gone wrong. Unlike many others, however, he has also suggested solutions to his ideas and supported them with references throughout his book for the interested reader.

This is not a read for the timid. He challenges many of the values that Americans hold as true today, and he suggests that our government is intentionally and incrementally taking away our freedoms and circumventing the Constitution. Dr. Martingano leaves no or very few stones unturned with respect to today's media and government in a way that empowers the average American in making better political decisions to ensure that we retain our freedoms.

A MUST READ!! Insightful and illuminating
Dr. Peter Kevorkian

Dr. Martingano has created an extraordinary book. It is thoroughly researched and well thought out. It is based on facts and brings to light how so many of the tenets that built the United States are slowly eroding. Sal offers clear insight as to why. The book is a must read for anyone who wants to be part of recreating the "greatness" of the American dream. A well written book, *America's Democracy Betrayed: Solutions to Fight Back* should be in the library of every American citizen.

An Eye-Opening and Timely Book!
Dr. Patrick Milroy

This is an eye-opening and timely book that uncovers the truth of an American political system gone awry—a system controlled by greed, big oil, big pharma, and corrupt politicians, with the average citizen unaware and duped. What is happening in the country of my birth is shocking, and we've got to stop the "Oh, that's just conspiracy" attitude, which this book does! Dr. Martingano's writing style is excellent and courageous, and the research that went into the book was thorough. I'd like all of my family members to challenge their understanding of US politics with this book. Thank you, Dr. Martingano.

Education Is the Key to Our Freedom. A Must Read.
Bleeding Heart Liberal . . . Anonymous

Dr. Martingano is a clear thinker. Well done treatise of a complex subject. A great steppingstone to the subject of our freedoms and our country. I am a bleeding-heart lifetime liberal Democrat, and I agreed with this book's premise and followed the logic. I would hope more people read this and become educated to the fact that there may be forces hidden from our view that just may be directing us to a submissive and less free world.

William J Federer, best selling author
Dr. Sal Martingano's book, America's Democracy Betrayed, is a must-read. It is hard-hitting and eye-opening, yet written in an easy-to-understand, down-to-earth style. Dr. Martingano has done the hard lifting, researching decades of information to be able to lay out in plain sight what has been going on behind the scenes. From his family's background, being Italian immigrants leaving a failed socialist country, Dr. Martingano strips away the media's façade to reveal what is really going on. You will be awakened and challenged by reading *America's Democracy Betrayed*.

America's Democracy Betrayed

America's Democracy Betrayed

Solutions to Fight Back

Dr. Sal Martingano

credo
house publishers

Contents

Author's Note

America is like a healthy body and its resistance is threefold:
its patriotism, its morality, and its spiritual life.
If we can undermine these three areas,
America will collapse from within.[1]
—Joseph Stalin

America was born from the ashes of lost freedom, paid for with the lives of countless millions exterminated in the name of world dominance. While America was at the height of its prosperity, enjoying the precious fruits of religious, social, and economic freedom, Europe was being carved up by vicious dictators, hell-bent on the destruction of any remnant of a civil society. Power and control left little room for individual freedoms. Life meant nothing unless it was an asset to the state. It was Joseph Stalin who understood that freedom is the nourishment of rebellion. As the supreme dictator of the Union of Soviet Socialist Republics (USSR) from 1929 through 1953, he ruled by terror, crushing freedom from wherever it arose. Stalin realized that to gain loyalty, there can be no room for individual thought. In coming to power just five years after Lenin's death, Stalin secured his supreme position by executing all who disagreed with his rule. Millions of peasant farmers were shot or exiled to work camps in Siberia for not agreeing to yield control of their farms to the government.[2]

During the same era, Adolf Hitler mimicked the impressive loyalty that Stalin achieved through the extermination of all dissidents and proceeded to do the same to past government officials to ensure a clean slate, free from opposition to the newly formed Nazi Aryan state.[3] Benito Mussolini defined fascism with equally ruthless extermination of millions of freedom-loving people. Fascism viewed political violence, war, and conquest as means to achieve national solidarity.[4], [5] Freedom soon became a footnote in European history, but in a strange twist of fate Stalin became the target of the German Nazi expansionism and realized that the only way to ensure an independent Soviet Union was to join in alliance with the Allied leaders FDR and Winston Churchill. Stalin did not suddenly embrace freedom, but to the extent that freedom existed in the US and Great Britain, it had the unwavering resolve to match the German war machine. However, Stalin knew that the only way to defeat large, freedom-loving nations was not with force but through the relentless erosion of traditions and morality.

Some seventy-five years after Stalin's words about America's destruction, freedom is slowly becoming attached to relentless government regulations, in which the illusion of freedom is more dominant than freedom itself. The purpose of this writing is to give meaning to historical events in an attempt to make evident that for history to repeat itself, it needs the cooperation of ignorance of facts, a lost sense of patriotism (as it relates to what gave birth to the freedom America has enjoyed for over two hundred years), and the unwillingness to act in the face of government oppression. Our founding fathers gave us a blueprint for assuring freedom in the form of our Constitution and Bill of Rights. Much of what you will read in the pages that follow are not-so-subtle reminders that the overwhelming evidence of oncoming, centralized government oppression is upon us now and growing exponentially. Pointing out inequities in our way of life for its own sake does not take courage; developing viable solutions that stand fast to what is "right" and not what is "expedient" binds the collective wisdom of freedom-loving people. One only needs to ask, "are we better off today than we were last year or five years ago"? If you hesitate in your response, the answer is obvious.

Freedom is not free: it requires responsibility, vigilance, and a keen eye to recognize those who enjoy our freedom but seek its destruction from within. Only swift action can stop oppression. Entitlements remove "fair exchange" in a society and burden the economy with inequity, all in the name of equity. Freedom is nothing more than common sense with a plan that respects individual rights. The following summarizes the death of common sense and the insidious decay of the moral and spiritual character of this country:

The Death of Common Sense?[6]
Lori Borgman, March 15, 1998

Three yards of black fabric enshroud my computer terminal. I am mourning the passing of an old friend by the name of Common

Sense. His obituary reads as follows: Common Sense, aka C. S., lived a long life, but died from heart failure at the brink of the millennium. No one really knows how old he was; his birth records were long ago entangled in miles and miles of bureaucratic red tape. Known affectionately to close friends as Horse Sense and Sound Thinking, he selflessly devoted himself to a life of service in homes, schools, hospitals and offices, helping folks get jobs done without a lot of fanfare, whooping and hollering.

Rules and regulations and petty, frivolous lawsuits held no power over C. S. A most reliable sage, he was credited with cultivating the ability to know when to come in out of the rain, the discovery that the early bird gets the worm and how to take the bitter with the sweet.

C. S. also developed sound financial policies (don't spend more than you earn), reliable parenting strategies (the adult is in charge, not the kid) and prudent dietary plans (offset eggs and bacon with a little fiber and orange juice).

A veteran of the Industrial Revolution, the Great Depression, the Technological Revolution and the Smoking Crusades, C. S. survived sundry cultural and educational trends, including disco, the men's movement, body piercing, whole language and new math. C. S.'s health began declining in the late 1960s when he became infected with the If-It-Feels-Good, Do-It virus.

In the following decades, his waning strength proved no match for the ravages of overbearing federal and state rules and regulations and an oppressive tax code. C. S. was sapped of strength and the will to live as the Ten Commandments became contraband, criminals received better treatment than victims and judges stuck their noses in everything from Boy Scouts to professional baseball and golf.

His deterioration accelerated as schools implemented zero-tolerance policies. Reports of six-year-old boys charged with sexual harassment for kissing classmates, a teen suspended for taking a swig of Scope mouthwash after lunch, girls suspended for possessing Midol and an honor student expelled for having a table knife in her school lunch were more than his heart could endure.

As the end neared, doctors say C. S. drifted in and out of logic but was kept informed of developments regarding regulations on low-flow toilets and mandatory air bags. Finally, upon hearing about a government plan to ban inhalers from fourteen million asthmatics due to a trace of a pollutant that may be harmful to the environment, C. S. breathed his last.

Services will be at Whispering Pines Cemetery. C. S. was preceded in death by his wife, Discretion; one daughter, Responsibility; and one son, Reason. He is survived by two stepbrothers, Half-Wit and Dim-Wit.

Memorial Contributions may be sent to the Institute for Rational Thought. Farewell, Common Sense. May you rest in peace.

Author Asserts

It is always my intent to give accurate, referenced information to my readers, well-rounded information that allows for good decision making.

Be advised that the media is no longer independent and often offers its own agenda at the expense of constitutionally guaranteed freedom of speech and access to public information.

It has come to my attention that certain footnoted references listed in this book no longer exist in web searches. Not surprising; most of these deletions are intentional and relate to controversial topics unfavorable to recent government actions.

Let it be known that the information stated in this book was, and still is, true despite being scrubbed from public view. The informational content will not be removed, as it represents this author's First Amendment right to free speech.

Preface

Americans are enamored by the story of the founding of our Constitution, as though it is a story from a good novel, yet never fully grasping the price in blood that our Constitution required. Our founding fathers left us with a sacred trust never before experienced in human history. "We the people" are attempting to make sense of what has happened to this glorious country after decades of reflection on the historical events that have transformed not only the economics of this country but the terminology as well. The basis of my writing this work lies in the premise that *words have meaning.* Many in our society are totally unaware that when words change, so do their implications. Society in this country has been sheltered from changing terminology.

One example of changing terminology in our Constitution is in the initial intent of a *free enterprise* system of economics. Arthur C. Brooks, political commentator for the *Washington Post,* wrote an editorial column on May 23, 2010, titled "America Faces a New Culture War: Free enterprise vs. government control." He stated,

> It is a struggle between two competing visions of the country's founding and future. In one, America will continue to be an exceptional nation organized around the principles of free enterprise—limited government, a reliance on entrepreneurship and rewards determined by market forces. In the other, America will move toward European-style statism grounded in expanding bureaucracies, a managed economy and large-scale income redistribution. These visions are not reconcilable. We must choose.[7]

In today's society, free enterprise now includes governmental meddling as the basis for its survival.

America was born, in part, from the dreams of immigrants worldwide who were eager to break the ties of moral degeneracy and class distinction. These people wished to test their humanity with millions of others in the competitive world of a capitalist society. Surely my grandparents had no real grasp of capitalism or what freedom really meant, coming from the socialist and pre-Fascist society of the Mussolini dictatorship in Italy. At the turn of the twentieth century, Italy was in economic ruin due to failed socialist policies and environmental challenges, and this was about to worsen drastically under the ideas of fascism, in which the individual existed only to strengthen a powerful governmental dictatorship. My grandparents and over 4 million other Italian families were willing to take the risk to escape from the land of their ancestors to find what is inherent to the human experience: freedom. An estimated 100 million Americans have at least one ancestor who came through legal immigration to the US during the 1900s.

My parents, the products of immigration, were charged with building a new world for their families with the promise of relatively high-wage jobs generated by industrialization and the opportunity for upward social mobility. Instead, they came face-to-face with the Great Depression. Survival was a matter of persistence and the clear vision that it was up to them and not some governmental regime to save them. It was World War II and the need for a change from isolationism that tested the resolve of our nation; it also effectively ended the Great Depression.

Born into the initial class of what has become the Baby Boomer generation, I grew up in a world where pride, integrity, and individuality were not considered "racist" or discriminatory (as they are today) but were the keys to success. Individual success and competence, in whatever your chosen field, led to the cumulative success of society. The concept of *class distinction* did not arise from intentional, societal wrongdoing but was the motive to become a better and more productive member of society as a whole. America was known as the *land of opportunity* because class distinction was neither a deterrent to personal success nor an anchor to the social structure of society.

As a young boy I was fascinated by how things were named, and, more importantly, why they were named. It took most of my elementary school years to understand why I was there. All I can remember was that school was about the memorization of facts, studying for the sake of passing exams, then just as quickly forgetting what I had learned in order to absorb new facts. My teachers were masters of teaching what to learn but never how to learn. The result was that I became a mediocre student at best and bored at worst.

There is a Buddhist proverb: when the student is ready, the teacher appears. I wasn't prepared for my teacher to appear, but the universe had other ideas. At age nine, I disobeyed my father's orders not to ride my new bicycle to a different neighborhood and promptly found myself staring at my right elbow protruding from my skin. Neighborhoods in Brooklyn, New York, in the 1950s were filled with huge maple and oak trees, left over from vast farmlands and forests of the late 1800s. I ventured into unknown territory and promptly ran my bike into a gaping hole where one of these behemoths used to stand. I bounced out of the hole but landed, out of control, on an up-slanted concrete driveway, elbow first. Oddly, the sight of my compound-fractured elbow, sticking out of my skin, was less painful than the thought of what my father would do to me at the sight of the destroyed front wheel of my new bicycle. Instinctively, I jerked my right arm straight, and the bone went back into the hole in my skin; I calmly walked my bike with my arm hanging at my side back to my house, prepared to face my father's wrath for my disobedience.

What followed was eleven months in a full hand-to-shoulder cast and finding myself homebound due to school safety regulations at the time. This single event started my transformation in learning with the appearance of a home school teacher. Suddenly, I was captive to a caring human being who was concerned in teaching me *how* to learn rather than just *what* to learn, opening my world to critical thinking at age nine. When I returned to school the next year, I found myself far ahead of my fellow students. Even the dreaded subject of history bristled with excitement. Gone were the boring days of memorization in favor of "living" the experience of learning.

I spent nearly two decades in the Boy Scouting program, moving through the ranks of self-reliance until I reached assistant scoutmaster. That was where I built character and the understanding that integrity, responsibility, and knowledge are ideals earned and not given. Why were our standards in life being so watered down? Where were the men in my life? It was clear that our country had changed, and not in a good way. The world was getting uglier. The conflict in Vietnam raged for over a decade. The respect for those who made America happen was being trashed in favor of an ever-growing government entity that seemed to be removing our freedoms rather than protecting them. The entitlement generation was born. I finally had enough and decided to reevaluate my life.

Going through college, I found that professors were spewing information totally foreign to me. I enrolled in a liberal arts degree program, thinking this meant a general, broad-based education in which I could expand my critical thinking skills into what would eventually become my life's work. In the midst of the 1960s, I quickly found that this degree program was instituted to indoctrinate students into following the political trends and getting on board with causes because they were revolutionary, and as such opposed to the American lifestyle to which I was accustomed. My thinking did not lend itself to the hippie mentality of revolting against social values. Realizing my error of not being the critical thinker I thought myself to be, I changed degree programs to pursue an engineering career, specializing in architecture. Apparently, engineering was the key to the future. After one year of torture and a basic course in psychology 101, I realized that my tendencies were toward intuition, thoughtfulness, and vitalist thinking, as opposed to the analytical and abstract. Leaving engineering behind, I came to recognize that my interests were in understanding complex principles and making them easy to understand. I was a teacher! Once I understood that I could be both student and teacher, I realized that I had passed my test in critical thinking, that I would never again be dependent on what others decided to say or do.

By the 1970s, our country was experiencing shortages that we had never experienced before. Gasoline shortages because of a country called Iran. Who the hell were they? Why did a mob of young Islamic revolutionaries on November 4, 1979, overrun the US Embassy in Tehran, taking more than sixty Americans hostage for 444 days? And who was the Ayatollah Khomeini? Little did I know that the seeds planted in a liberal arts degree would someday be the fruit of the destruction of this country.

My journey to find the real meaning of my life exploded in many directions. On one side there were people hell-bent on change, even if they did not know or care what that change was. On the other side were the traditional thinkers, seeking to build our country—the engineers, if you will. I found myself asking the age-old question, Who am I?

For the next sixteen years I was in heaven; I had found my niche in life. Then, out of nowhere, change was yet again becoming ugly. Why was an inner-NYC high school changing its curriculum to totally accommodate English as a second language? Why were academic courses being broken up into regular and remedial classes? Why were kids being talked about as though they were the "property" of a school system, speaking of them in terms of what daily attendance meant to school funding? Why did the school system have to deal with the teachers' union rather than the teachers? Why was there a movement to dumb down our school system in general? Why was there open enrollment in colleges? I had thought that either you made the grade, or you did not . . . and what the hell was *New Math?*

Part of the answer was firmly entrenched in actions of the 907,000-member American Federation of Teachers (AFT), headed at the time by its union leader, Albert Shanker. Mr. Shanker's outward rhetoric was always tempered around better education for children. The sheer size of the union and the clout it carried through its union dues and retirement funds became the cornerstone for the progressive takeover of the educational system that led to the dramatic changes in the mid 1970s.[8]

The AFT fought for better teachers, smaller class sizes, and union employee benefits that amounted to massive entitlement programs that NYC had to bear or face the wrath of a 904,000 teachers' union strike. During Shanker's presidency, teachers were no longer judged on their merit based on supervisor reviews but by their negotiated three-year tenure rule. After three years, aside from insubordination, a teacher could not be fired. Teachers were guaranteed pay raises based on years of service rather than ability.

By 1975, NYC was in grave financial trouble and unable to meet its salary and benefit obligations to the members of the AFT. Shortly thereafter, Shanker and the AFT whipped its membership into a frenzy over pay raises, benefits, and the need for smaller class sizes and new teacher salary parity. NYC responded by refusing to negotiate, resulting in a five-day AFT strike, shutting down the entire NYC school system. NYC imposed an ordinance forbidding *all* city workers from striking, but Shanker called the strike anyway. As I walked the picket line, it was clear that we could be sued by the city for striking. After five long days, Shanker announced a settlement. Existing teachers would receive less than a one percent pay increase, stating that higher paid teachers needed to share incomes so that new teachers would receive benefits. Teachers would not be sued for striking against the city but would not be paid for days lost. Somehow this was portrayed as an equitable win for striking.

Several years later it was discovered that Shanker and the AFT had struck a deal with NYC to float a $150 million dollar stimulus loan from the huge teachers' retirement fund for a hefty return. The five-day strike was staged as a show of strength by the AFT, when in fact the progressive mindset of the powerful union was neither for the school children nor the teachers. It was about building a bigger financial base for the union, sacrificing teacher salaries to bail NYC out of its financial crisis. Shanker indeed duped the teachers. In an unconfirmed Shanker quote in 1985, he may have secretly revealed his true intentions as union boss: "When schoolchildren start paying union dues, that's when I'll start representing the interests of school children."[9]

Leaving teaching and starting over to become a chiropractor with a family in tow was the single greatest experience/experiment of my life. I finally had the chance to find out what I was made of. In chiropractic school, I was introduced to the philosophy of life. I had always tried to answer the *how* as well as the *what* in life, but I had never considered the *why*. One of my initial assignments in chiropractic philosophy introduced me to the writings of Ayn Rand and a book titled *The Fountainhead*. To say this was an eye-opening experience is an understatement. The author was a refugee from communist Russia to the US, just as my grandparents were refugees from socialist Italy. Rand used metaphors to communicate truths and lessons of life. *The Fountainhead* was about an architect, which captured my attention since Architecture had been my major in college before becoming a teacher. After reading Rand's book, I found the message to be far deeper than architecture. She wrote of integrity, humanity, and freedom vs. coercion; Rand used architecture as a metaphor for one's philosophy of life. I was beginning to understand the *why* in life.

What makes my writing different in this book is not the information it contains but the enablement it provides to make the "complex" easier to understand: the fruition of my life's quest.

It is my intent to help empower the average American with the ability to stand for what is right and not for what is expedient. Taking back our country is not for the faint of heart. We are well past critical mass in terms of the damage created by years of neglect of our founding principles. If there is a collapse of the economic and political structure of this country, those who survive the inevitable rebuilding process will be totally dependent on the memory of what made this country independent. It is my hope that my contribution will be remembered.

Once exposed to the light, you can never return to the darkness.

Introduction

This is not the forum of a conspiracy against the federal government, nor is it an attempt to rally a revolution. This is an attempt to enlighten our citizenry about what is to become the future of the United States of America. The framers of our demise as a nation were fortunately socialists and not communists. Socialism takes over a country by ignorance and ever-increasing public entitlements; Communism takes over a country at the point of a gun; however, both government models achieve the same goal: loss of freedom, which is the antithesis of the framers' design. It is my belief that what we have been incrementally experiencing since the onset of the "progressive" movement, initiated openly during the Woodrow Wilson administration, is the intentional bastardization of our representative republic and the demise of the very freedoms envisioned by our founders. First and foremost, freedom to express one's views openly in an open society and without fear of retribution is the quintessential difference between a representative republic like America and a dictatorship, where freedom of expression is allowed as long as it is in agreement with the state. The illusion of freedom was uniquely expressed by Ayn Rand: "There's no way to rule innocent men. The only power any government has is the power to crack down on criminals. Well, when there aren't enough criminals, one makes them. One declares so many things to be a crime that it becomes impossible for men to live without breaking laws."[10]

Sadly, the insidious deception of freedom of expression, as guaranteed by the First Amendment of our Constitution, is becoming our reality. The progressive movement understands that public opinion can be changed or permanently altered simply by changing the meanings of words. In America it should not matter what one's belief or acceptance is of gender, race, or sexual orientation; however, over the years political influence has imposed its will on the people. America, as a country, is appalled by the treatment of women in the Arab culture, where for a woman the simple act of driving a car in Saudi Arabia can be punishable by imprisonment.[11] However, in America, it was not until 1920 that women obtained the right to vote.[12] Freedom is free only if people remain vigilant. Once people acquiesce to political or governmental influence, freedom is but an illusion.

Over the past twenty or more years our country struggled with the growing awareness of the gay movement. Words have meaning; how many words have been used to describe homosexual individuals? As a boy in the 1950s, I was taught that *queer* was the correct terminology and thought nothing more of it. With political correctness came the terms *lesbian* and *gay,* essentially describing the same thing, each occurring with its own political agenda.

The progressive movement has put intent behind each word change it wishes to vilify, thus challenging freedom of speech. Presently, it is okay to speak of gay marriage but not politically correct to express one's thoughts on gay marriage. The point being made here is that when intentional word changes occur, the meanings of those words also change, and this change in meaning is unchallenged. America has the freedom to express itself without political retribution. The gay rights issue is classic progressivism at its worst. The president and CEO of Mozilla, Brendan Eich (creator of the Firefox Web Browser), was recently forced to step down from his position because of political correctness—in other words, his views on gay marriage.[13] In 2008, Mr. Eich exercised his freedom of speech and expression as an American citizen by making a personal financial contribution to oppose the gay marriage issue in California, known as Proposition 8. Ironically, in that same year presidential candidate Barack Obama apparently shared the identical view, stating publicly that he believes marriage should be between a man and a woman; it would have been potential political suicide not to have done so. However, in 1996 then Senator Barack Obama publicly supported gay marriage. In 2013, Obama once again supported gay marriage.[14] His statements reek of hypocrisy, yet the progressive movement has made gay marriage the focus of political attention, whereas Mr. Eich is now considered an enemy of the state because of his 2008 anti-gay marriage stance.

If this type of political behavior can continue chipping away at our freedom of expression, the progressives will have free rein to place other politically sensitive issues into the category of criminality, thus making freedom a footnote in American history. Certainly, there are common sense limitations to freedom:

Freedom of speech is the political right to communicate one's opinions and ideas, using one's body and property, to anyone who is willing to receive them. The term freedom of expression is sometimes used synonymously but includes any act of seeking, receiving, and imparting information or ideas, regardless of the medium used. In practice, the right to freedom of speech is not absolute in any country, and the right is commonly subject to limitations, as with libel, slander, obscenity, sedition, copyright violation, and revelation of information that is classified or otherwise protected.[15]

Remember democracy never lasts long.
It soon wastes, exhausts, and murders itself.There never was a democracy yet that did not commit suicide.

—John Adams, April 15, 1814

Whoever thought that this glorious land, the destination of millions fleeing from the tyranny of their homelands, would ever succumb to the same trappings that forced these people to leave everything and try to start anew? This country was truly the land of opportunity. Personal freedoms, risk taking, education, and the result of the Industrial Revolution transformed this country into the model for the world to emulate. It also started the movement that our enemies wanted to destroy. The power and might of the US were unrivaled. No country wanted to go head-to-head with a country with unlimited resolve. World War I and World War II proved that we were able to stand for what this country was founded upon and created our country's greatest generation: the men and women of the World War II era. However, considering our history and all that is happening now, is it possible that in just under two generations our country could have changed this much? It was President Ronald Reagan who said, "Freedom is only one generation from extinction."

What we did not know, as our country experienced the innocence of childhood and going through the adolescent years, was that there were forces at work to tame these freedom seekers. The rebellious forces in the US that dominated the 1960s were the precursor of a country about to change. Where did these people come from? They were not coming from neighborhoods we grew up in; they seemed to just appear on our college campuses and in the workplace. The truth is that, while most of us were still enjoying the *Jackie Gleason Show* and *Father Knows Best,* our history books, business corporations, banks, and colleges were being infiltrated by a dissident movement, planned by a "Grand Design" years earlier, to bring the US back into a world filled with centuries of despots, rulers, kings, tyrants, and monarchs; where *freedom* was a dirty word and the one weapon that could emasculate the likes of Stalin, Lenin, Hitler, and their predecessors back into history. Little did we know that this country was about to change, perhaps forever. The age of isolationism was over. Things were about to get ugly.

For the Baby Boomers, this was the age of awakening. College professors were spewing information totally foreign to those who were the product of our *greatest generation.* This was the first time the word *liberal* euphemistically substituted for a philosophy of education that empowered individuals with a broad knowledge base and transferable skills, while at the same time minimizing the need for self-reliance and the individual. Communal thinking and less reliance on entrepreneurship were becoming fashionable. The politics of today demonstrates the liberal ideology as demonstrated in the 1995 book by Hillary Clinton, *It Takes a Village to Raise a Child.* Similarly, in a 2012 campaign speech, Barack Obama stated that "If you've got a business, you didn't build that." Both statements seem innocuous at first glance, but the issue is not in the statements but in the ideology it portrays. After further analysis, the real message implies that it takes a strong, centralized government to secure the means to achieve success.

Liberalism morphed into what is presently portrayed as "progressivism," a subtle terminology change with destructive consequences. Progressivism is a type of thinking that has been lost or conveniently removed from the teaching of world history in our schools. In fact, progressive ideology became the mainstream with the Nazis during the reign of Adolph Hitler. Nazism was sold to an unsuspecting German population as the *National Socialist German Workers' Party,* with the only requirement being the belief that the state has supremacy over individual rights, all in the name of social progressive justice. Americans are similarly accepting the ideals of progressivism at face value because Who does not want social justice for all?

William Lafferty, in his article *Historical Parallels between Progressivism, Nazism, Fascism & Marxism Are Not Accidental* states that "Progressives, I suggest, have three main characteristics. They see themselves as morally superior and feel it is their duty to tell others what they should do. They are experts at lying. And, finally, they use the government to force their views on others."[16] These characteristics are readily apparent in the massive consolidation of power in Washington in the name of social justice, along with its signature program Obamacare.

The concepts of Ayn Rand's writings in both *The Fountainhead* and Atlas Shrugged are introspection into what is becoming mainstream America. However, these concepts became very real when I was introduced to author G. Edward Griffin, in Cancun, in 1990. That entire weekend, known as The Global Summit, was about what is in store for the future of the world based on those who have the power to control minds. Griffin's book, *The Creature from Jekyll Island: A Second Look at the Federal Reserve System,* is a factual and historical account of the 1910 Jekyll Island, South Carolina, meeting among seven international men of banking and government who were tasked with the challenge of creating the blueprint that would serve as the precursor for what is now known as the New World Order.

Griffin's book mentioned that the US was the last stronghold of freedom and the only entity standing in the way of world domination by a totalitarian government.

The seven men at the Jekyll Island meeting knew that it would take at least two generations (approximately one hundred years) to complete the takeover of the US. This takeover began in two ways: Woodrow Wilson's 1913 election and ending US isolationism by way of WWI. Germany implemented unrestricted submarine warfare on all merchant ships. Although President Woodrow Wilson declared the United States to be neutral, on August 4, 1914, he secretly approved shipping small arms and high explosives to England, hidden in the belly of the passenger ship *Lusitania,* destined for Liverpool, England.[17] Whether by chance or design, Germany torpedoed the passenger ship, killing 1,959 innocent people, including 159 Americans. This was seen by the US as an overt act of war. What actually happened was not revealed until decades later when the wreck revealed evidence of military arms and explosives. However, this incident was the United States' introduction onto the international scene.

In line with the message of *Atlas Shrugged*, the age of disinformation began in the US. Everything done by future presidents, both Republican and Democrat, had one goal: to get the US to abandon its founding fathers' constitutional genius (which Ayn Rand spoke of) and to foster an ever-growing centralized government. This centralized government would constantly be on the lookout for ways to help those who did not contribute, while blaming those who did for their selfishness. As we see now, we have one political party posing as two. Whoever is in power moves the country closer to tyranny, resorting to legislation to implement their agenda on the population. Those individuals who can produce while encouraging independence and freedom find themselves outside the established mainstream. To become part of the *collective* comes right from the Communist Manifesto, a fact intentionally implied in *Atlas Shrugged*. Trade unions were sold as collective voices for the common man but have become containment compounds for the working man, dictating what one can or cannot do. One cannot be almost free, just as one cannot be almost pregnant!

The Federal Income Tax officially began in 1913 (surprise, surprise), ensuring that no one would escape the power of a centralized government. The Federal Income Tax was originally sold to the people as a tax on their investments, not their earnings. For example: if you earned $1,000 and invested 50% of it in a bank, stock market, or land, the income from those investments would be taxed—not your initial $1,000 earnings. However, by 1918, the centralized new federal government wanted more control over private enterprise, i.e., the wealth of the nation. To accomplish their objective, it was necessary to enact an 1871 ruling, which essentially transformed the "United States" into the "United States Corporation."

Ninety-five years after the founding of the original "united" States of America, a separate and different United States Corporation was formed in 1871, which controlled only the District of Columbia and its territories. The actual corporation (the United

States Corporation) is the legal entity that is our current government. The original Constitution still exists and has been clarified by Supreme Court Justice Marshall Harlan (Downes v. Bidwell, 182, U.S. 244, 1901) in two separate opinions: "Two national governments exist; one to be maintained under the Constitution, with all its restrictions; the other to be maintained by Congress outside and Independently of that Instrument." To this day Harlan's opinion is still intact; a fact that has never been spoken of publicly or ever taught in schools. The United States Corporation has the power to use its assets as collateral for loans and business deals. Those assets are the earnings of every citizen of the United States, as chattel, to be used as collateral for government spending, leading to a progressive income tax on earnings, period. The United States Corporation has no obligations or accountability to "we the people" except to make a profit as a corporation.[18]

Every president from Wilson to Obama, except Reagan and Trump (who were flukes, and not anticipated by the framers of "the plan"), was put there to move the country toward the New World Order. The latest recession/depression seen in the banking and mortgage loan industry was intentional. The truth behind the real estate failures is that the government forced banks to make risky loans, then bundle and sell them under the political fiction "with the full faith and credit of the United States." Fanny Mae and Freddie Mac stood behind every bad loan the banks made. In other words, the people themselves were being held responsible for the collapse because they made risky investments. Financial real estate collapse was inevitable. Magicians and politicians call that "sleight of hand."

Obama's 2016 election proved that the Jekyll Island plan was accurate and is being followed to the letter. It has been over one hundred years since the Jekyll Island meeting, and with the entire US in turmoil and on the verge of economic collapse due to colossal debt, the people still elected Obama.

There is evidence that the entire 2020 election process was rigged by moving to early voting under the pretense of the Covid-19 pandemic. With ballots being sent by mail and weak methods of voter identification, how difficult is it to report whatever the government wants? Thirty-five percent of the population chose to vote by mail. The rollout of the recent Healthcare Affordability Act was a total disaster due to what appeared to be incredible incompetence in designing www.healthcare.gov, including the lack of security measures to safeguard personal information. Deception comes in many forms. Touch screens provide the perfect cover for personal information to be stolen or elections to be rigged. This is the legal equivalent of tampering with the election process via the US Postal Service and the Federal Communications Commission, and there is no way to verify.[19] There also now exists scientific proof that the 2020 election was the biggest cyber-crime in world history.[20]

History is supposed to be the ultimate teacher; however, when lessons are not learned or are intentionally ignored, the result is emboldened repetition of the same activity. Elections laws are quite specific, yet since the "state" legislatures have the ultimate responsibility for regulating how their state elections are run or changed, it is not too difficult to imagine how politics can alter the election process. The most recent example was the 2020 presidential cycle. Regardless of your political stripe, the "irregularities" were blatant and intentional. Congress was left with the difficult task of following constitutional guidelines as it relates to the Electoral College certification, yet it was clear that what occurred was not within the purview of our framers. With thousands of signed affidavits and visual evidence of possible fraud and election tampering due to early voting and vote harvesting, Congress was left with investigations necessary to answer the questions posed by some 76 million voters, without the time to do so. It must be clearly noted that the need for political distractions is a requirement for election chaos. In the Obama era, it was the Affordable Care Act that provided the distraction. In the Trump 2020 election cycle, it was Covid-19. Both distractive scenarios were exploited to achieve the cover necessary for the yet unproven voter deception.

Resolution to these historical events is, in part, dependent on the political party in control of the government. Had Obama lost his second term, the Democratic party would have displayed the same politically disruptive response as did the Republican party in its loss in 2020, with politicians from both sides of the political spectrum spouting conflicting jargon, depending on their political needs. Upholding constitutional guidelines must never be influenced by subversive politics or current events.

Do you know of a corporation that functions without a budget? For that matter, what business or individual can function without checks and balances or a profit and loss document? The federal government is now borrowing forty cents of every dollar spent due to raising the debt limit on borrowing, under the guise of "with the full faith of the US government," as opposed to cutting spending. Adding to our debt is the ability of the Federal Reserve to simply print money without backing. It is estimated that the Federal Reserve prints 118 million dollars per day, or over 75 billion dollars per month, to pay down the interest from reckless borrowing.[21] These acts will bankrupt our country, completing the plans made at Jekyll Island.

The lessons of *Atlas Shrugged* have not gone unnoticed. Most people do know that we are being duped. They also know that the "uninformed" are being used as pawns to continue the rhetoric that taxing the rich will somehow save the poor. The poor will always be poor to perpetuate the lie. The poor depend on jobs or entitlements. If the government kills the job market, what is left? So, how do you save the poor by killing the rich?

Regarding the structural relationship between the twelve Federal Reserve banks and the various commercial (member) banks, political science professor Michael D. Reagan wrote:

> The "ownership" of the Reserve Banks by the commercial banks is symbolic; they do not exercise the proprietary control associated with the concept of ownership nor share, beyond the statutory dividend, in Reserve Bank "profits." . . . Bank ownership and election at the base are therefore devoid of substantive significance, despite the superficial appearance of private bank control that the formal arrangement creates.[22]

The bottom line is that the Federal Reserve Bank is not "federal" at all but a group of private corporations, named as such (federal) to give the illusion of confidence. The Federal "Reserve" has no reserves but is a depository set up by law, allowing it to reap (take) the wealth of the nation's private banking system and making its assets the assets of the corporation of the United States (and not the people who earned the assets). The Federal Reserve is not a bank.

The Federal Reserve banks issue shares of stock to member banks, stock that may not be negotiated or used as collateral for a loan. The Federal Reserve Banks pay no interest to member banks but instead allow member banks to offer "fractional banking practices." In short, a member bank can loan nine dollars for every dollar it takes in. These loans are guaranteed by the Federal Reserve Bank, once again using their meaningless statement "with the full faith and credit of the United States."

The Federal Reserve was created by Congress with the passage of the Federal Reserve Act of 1913 (surprise, again). It is privately owned by the Corporation of the United States. The corporation's Board of Governors is appointed, not elected; therefore, the Federal Reserve is autonomous.

So outrageous is this system for duping of the American public that its secrets can be easily hidden in plain sight. Those who dissent or try to expose the "Ponzi scheme" are labeled "conspirators" and "dissidents." They are dismissed by the uninformed as "kooks"—the perfect scenario for hidden agendas.

Let's do some fact checking on the status of our country and those who are attempting to change it. In 2008, Obama ran on a platform of "change," with the idea that in order to bring equality, changes had to be made—even to the Constitution itself. The US government was set up "by the people" and "for the people." So, let's see how Obama's plan worked out for us:

1. Obama instituted a single payer, government-run healthcare system, which effectively eliminates private enterprise, health insurance (as we know it), and free market healthcare by declaration that present healthcare policies are "junk" and not all-inclusive. In doing so, Obama's single payer system mandated coverages that are not needed by every person. For example: a single man is required to have obstetric coverage. Insurance and deductibles will nearly triple, instead of going down by Obama's stated $2,500. Obama publicly stated 27 times that "it is possible to keep your present doctors and healthcare plan" but failed to add "only if you can afford to do so." Obama's outright lies to the public and then chastisement of the public for not understanding his words border on tyranny. Obamacare requires an approved government drug program, whether or not needed by an individual. Fail-

ure to take advantage of this program results in a cumulative fine until compliance. However, Congress runs on a different healthcare system, which allows federal government employees and their families freedom from Obamacare. They have self-directed, independent, lifetime healthcare benefits apart from anything they impose on the citizens, including healthcare's biggest albatross: Medicare.

2. People must be responsible for their actions, both public and private, requiring regulations, permits, licenses, and malpractice/liability policies for business. Yet the federal government is exempt from most laws the citizens must follow. The government can impose Eminent Domain to acquire private lands and impose its privatization of "public" parks (and did so under FDR). Oddly enough, these properties are off limits to the public without permit since ownership belongs to the Corporation of the United States and not the people of the United States.

3. Citizens must have collateral to secure loans from banks at interest rates; these banks are often comparable to loan sharks. However, the federal government can simply borrow and spend money at its own discretion via congressional edict. Examples of these edicts are US bonds; debt ceilings; no-interest loans to itself by the Federal Reserve (paid for by altering the prime lending rate to the citizens); and worst of all, fiat money, created at the behest of the Federal Reserve chairman. Simply put, fiat money is the creation of money out of thin air.

4. Citizens are forced to pay federal, state, and sometimes city income taxes. Citizens also pay a myriad of hidden taxes under the guise of property tax and sales taxes on almost everything we purchase. These funds are all directed to the federal government, under penalty of law. Yet the federal government (as a private corporation) is able to be totally unaccountable for the money it receives; pays no interest on what it collects from the people; uses employers as tax collecting agents of the US government without compensation; and has no federal budget, profit and loss statements, or reporting of any income on its investments. In short, the corporation of the US functions as a totalitarian "benevolent" dictatorship hiding behind the cloak of *socialized democracy.*

The mere expressing of what is public knowledge can label a person as a dissident or, in extreme circumstances, a terrorist (therefore subjecting that citizen to potential Patriot Act consequences), ensuring that government secrets never become known.

Ayn Rand was a product of Communism, and her writings in *The Fountainhead* and *Atlas Shrugged* portray scenarios totally unfamiliar to a naïve, freedom-loving country. However, those in power know full well the power of her words and resort to the censure of all media outlets to ensure the demonization of her message. Sadly, it took fifty years for the message of *Atlas Shrugged* to resonate with the citizens of the US and the world, not because we understand the message any better but because entitlements are slowly going away, leaving the uninformed in a state of panic.

Any country where the producers are penalized by regulations and taxes while the non-producers can use or make laws to inhibit competition enslaves itself into universal mediocrity. It is a country doomed.

> For the great enemy of the truth is very often not the lie—deliberate, contrived, and dishonest—but the myth—persistent, persuasive, and unrealistic. Too often we hold fast to the cliches of our forebears. We subject all facts to a prefabricated set of interpretations. We enjoy the comfort of opinion without the discomfort of thought.[23]
>
> —John F. Kennedy

For Further Reading

"The Collapse of The American Dream Explained in Animation." YouTube. http://youtu.be/mII9NZ8MMVM (accessed July 21, 2014).

Griffin, G. Edward. *The creature from Jekyll Island: a second look at the Federal Reserve.* 3rd ed. Westlake Village, Calif.: American Media, 1998.

Hunter, Greg. "Never Ending Money Printing." Greg Hunter's USAWatchdog. http://usawatchdog.com/fed-money-printing/ (accessed June 15, 2014).

Murphy, Robert. "The Fractional Reserve Banking System Explained." The Market Oracle. http://www.marketoracle.co.uk/Article20300.html (accessed June 15, 2014).

Williams, Walter E. "Walter E. Williams—Liberals, Progressives and Socialists." townhall.com. http://townhall.com/columnists/walterewilliams/2012/08/08/liberals_progressives_and_socialists/page/full (accessed June 11, 2014).

Chapter 1

Hypocrisy

Oxford online defines hypocrisy as "the practice of claiming to have moral standards or beliefs to which one's own behavior does not conform."[24] Hypocrisy is now the norm, as is evidenced by the attack on our Second Amendment right to bear arms. Guns, knives, or baseball bats are inanimate objects of pleasure or defense and are incapable of anything unless directed by the user. The uninformed are taught that these objects are, in effect, real unto themselves and that safety should be in the hands of trained individuals—of course, for their own safety. However, even the uninformed soon realize the hypocrisy when they are denied Second Amendment rights. The very politicians who seek to disarm are themselves armed. Your children are sent to schools as "gun free zones," yet former President Obama's children had thirteen armed officials in their schools. Those politicians (tyrants in training) presently in Congress each is protected by a privately armed security force above the Secret Service. Even Nancy Pelosi, a staunch advocate of strict gun control, has a concealed weapons permit.

What better way is there to remove competition and gain compliance than to disarm your adversaries, both mentally and physically? Lord Acton, of the British monarchy in 1887, said, "Power tends to corrupt, and absolute power corrupts absolutely." The Greek mathematician Euclid, in 300 bc, used mathematic principles to prove that "Things that are equal to the same things are equal to each other." Therefore, it can be realistically stated that corrupt governments corrupt totally. Sadly, to corrupt our "inalienable right" to freedom is a travesty and by itself would never occur unless cunningly influenced by those in total power.

Our First Amendment right of Freedom of Speech is being hijacked by the relentless pressures of socialism within our government and, most recently, social media. Socialism's version of freedom of speech is based strictly on the "collective." It argues that anyone is free to speak what is acceptable to the state.[25] Of course, the "state," in their world, is one that is driven by large leftist groups that deem anything conservative to be "hate speech."

Have you noticed that the latest insult to our First Amendment right is to be labeled a "racist" if that speech is politically directed toward a Democratic official? The term racism is no longer limited to discrimination or prejudice against a particular race but is instead now used to shut down intellectual conversation.[26] President Trump, for example, has been called a racist to inject political bias. How do you defend yourself against such accusations? The offending person need not prove his statement since he, too, has a First Amendment right to free speech; therein lies the intentional misrepresentation and use of free speech. Just for the record, before Trump ran for president as a Republican, he donated $1.5 million to high profile Democratic candidates, including Hillary Clinton, Joe Biden, and Andrew Cuomo, none of whom would have accepted a dime from him, for political reasons, if he were truly a racist.[27]

Much time has passed since Lord Acton and Euclid, but human nature has changed little. Our democratic republic was founded on the freedom denied to the rest of the world by monarchs, kings, and tyrants. These absolute leaders proved that the total power they wielded corrupted totally. Democracy has inherent "checks and balances" and offers its citizens the choice of elected officials. Most all other forms of government are chosen, not elected. Their population has a choice of "one." The day our country was founded also started the process of its eventual demise. No democracy has survived for more than two hundred years. The reason is that freedom comes with a price—diligence. Once a democratic population relinquishes its "due diligence" to career politicians, not long thereafter the rumblings of another revolution emerge.

I mention this because we are presently into our 245th year since our founding, and history is catching up. The dumbing down of our society has left us vulnerable to deceit. Our most precious right of self-defense, prominently displayed by the Second Amendment of our Constitution, was put there not so much to defend from each other but to ensure defense against government tyranny. Our present federal government has demonstrated by its actions that socialism has arrived. To accomplish the two hundred plus-year destiny of this democracy, it must make "population controls" appear as "freedom." To the uninformed who are experiencing ever diminishing freedoms, this twisted idea of freedom breeds panic and chaos as the norm. To the oppressors (our elected officials), under-delivering promises can be blamed on the very freedoms they appear to protect. The result is "socialized democracy, a political movement advocating a gradual and peaceful transition from capitalism to socialism by democratic means."[28]

Once a movement begins, be it good or cynical, it can quickly gain momentum. From the political liberties taken against the constitutional laws of this country come those who feel that they too can interpret constitutional law. On December 29, 2011, the reality of our individual rights gone wrong became apparent when dealing with a legitimate firearms company, American Spirit Arms, and Bank of America. With our Second Amendment rights now in jeopardy, American Spirit Arms, as well as other, similar companies, experienced a five hundred percent increase in internet sales. American Spirit Arms' deposits were funneled to Bank of America (BOA), as has always been the practice. Suddenly American Spirit Arms was receiving no revenue from BOA to pay for their sold inventory. It was learned that BOA had decided to hold the deposits for further review. The manager at the bank told the owner of the company, "We believe you should not be selling guns and parts on the Internet."[29]

Further evidence of hypocrisy can be seen in the social media arena. Facebook is nothing more than a tracking system disguised as a way of sharing information. Recently, conservative bloggers or those who openly speak of conservative values as a way of exercising their right of free speech found this out. The "overseers" (federal government agents) are censoring true conservative dialogue by literally removing all postings. Further, your account can be targeted for further scrutiny at any time. I suggest that Facebook become a place for sharing recipes! Targeting and censoring conservative speech is not only a violation of our First Amendment rights but is in violation of the very Constitution the federal government is sworn to uphold, via every elected federal government official's sworn "Oath of Office" affidavit. All social media platforms are influenced by advertising dollars. Large corporations put their massive advertising dollars behind platforms that increase their profits; that's called capitalism. When independently owned social media platforms are bought or influenced by the highest bidder for purposes of restricting/controlling public discourse, that's called socialism.

The biggest and most obvious piece of hypocrisy displayed by our government is the fact that they have created one set of laws for the citizens and another set of laws for themselves, in essence granting themselves immunity from the laws by which *all* Americans are supposed to abide:

1. Healthcare: The government healthcare program is totally different from the healthcare program delivered to the people, including Medicare.
2. The Food and Drug Administration can actually test and approve only a fraction of the 1,200 new drugs presented to the market each year by the pharmaceutical companies, often relying on data from the pharmaceutical companies themselves. The AMA admits to over 200,000 deaths per year from "adverse reactions"—third leading cause of deaths in America,[30] more than all the deaths of WWI and WWII combined, yet the federal government offers immunity from prosecution or lawsuit to drug manufacturers.
3. Fanny Mae and Freddie Mac: These government programs have successfully brought down the housing market, operating against constitutional and state laws with impunity, yet not a single federal employee has been prosecuted.
4. The Federal Reserve, which is neither federal nor a bank and certainly has no reserves, operates autonomously and with impunity, answerable to no individual and no agency. It can print money out of thin air (fiat money), while controlling the value of the currency, without the House of Representatives, the congressional entity responsible for the financial security of the country.
5. Federal government employees are totally exempt from prosecution for any actions they take that may harm the country as a whole.

In fact, according to Louisiana State University, there are over 1,300 federal agencies that operate outside the laws that bind the citizens of the US. The hypocrisy is that we have allowed our government to run amuck, tacitly giving approval for their actions by not offering any meaningful opposition. In fact, opposition to federal control is punishable by the very laws they have passed. We have been lulled into submission and have forgotten "we the people."

In a twist of governmental hypocrisy, "we the people" got the chance to see how government officials react when subjected to the same invasion of privacy by CIA spying. Diane Feinstein, the California Democrat, complained that the CIA had searched the committee's computers and that the search was potentially criminal and may have violated the Fourth Amendment.[31] At the same time, she tolerates government spying on private citizens. Feinstein stated that the search came as the committee was investigating the CIA's use of secret detention and enhanced interrogation during the Bush administration. Feinstein gave a clear example that an elected official does not care at all that the rights of millions of ordinary citizens are violated by our spies, but suddenly it's a scandal when a politician finds out that the same thing happens to them.

This gives fair warning: being uninformed, passive, or compliant with this unconstitutional tyranny, from whatever source, is hastening the transformation of our democratic republic to socialism. President Reagan said, "Freedom is only one generation from extinction." Tyranny expands on the ignorance of the electorate. Over-promising "nirvana" to the uninformed brings only entitlements, not freedom. Once gone, freedom is gone forever.

Chapter 2

Healthcare, Covid-19, and the Medicine Man

Throughout time, human illness or the lack thereof has captivated humanity. In the years before organized medicine, human illness, optimal functioning of the body, and enhancing the survival of the species became the work of centuries of observation, trial and error, and experimentation. Each culture based its existence on its ability to adapt to its environment or perish. Many early cultures did perish. This is not the forum for a history lesson but suffice it to say that not much has changed in the human species except our ever-increasing technology and understanding of our environment. What has changed is the relentless pursuit to control how the entity of healthcare is delivered, separate from the entity of health itself.

Have you ever wondered how we ended up in a healthcare system that is riddled with errors and inconsistencies, priced beyond everyone's means, centered on the use of toxic chemicals, and with a track record of iatrogenic injuries that is beyond the carnage of all our wars? What happened to the "first do no harm" motto of early medicine? Who has taken us from the laws of nature to the practicality and ever-changing status of science? Most importantly, how have the healing arts become a government-controlled issue? My purpose is not to disparage or discredit what has been accomplished in medicine over the years but to instead demonstrate the intentional enhancement or misrepresentation of medical findings and products to enrich the "business" of healthcare.

These are questions not for scholars but for the average citizen to ponder. It is an oxymoron to discuss "natural healing." Healing, by definition, is the natural process of the body improving its own health. With the advent of scientific advances and the insatiable desire to speed up or circumvent natural processes, we have slowly accepted the uncertainties of today's chemical healing over time-tested natural healing, in much the way we embrace the logic of winning the lottery. We all know the inherent dangers of toxic chemicals; we all have heard staggering adverse statistics of modern medicine, yet we have accepted these almost without question.

If you watch TV in America, you have certainly seen pharmaceutical ads for the latest and greatest new drug, which somehow you should tell your doctor about. The ads follow a similar pattern: Do you feel (specific symptoms)? Has the (ailment) been holding you back? This is followed by visuals of a dejected person, The message is to "talk to your doctor" about whatever the drug is, followed by that same person smiling as they're walking along some exotic beach or playing in their garden, while at the same time you begin to hear a litany of potential side effects, which could be as mild as muscle aches or as serious as sudden death. The list is sometimes so long that you wonder whether you are listening to a commercial or a comedy routine.

I'm certain that most viewers don't even think it's odd that patients are asked to recommend drugs to their doctors. The United States is the only country, besides New Zealand, that legally permits "direct-to-consumer" pharmaceutical marketing. America is amid an opioid epidemic fueled in part by prescription painkillers. In 1971 President Nixon publicly declared a war on drugs; today we encourage people to take drugs.

The "Business" of Pain

Our healthcare system is predicated on the collective wisdom of centuries of experimentation throughout the world. "Health care is the maintenance or improvement of health via the diagnosis, treatment, and prevention of disease, illness, injury, and other physical and mental impairments in human beings."[32]

Vital signs are a group of the four most important signs that indicate the status of the body's vital functions. These measurements are accurately reproducible and a consistent measure to help assess the general physical health of a person, give clues to possible diseases, and show progress toward recovery.[33] The four main vital signs routinely monitored by medical professionals and healthcare providers are body temperature, pulse rate, respiration rate, and blood pressure. Recently, an additional sign has been subliminally added to the list: pain. It has been added in the form of a "subjective" sign (not medically reproducible or tested), as opposed to the standard "objective" vital signs that are medically reproducible. The healthcare provider simply asks their patient to rate their "pain" level on a scale of 1–5 or 0–10, hardly requiring the expertise of medical school training. The scale is then used to determine the degree or strength of pain medication—a potential disaster looking for a place to belong. Subjective patient standards for pain are impossible to quantify.

Pain is not a vital sign but a symptom. The concept originated in the VA hospital system in the late 1990s and became a Joint Commission standard in 2001. Pain was allegedly being under-treated. Hospitals were forced to emphasize the assessment of pain for all patients on every shift with the (mistaken) idea that all pain must be closely monitored and treated. This is based on the (mistaken) idea that pain medication is capable of rendering patients completely pain free. This has now become the expectation of many patients who are incredulous and disappointed when that expectation is not met.[34]

Over the years, pain has become the unintended mainstay for the medical profession. Pain is not an illness or disease, yet with the ever-increasing "direct to consumer" TV advertising by pharmaceutical companies exploiting pain, the resulting windfall of pain medications has made pawns of medical physicians because of their prescription pads. Pharmaceutical companies cannot write scripts but spend billions of dollars in incentives for physicians to "treat" pain with their products. In fact, entire clinics have sprung up everywhere devoted to nothing but "pain management" via pain-reducing drugs.[35] A personal physician friend of mine openly stated his disgust over the treatment of pain. Many patients come to his office demanding strong pain medications, regardless of his professional workup or examination results. If he refuses or offers alternatives, they simply go doctor shopping. If pain is touted as the fifth vital sign, I do not see the situation getting better anytime soon.

During the 1960's Hippie Counterculture, experimenting with drugs got you high. Today, trivializing potent drugs or pain killers via TV commercials has, in part, left thousands susceptible to more dangerous experimentation with substances like Fentanyl. Fentanyl is fifty times stronger than heroin, so potent that an amount the size of three grains of sugar is lethal to an adult. The only acceptable, "on-label" use for Fentanyl is for severe pain in cancer sufferers. Today, the drug has two main sources: the prescription drug industry and the streets by Mexican drug cartels, under the main control of Joaquin "El Chapo" Guzman. The Mexican immigration issue in human trafficking pales in comparison to the Fentanyl being smuggled into the US.[36] On a personal note, a close friend and his wife lost both their children to a Fentanyl overdose—a far cry from "getting high."[37]

In the late nineties, OxyContin was introduced and touted to be a safe, "nonaddictive" medication for pain. One of the premises of this book series is that words have meaning. Effective marketing often requires the deliberate distortion of the truth or, worse, lying by using words that are intentionally misleading. This is the case for marketing OxyContin. Purdue Pharmaceuticals marketed OxyContin as an effective, nonaddictive medication for the chronic pain of cancer. The optimal deceiving marketing term is "medication." A *medication* is any substance that is designed to prevent or treat diseases, whereas a *drug* is designed to produce a specific reaction inside the body.[38] While there is overlap between the two types of substances, Perdue Pharmaceutical exercised deliberate misrepresentation of OxyContin in the minds of the consumer by allowing consumers to assume that their doctor prescribed OxyContin as a medication, when clearly it was being prescribed to create a "reaction" of pain relief, not disease "treatment."

The result has been an epidemic of drug dependence and destruction of human life. Its marketing was misleading enough that Purdue Pharmaceutical pleaded guilty in 2007 to a federal criminal count of misbranding the drug "with intent to defraud and mislead the public," paying $635 million in penalties.[39] This discussion is not to diminish the pain and suffering of the chronically ill or to admonish the compassion that medical doctors have for their patients but instead to underscore the lucrative "businesses of healthcare." Perdue Pharmaceutical received nothing more than a financial slap on the wrist for the destruction of lives due to addiction and deaths. On average, it has been estimated that, on a global scale, 100,000 people die from OxyContin abuse per year.[40] Purdue's income for OxyContin in 2011 was $3.1 billion. The original patent for OxyContin expired in 2013, reducing their revenues to a mere $1.9 billion due to generics. Pain drugs like OxyContin have an even greater value in the illicit street drug market. Purdue has taken steps to eliminate the possibility of crushing the pills for illegal street sales, but in doing so it may make doctors more comfortable prescribing it, an outcome Purdue is hoping for. The result could be an even greater number of invisible addicts.[41]

The "Business" of Healthcare

It makes one wonder if this blatant misuse of logic and common sense is part of the marketing strategy of a larger game. Magicians are famous for their "sleight of hand." Can we be participating in an elaborate illusion where the reward is always held just beyond our grasp? We have been trained to adhere to the tenets of conventional medicine yet not question who or to what extent these tenets benefit us. I would think "brainwashing" would be an acceptable reason, but no one seems to be held against their will. So, how can one explain the predicament of logic and common sense not playing a part in the demise of our healthcare system? People seem happy complaining about not being able to afford healthcare without huge subsidies. They often use their healthcare misfortunes as a "red badge of courage," more concerned that they are not as bad off as their neighbor. Fear of the unknown has overcome common sense when dealing with our healthcare system.

We are in a place in time where right and wrong somehow have no meaning because of the numerous shades of gray in healthcare. We have all heard the arguments and have witnessed the proof of the demise of our present healthcare system, yet we can't seem to move toward the logical direction of a non-chemical approach to healing or the dictatorial principles of a single payer, government-run healthcare system. It is my opinion that there are forces at play that keep us content arguing over the type of technology, the generation of new drugs, or the degree of insurance coverage. In other words, we are content discussing the "candy" while the issue of running the "candy store" is ignored.

It has been said that all things of value must make sense. Our present healthcare system direction seems to lack that basic component. Individual physicians are losing their identity in favor of a corporate approach to healthcare. Individual doctors' offices are becoming a thing of the past. Physicians are being faced with insurance participation requirements that stifle their income and compromise their practice abilities. The resulting conclusion is that the present direction of healthcare has less to do with delivering better health than with providing for the "business" of healthcare. We must understand that, continuing to stay the course is not in our best interest. We can start by asking some basic questions:

1. If our government is truly interested in healing and in the safety of its people, how can they justify one quarter million related medically induced deaths per year?[42]

2. If our government is really interested in bringing economic sanity to healthcare, how can they justify allocating 17.9% of GDP in 2012, rising to 20% of GDP in 2021?[43] By comparison, all proven natural healthcare technologies and treatments combined make up only 1.9% of the total healthcare bill?

3. If our government is truly for medical and personal independence (our constitutional rights), why legislate healthcare mandates that remove individual healthcare choices? Example: Every person over sixty-five becomes dependent on the government entitlement program "Medicare," a one-size-fits-all entitlement that discourages independent thinking and freedom of choice.

4. In 1909, Henry Ford inadvertently gave the best analogy after producing the Model T Ford, the first mass-produced automobile in America: "Any customer can have a car painted any color that he wants so long as it is black." Hmmm!

5. If we are truly a democratic republic, why do all medical mandates stem from the World Trade Organization, which is an international organization instituted for the purpose of controlling world activities? The US agreed to the WTO's "General Agreement on Trade in Services" (GATS), which establishes binding legal obligations limiting local policies regarding healthcare services.[44]

6. If the FDA was truly established to protect us from harmful products, why have so many approved drugs been removed due to their harmful and sometimes deadly effects, in some instances only to be replaced by even more harmful drugs?

7. If health is dependent on the body better adapting to its environment, why are vaccines being created to stop every living adaptive process?

- Vaccines stop natural body adapting via chemicals and toxic microbes.
- If vaccines truly work, why does the government have to mandate them with dire consequences (i.e., no shot could mean no school or social services taking children away from parents)?
- If vaccines cause harm in up to 10% of the cases, how come the pharmaceutical companies that make them, the medical personnel who administer them, and the governmental agencies that approve and mandate them (FDA) are totally immune from prosecution or to malpractice or wrongful death claims?

These are just of a few of the questions that should be asked about our healthcare system. If appropriate questions are asked, certain facts will become clear:

1. This system is designed to discourage natural healing with disincentives to the open marketplace. Private companies cannot get their products or research to the open market.
2. This system decentralizes related healthcare industries by legislating the profits out of a free enterprise system.
3. This system controls the flow of money to the industry through the World Trade Organization, the Federal Trade Commission, and even the Internal Revenue Service.
4. This system slowly disarms the masses and dominates the direction of healthcare.
5. This system produces government entitlement programs for everything in healthcare.
6. This system forces people to get used to "someone else" paying for their health needs.
7. Once government has total control over healthcare, they can easily begin to remove more and more freedoms, very slowly under the guise of the "common good."
8. Soon you will realize that you have no freedoms left—only government programs.

Does this sound like the "democracy" that our founding fathers wrote about in the Declaration of Independence and spelled out explicitly in our Constitution? I think not. Government was never designed to "own" any part of the sovereign rights of the states or the people. It was not designed to interfere with everyday life. Government was to provide for the "Common Defense" and uphold the laws of the land.

Government in Healthcare

Those who have studied world economics and world politics know that these are not the actions of a democratic republic but are in line with socialism. Socialism is the slow, nonviolent government takeover of all goods and services to its people. Socialism pretends to protect and "father" its people by offering entitlement programs in all aspects of the economy for the good of the people. It slowly tries to separate and redistribute the wealth of the nation so that there is no "power base" left to bargain from. Socialism offers a government-controlled centralization of all activities, including healthcare. Unfortunately, in the end, socialism leaves no room for personal freedom—the very freedom we, as a country, have fought to protect for over two hundred years.

This discussion is not only about healthcare but about the basis of our understanding of the American healthcare system. Democratic forms of government do not seek to control but instead encourage the marketplace to set the benchmarks. When the American medical marketplace becomes alien to the other American economic marketplaces, one must question why. Why destroy the competitive insurance marketplace in healthcare in favor of a massive centralized single-payer system, void of competition? How democratic can "controlled" insurance be? Obviously, it is not intended to save money, as it was presented. Medical costs have skyrocketed with the addition of the federal Affordable Healthcare Act. In fact, medical doctors are mere pawns of this system, needed only for their licenses to secure business profits. They are paid stipends for their services based on governmental allowances (codes). They have mandates as to how to practice and what to prescribe based on timetables, not patient needs. Prevention is merely a euphemism for treatment. One cannot practice prevention in a system requiring disease to survive.

History is very clear: those who give in to others controlling their daily lives will ultimately lose their freedoms to those forces.

This is not only about our medical healthcare system; it is about our freedom to maintain our democratic way of life. Too often discussions of this type are ushered out as conspiracy by "kooks" who can't make it in society. This is the very reason informed people prefer to maintain silence; the very weapon used by socialism.

Government agencies have no business in healthcare. A centralized governmental control over healthcare is about control over the money and direction in healthcare, not the healthcare per se. The motives of a large, centralized government are clearly to control the wealth and power our healthcare system generates. The financial gains of the vast pharmaceutical reserves and resources are no different from the financial gains from energy reserves and resources. America is on course to spend over two hundred billion dollars on pharmaceutical medications and prescription drugs. To put this in perspective, that is more money than the federal government spends on education, agriculture, transportation, and the environment combined. What industry can you name that can increase its profits fifteen to twenty percent a year, doubling every five years? Our government allows pharmaceutical companies to control the testing of new drugs, designing trials to suit its interests, not the consumers'. According to the FDA, "It is the responsibility of the company seeking to market a drug to test it and submit evidence that it is safe and effective."[45] It is the job of the FDA to "review" the data presented by the pharmaceutical company's drug approval application and propose appropriate labeling. We were led to believe that the FDA has massive testing facilities, where each drug is thoroughly tested before approval. The FDA has no such testing labs

In 2015, the FDA approved 55 new drug applications, some with an annual market value, per person, of $14,000.[46] As you might imagine, there is a lot of critical data to be analyzed. The reality is that clinical data alone does not ensure safety. To assist in the approval process, the FDA employs "Bayesian" statistical analysis, which provides a formal mathematical method for combining prior information with current information at the design stage, during the conduct of the trial, and at the analysis stage.[47] In simple English, Bayesian analysis is the "best guess" outcome analysis, based on statistics rather than on actual patient clinical trials. So how safe are approved FDA drugs? One only has to look at the one-third failure rate of some pharmaceutical drugs to understand why the FDA, the pharmaceutical companies, and the doctors who prescribe the drugs are immune from prosecution.

Drugs getting pulled from the market are the result of "human guinea pig" experimentation. The one factor not predicable in Bayesian statistical analysis is how a particular drug will react in the human body. This factor is determined, after years of medical use, by adverse reactions rates or deaths that override clinical benefits. *All* pharmaceutical drugs are synthetic; many of them are toxic to the human species yet demonstrate "some" therapeutic benefit in pharmaceutical company clinical testing with lab animals. Is it fair to say, therefore, that there is a dangerous "benefit to detriment" relationship in all pharmaceutical prescription drugs?

Apart from the astronomical cost of some pharmaceutical drugs, one can say that drugs potentially can save lives. Medical costs have skyrocketed, in part, due to the enormous costs involved in research and development (R&D) of the drugs. The perceived notion is that pharmaceutical companies need to recover their initial investments in producing drugs. The hidden secret is that virtually all research and development costs for new drugs are paid for by investor groups prior to the FDA drug approval. Pharmaceutical companies are therefore partnered with investors, who attain huge returns on their investments. The ultimate market pricing of the drugs is based on what the market will bear. What price would one pay for a possible lifesaving drug? Drugs have become the default treatment in medicine.

Our medical healthcare system reeks of socialism, where the government controls the reserves and resources as the means to control the masses. Administrations have come and gone, filled with the rhetoric of nondemocratic ideals, especially in healthcare. With the election of Donald Trump came a glimmer of hope for repealing "the (not so) Affordable Care Act." As of this writing, the repeal and replacement of Obamacare has proven to be as elusive as ever due to entrenched government strongholds. With the total Republican takeover of the Senate, the House of Representatives, and the Presidency, the "elites" within each party continue to protect the financial government windfall that is medical entitlement programs. Of course, "we the people" are treated to a daily dose of human hardships rather than the return of "freedom of choice" that represented "free market capitalism." The socialistic mantra is to utilize compassion as a replacement for critical thinking, resulting in an appeal to the "heartstrings" rather than the intellect. Without the controlling factors required for socialism to take over; when the distribution of wealth no longer has a vehicle of implementation, socialism ceases to exist. The interesting part is that the average person does not even know what is happening.

Modern medicine is forming a disconnect between science and the universal forces of life itself. We have gone from a culture of observation to one of intervention. To be able to change life's rhythms to suit a hypothetical outcome is not within the purview of scientific method, yet it exists at every level of our medical system. Below is a review of the facts of just two significant components of our healthcare system never openly revealed to the public: vaccines and cancer.

Vaccines

To challenge the veil of "microbial mystery" that today's "Medicine Man" and pharmaceutical industry push on society is considered by the medical establishment as conspiracy theory or even heretical. In general, there are no mysteries about microbes. As a species, we are put on this planet to live harmoniously with all other living creatures. Fortunately, we don't live in swamps or thrive on organic waste, but microbial species do. It is the job of microbes to stabilize the waste products of our existence, while we benefit from their byproducts. Perfect examples of this synergy are that there is no possible way that we can digest food without bacteria or produce vital hormones in the absence of certain microbes.

There are reasons that some species of microbes are harmful to humans and will infect us. Yet even this has a benefit to humans. We have an immune system capable of producing almost any antidote; however, we must first be exposed to the harmful bacteria or virus naturally before the human immune system can send it to our internal lab. In other words, you must get infected first to get healthy for life (adaptive). Once the body figures out what the DNA structure of the microbe is, it produces an antibody against that specific harmful bacteria or virus, in effect exposing the microbe to its own death machine. This goes under the title "survival of the species." Those within the species strong enough to recognize and produce antitoxins against invading microbes survive, and those that do not, perish. It's nothing personal, just the ways of life. We are led to believe that life is always "good," as though there are good and evil inherent in life. The truth is that life is about thriving or surviving. In death, life finds the most expeditious way of termination.

Having made the above statements, we can now discuss what the modern Medicine Man has to say about it. The Medicine Man wants us to believe that microbes are our enemies, that modern medicine has a chemical antidote to every microbe, thus ensuring the wellbeing of the human species without depending on the immune system. Nice marketing strategy, but it is simply not true.

The concept of injecting a microbial toxin (vaccine), attenuated (weakened) or otherwise, directly into the bloodstream is a misunderstanding of nature itself. This process bypasses the normal mode of entry into the body, hoping that the body will respond in the same way it does when contracting a microbe naturally. To the Medicine Man, it is heresy to challenge the use of vaccines, a favorite tool used to discourage critical thinking.

The Father of the Germ Theory is actually Robert Koch, yet it was Louis Pasteur who got the credit. Pasteur himself, in one of the most quoted deathbed statements perhaps of all time, stated that "his rivals had been right, and that it was not the germ that caused the disease, but rather the environment in which the germ was found."[48] Further scientific evidence was presented by Professor Antoine Bechamp, who stated that Pasteur's Germ Theory was inaccurate because it did not take into account that germs mutate depending on the acidity and toxicity of the body. Therefore, vaccines are adding microorganisms and contributing to the toxic internal environment left behind by vaccine components, which allow the organisms to further mutate into more serious disease entities.[49] To this day, the charade of the Germ Theory still prevails and makes for great pharmaceutical marketing and a source for fear leading to compliance within the population.

One needs to look no further than the Covid-19 pandemic to understand how microbes can be used by Big Pharma to alter life itself. For the first time in modern immunology, a virus has been blamed for a worldwide pandemic without ever isolating a single, intact virus. Simply put, the Polymerase Chain Reaction Test (PCR) was approved by the World Health Organization (WHO) to test for a virus that had not yet been isolated. This is not just medical deception; it reeks of deep criminal intent. According to Dr. Anthony Fauci, the PCR test is performed by running the viral sample through a series of up to thirty-five "cycles" (sensitivity cycles). More than thirty-five cycles renders the PCR test meaningless because the test picks up inactive or nonrelevant viruses.[50] However, the WHO approved the PCR test to be performed by labs at up to thirty cycles, thus yielding "pandemic level" false positives.

The pandemic led to unrealistic levels of population compliance that literally destroyed the middle-class economy in most major cities. It should be noted that on the same day that the CDC approved the Pfizer Covid-19 vaccine (December 14, 2020), the WHO revised its PCR testing protocols in recognition of the false positives that led to unnecessary lockdowns and quarantines.[51] In doing so, the WHO intentionally "saved face," appearing to be sympathetic to the suffering of the people, while the actual intent was to dramatically reduce the number of Covid-19 cases, making the vaccine look very effective.

The developer of the PCR (Polymerase Chain Reaction) test was Kary Mullis, PhD. In June of 2019, Mullis made a "jaw dropping" statement upon realizing that his PCR test was being used to "diagnose" the presence of the Covid-19 virus. He stated that, "This test should NEVER be used to diagnose ANY viral infection. It was designed to amplify your DNA samples to find ANY past viral fragments."[52] In doing so, Mullis put the entire Covid vaccine protocol in question. Mullis was attempting to protect his name and PCR test from possible liability, since it was being used for an unintended purpose. This didn't sit well with Big Pharma, the CDC, FDA, nor the AMA, who pressured all media sources to bury the Mullis statements. Mullis continued to find venues to expose the truth, and on August 7, 2019, Kary Mullis suspiciously died, just two months after making his statement. Kary Mullis was a noted critic of climate change and Dr. Anthony Fauci.[53]

The Covid-19 vaccines are the first vaccines in history containing NO VIRAL or MICROBIAL components designed to give the body's immune system a weakened version of the disease in order to assist building antibodies against the real thing. Covid vaccines are 100% experimental "spike proteins" that alter how the body responds to immune challenges. In a recent MIT study, researchers called "To Suspend Covid-19 Vaccinations Upon Discovery of Spike Proteins in the Nucleus (DNA) of Living Cells." The implication of this study is that once DNA is altered by a spike protein, the change is permanent, can be passed on through childbirth and could alter life itself in ways still unknown.[54]

According to the World Health Organization's chief scientist, Dr. Soumya Swaminathan, "At present we are not confident Covid vaccines prevent the transmission of Covid-19; even people who have received the vaccine could infect others."[55] The CDC states that the Covid vaccines are not designed to prevent the person from getting Covid but will possibly reduce the symptoms of Covid.

In case the message is not clear enough, consider the following: The 2020 Seasonal Flu Has Dropped by 98% Worldwide as It Is Re-labeled Covid-19:[56]

Worldwide, seasonal influenza is around 98% lower this year than in earlier flu seasons. The CDC says: "The percentage of respiratory specimens testing positive for influenza at clinical laboratories is $1/10^{th}$ of 1%." It is clear from this that the common seasonal flu merely is being called Covid-19. This fraudulent increase in Covid "cases" has led to mass hysteria, lockdowns, quarantines, mask-wearing, social distancing, and economic collapse.

As of this writing the US death toll from Covid-19 is approximately 700,000. It should be clearly noted that CDC and FDA have fraudulently altered the definitions of "herd immunity" by stating that herd immunity is acquired by the number of "vaccinated" individuals in a population instead of the number of an "exposed" population to a virus, acquiring natural immunity. Similarly, death certificates have been altered to list Covid-19 as the primary cause of death, even if the actual cause of death was due to an auto accident but the person also tested positive for Covid-19. By comparison, the World Health Organization estimated the 2018–2019 seasonal flu deaths at 49,000. The World Health Organization states that the actual deaths from Covid-19, without any comorbidities or definition tampering, is 6% of the 700,000 or 42,000 deaths, which is less than the 2018–2019 seasonal flu deaths.[57]

Quarantines, lockdowns, and social distancing are unique to the Covid-19 pandemic. Prior pandemics simply ran their natural course without major interruptions in everyday life. Infected people stayed home until the virus passed, allowing natural (acquired) immunity to end the pandemic. It should be noted that during the 1969 Hong Kong Flu pandemic, the big event of the year was Woodstock, with over 400,000 people attending and where literally none of the present Covid restrictions were observed. Times were certainly different, but pandemics have one thing in common: they kill the most vulnerable; it's not personal, it's life.[58]

Chairman of Reform California, Carl DeMaio, is calling for an audit because, in a typical year, San Diego County gets over 17,073 reported cases of influenza. This year, however, which is well into the flu season, only 36 cases of the flu have been reported. He says that, if Covid stats are used to shut down the economy and to take people's livelihoods away, the data should be audited.

The media, in conjunction with the Medicine Man, influences popular thought when it comes to vaccines. In July 2013, the pro-vaccine forces got their chance to flare up with the hiring of Jenny McCarthy on the popular TV program The View. Within one day, the media gossip writers came out with: "Jenny McCarthy's "View" Hiring Met with Outrage Due to Her Anti-Vaccine Views." The *Huffington Post* ran an article by Jack Mirkinson stating, "Executives at ABC should be ashamed of themselves for offering McCarthy a regular platform on which she can peddle denialism and fear to the parents of young children who may have legitimate questions about vaccine safety." Presumably, those executives have decided that the revenues Jenny McCarthy might generate are worth more than the truth.[59] The truth is that Jenny McCarthy has an autistic child as the result of a vaccine and that no serious effort has ever attempted to answer the vaccination/autism connection, nor will it ever. That same year (1993), British surgeon and researcher Dr. Andrew Wakefield published his report on the MMR/autism connection in *The Lancet*. He too was met with outrage for suggesting such a connection (discussed in depth later on in this chapter).

Many assume that vaccines and "shots" against microbes attack the right microbe. What is never considered is that no microbe falls for the same trick twice. Even if the vaccine hits its mark, the microbe, being a living entity as we are, adapts to the onslaught and mutates to another form that is not affected by the shot. The microbes that adapt are called vaccine-resistant microbes. The Medicine Man counters resistant microbes with "herd immunity," a belief that if enough of a population (95%, says the CDC) is vaccinated, the infective microbe will somehow go away. Vaccines, at best, offer temporary immunity.[60] Therefore, regardless of herd immunity, the protection vaccines offer is short-lived. Vaccination is not a permanent solution but falls under the category of a good medical marketing tool. A review from the Cochrane Collaboration, a widely respected research-analysis team, went over all the available flu vaccine evidence and entered its exhaustive and astounding conclusion:

1. In healthy adults, no flu vaccine delivers protection from the flu. It doesn't protect against transmission of flu viruses from person to person, either (herd immunity). How can the group be immune when vaccines are doing nothing to prevent the free movement of germs from person to person?
2. The promotion, pandering, scare tactics, media coverage, and "expert medical opinions" are all useless, worthless, and irrelevant, due to poorly constructed, pharmaceutically biased and misleading data.
3. Billions of dollars of financed lies about flu vaccines were just that—lies.
4. Since flu vaccines do not protect against flu or even stop the transmission of flu viruses from person to person, the so-called "rehearsing" of the immune system via the "flu shot" is merely somebody's fantasy story—a legend, a myth.[61]

It is widely accepted that vaccines are not perfect, but few have any knowledge of why. The flu shot does not work on sixty percent of people because the flu shots do not produce the right antibodies; therefore the body doesn't even recognize it is there. Worse, by adding an unfamiliar microbial concoction directly into the bloodstream, bypassing all the body's natural "T" and "B" lymphocyte and Immunoglobulin A (IgA) defense systems (which are designed specifically to categorize incoming microbes), the shot leaves the body totally vulnerable to a microbial infection it would not have developed if the lymphocytes had been allowed to do their job. In other words, the shot can potentially give a vaccinated person the flu, *which would ordinarily happen in sixty percent of cases.* The Medicine Man (which includes the pharmaceutical industry) knows this and counters the argument by attenuating the virus (partially or totally killing it) to the point that its DNA is rendered useless before putting it into a shot. The result is that you cannot get the flu from the shot anymore (because it is a dead microbe); however, they neglect to mention that you can't produce any antibodies, either.

Flu vaccines take one year to cultivate in sufficient quantities to make mass vaccines. Vaccines are specific to one microbe. That means that a vaccine for one microbe will not work on another. Let's do the math. There are 16 known strains with 144 possible subtypes for Influenza "A" viruses alone, according to CDC estimates.[62] A year in advance, vaccine manufacturers have to choose which virus and subtype will be the culprit that produces the flu the following year. Their chances of getting it right are not always predictable. Prior stats on the flu were that 65–75% of people who got the flu shot got the flu anyway (no real surprise here). To increase their odds of getting it right, vaccine makers now have a trivalent vaccine, meaning that they mixed the top three predicted viruses the year before and hit you with a triple whammy vaccine. That decreased their odds of missing the right microbe but did nothing to stop the flu, since these new concoctions were also killed viruses. But, hey, it makes for good Research and Development marketing to the public. Surely the flu kills people; so do asthma, pneumonia, and just about any other diseases, *if the body's immune system is not up for the challenge.* To perpetuate the inconsistencies, myths, and outright lies, legislation and "slick marketing" are the only recourse. Here's a stat you will never hear: "baby aspirin kill 5,000 babies per year due to intestinal bleeding from the aspirin."[63]

To pacify a concerned public, each state government developed "vaccine waivers" to cover possible reasons individuals may choose not to receive a vaccine. Originally there were three possible vaccine waivers: medical, religious, and philosophical. Presently, only the medical waiver is recognized in all fifty states, with the religious waiver acceptable in almost all states. Oddly, the actual reason for vaccine waivers is not for your protection at all but for the Medicine Man. Diseases like Guillain-Barre syndrome, Tourette syndrome, Tardive Dyskinesia— and even death—are documented effects stemming from the vaccine program; it is the waiver that protects the Medicine Man from prosecution.

During the rapid development of new vaccines also came increased adverse reactions of varying severity. Pediatricians were at a loss to adequately explain why these severe reactions occurred, since the vaccine makers had assured the medical establishment that their products were safe and effective. Mounting lawsuits against the vaccine makers resulted a petition to Congress by the pharmaceutical companies providing the vaccines to provide legal protection from lawsuits. The pharmaceutical position was that they would no longer be able to supply vaccines to the public if they continually faced lawsuits. As a result, the Centers for Disease Control, along with Congress, granted total immunity from product liability, not only to the pharmaceutical industry but to the doctors, including the pediatricians who dispense the vaccines. In short, vaccines are the only industry that can produce products without oversight or prosecution.

If a child had a life-altering reaction to a vaccine, parents had no recourse, since all involved in the vaccine industry are immune from prosecution or product liability. Further, pediatricians had the ability to tell parents that they had the option of a vaccine waiver but could choose not to apply for one. Of course, the same pediatricians told parents that if they did not follow the CDC's vaccine recommended program, the pediatrician would not see them as patients ever again. The vaccine programs are sold not by their virtue but based on fear.

America has followed CDC guidelines based on their testing of drugs for safety and efficacy. Would it surprise you to know that the CDC does NOT have any testing labs or facilities to actually test vaccines or drugs? So how can the CDC approve vaccine or drug safety? Before the CDC and FDA licenses (approves) a vaccine, the vaccine is "tested extensively by its manufacturer." CDC scientists and medical professionals carefully evaluate all available information about the vaccine to determine its safety and effectiveness.[64] So, we have the equivalent of the pharmaceutical "fox" guarding the henhouse. So, we have the equivalent of the pharmaceutical "fox" guarding the henhouse. It must be clearly understood that there is no "arms-length" relationship between the CDC and vaccine manufacturers. Robert F. Kennedy Jr. stated that "the CDC is not an independent agency. It is a vaccine company. The CDC owns over 20 vaccine patents and sells about 4.6 billion dollars of vaccines every year."

To pacify the population, the government set up the National Vaccine Injury Compensation Program, designed to deflect liability from vaccine makers and doctors and provide monetary compensation for vaccine-induced debilitating illness or death. The pharmaceutical industry applies to the program seventy-five cents per dose of vaccine. To date over 3.5 billion dollars has been awarded to vaccine-injured children. To recover lost income, the pharmaceutical industry simply doubled or tripled the cost per dose of most vaccines. Common sense would dictate that if all vaccines are safe and effective (as stated by the CDC), there would have been no reason to award 3.5 billion dollars to families affected by vaccine-induced debilitating illness or death. In 2006 the drug research unit at Southampton University published a survey of reporting incidence in the international journal of toxicology and drug experience (Drug safety 2006; 29(5):385-96). "In total," state L. Hazell and S. A. Shakir, "37 studies using a wide variety of surveillance methods were identified from 12 countries. These generated 43 numerical estimates of under-reporting. The median under-reporting rate across the 37 studies was 94%." Incredibly, then, 94% of vaccine side-effects are consistently not reported around the world.[65]

Pediatricians are required to follow the CDC's vaccine schedule for their patients and are punished financially if they do not. Insurance companies like Blue Cross/Blue Shield (BC/BS), in conjunction with pharmaceutical financial backing, set up the Pediatrician Incentive Program that rewards pediatricians who fully follow vaccine guidelines. The incentive program requires that the pediatrician have a 63% compliance rate for patients receiving *all* required vaccines. If just one vaccine is missing, the pediatrician's score is "0" for that patient. If compliant, BC/BS will pay the pediatrician $400 per patient. The average American pediatrician has 1,546 patients. If all patients are fully vaccinated, the pediatrician will receive $618,400 just for being compliant. Additionally, the pharmaceutical companies will pay $18/vaccine dose ($1,242 per patient) to the pediatrician if his patients have received all 69 required doses. So, let's do the math. BC/BS will pay the average pediatrician $618,400 if they have a 63% vaccine compliance ratio, while the pharmaceutical industry pays the pediatrician $1,920,132 if all their patients receive the required 69 doses. That is potentially a whopping $2,538,532 dollars just for administering all vaccines. Of course, this does not include the pediatrician's office visit charge. Is it any wonder that pediatricians require vaccines, regardless of their personal views or your desire for exemption?[66]

Ever wonder why the various strains of flu seem to have strange names attached to them or why each flu season is touted as the worst season in decades? The Hong Kong Flu, Russian Flu, Asiatic Flu, Swine Flu, and Bird Flu are just a few. Why not the Brooklyn Flu or the Idaho Flu? The reason is that giving foreign names that are known antagonists to American thinking suggests artificial danger from the flu. The Swine Flu, for example, never actually happened in the US and had almost nothing to do with pigs. The Chairman of the Health Committee of the Council of Europe, Dr. Wolfgang Wodarg, started a hearing about the relationship between vaccine manufacturers and the World Health Organization. Dr. Wodarg stated, "The swine flu was a falsified pandemic, a mild flu, with the aim of increasing the profits of the vaccine producers by tapping countries for their meager health budgets and exposing people to risks with untested vaccines." He calls it one of the "greatest medical scandals of the century."[67]

To further secure the secrecy of possible vaccine-induced diseases and halt any legal or moral challenge to their administration, the Centers for Disease Control "stacked the deck" with its reporting of adverse reactions to vaccines. Section 42 300aa-25 in the Vaccine Injury Table states, "If the first symptom of these injuries/conditions occurs within seven days, it is presumed that the vaccine was the cause of the injury or condition unless another cause is found."[68] It is this author's opinion that the CDC utilizes "crystal ball" science, stating in effect that adverse reactions cannot occur outside the time specified in the Vaccine Injury Table. The United States' legal standard defines vaccines as "unavoidably unsafe products that are quite incapable of being made safe for their intended and ordinary use."[69]

Apparently, the CDC is unable to answer the overwhelming yet "anecdotal" evidence of the occasional sudden onset of horrific adverse reaction or diseases after vaccine administration. It should also be clearly understood that no matter how overwhelming the evidence, vaccines are at best "incapable of being made safe for their intended and ordinary use." Vaccines will nonetheless be a mainstay and required component "covered" (without copay) by Obamacare and most likely any future revision or replacement healthcare system. Vaccines will become part of the "nationalized" healthcare system and, as such, will be bought and sold under US government guidelines. Vaccines will become tied to participation in government programs, making their increased usage dwarf present levels. With the US government becoming a sole distributor of vaccines (massive purchasing power), vaccines stocks could potentially quadruple according to CDC predictions, giving vaccines inflated market shares having little to do with their intended usage.

Since vaccine makers are no longer liable for product failures, there is little government oversight other than the review of pharmaceutical vaccine data produced by the vaccine manufacturers. Product safety and efficacy are of major concern in all industries. Pharmaceutical drugs must go through stringent clinical trials using double blind, placebo (a substance that has no therapeutic effect, used as a control in testing new drugs) control groups; however, vaccines are put to market under different standards. Almost all clinical vaccine trials *do not* use placebos but instead use substances already found in the vaccine or previous versions of the vaccine. As counterintuitive and unscientific as this sounds, vaccine makers can legally skew safety and efficacy results. For example, the Gardasil vaccine, which contains the most "aluminum" adjuvant (nonmicrobial preservative or molecular enhancer) of all vaccines, uses "aluminum" as the placebo during clinical trials. The result is that the vaccine and the placebo react similarly, giving the appearance of product safety. The Prevnar 11 (Pneumococcal pneumonia vaccine) used its previous version (Prevnar 9) as the placebo, thus removing any validity to the purported safety of the vaccine. This is total insanity but explains why the CDC and pharmaceutical companies can claim that vaccines are safe and effective.

It must be clearly understood that there is no "arms-length" relationship between the CDC and vaccine manufactures. Robert F. Kennedy Jr. stated that "the CDC is not an independent agency. It is a vaccine company. The CDC owns over twenty vaccine patents and sells about 4.6 billion dollars of vaccines every year."[70]

A final historical observation was revealed in Death Rates from Infectious Disease in Australia and in the text, "Immunization Theory vs. Reality," infectious disease killers like Polio, Smallpox, Whooping Cough, Measles, Tuberculosis, Scarlet Fever, and others were all at their most virulent between 1890 and 1930. On average, the death rates for every listed infectious disease were at their lowest levels (down 95%) when respective vaccines were introduced. Conveniently not mentioned is that local health departments were formed and made substantial progress in disease prevention activities, including sewage disposal, water treatment, food safety, organized solid waste disposal, and public education about hygienic practices.[71] All tables and graphs rating the effectiveness of vaccines against infectious diseases begin when the vaccines are first administered, ignoring the plummeting tendencies of the infectious disease that have occurred prior to the vaccine. Another coincidence, I presume!

Autism
In the 1950s, 1 in 10,000 children was diagnosed with autism. In the 1970s and 1980s, about 1 out of every 2,000 children received this diagnosis. By the late 1990s it was 1 in 1,000, then 1 in 150, 1 in 88, and now a new government survey suggests that the prevalence of autism is 1 in 50.[72] This is beyond tragic, illogical, and a shocking testimony that our modern healthcare system has ignored obvious correlations, including the relationship between the massive increase in mandatory vaccines and multi-dose vaccines like the Measles, Mumps and Rubella (MMR) shot with autism.

Early research in virology and childhood infectious diseases revealed that when the Measles and the Mumps were contracted naturally within close time proximity, the rate of Irritable Bowel Syndrome (IBS) skyrocketed. One of the signature markers for autism includes Irritable Bowel Syndrome. Japanese researchers tested this theory and found that the MMR shot did, in fact, increase the rate of IBS because of the introduction of the Measles and Mumps viruses simultaneously, similarly to a natural event of Measles and Mumps within an abbreviated time span. However, it should be noted that unless the person is extremely immune compromised, contracting Measles and Mumps at the same time statistically never occurs. Japanese researchers found that when administering the Measles and Mumps vaccines separately, over time and after the age of three, the rate of IBS dropped dramatically, as did autism rates. Japan has since given the MMR shot as separate components. Dr Hiroki Nakatani, director of the Infectious Disease Division at Japan's Ministry of Health and Welfare, said that "giving individual vaccines cost twice as much as MMR but we believe it is worth it."[73]

In 1993, former British surgeon and researcher Dr. Andrew Wakefield published an extensive study in the British medical journal *The Lancet* on the relationship between the MMR shot and IBS and found that when the MMR shot was given separately the rates of IBS and autism dropped dramatically. His conclusion was not that the MMR shot caused autism but that it was statistically safer to administer the MMR components separately and after age three, similar to the Japanese findings. Dr. Wakefield is a proponent of vaccines but sought only to make them safer.

As a result of Dr. Wakefield's study, the pharmaceutical giants essentially ignored Wakefield's conclusions and proceeded, instead, to discredit Dr. Wakefield's research as fraudulent. In 1998, the US government asked a federal court to keep thousands of documents that allegedly linked autism to childhood vaccines away from public view to ensure that no actual or casual cause/effect relationship could ever be documented. *The British Medical Journal* (BMJ) attempted to further discredit Dr. Wakefield by printing a retraction of Dr. Wakefield's research, simply claiming that his work was fraudulent and that he had ulterior motives. In essence, Dr. Wakefield was guilty by fiat, losing his license to practice medicine and having his reputation ruined. Dr. Wakefield never had the chance to refute the BMJ claims officially. The truth will never be told, since the Medicine Man's unholy monetary alliance with the pharmaceutical industry trumps justice.

In 2003, the US Congress commissioned the CDC to do a study attempting to link the MMR shot to autism. The result of the study demonstrated no link between the MMR shot and autism. In 2005, Dr. Brian Hooker, one of the lead researchers in the CDC study, expressed his awareness that the CDC study was intentionally altered by excluding critical data that actually demonstrated a 300% increase in the rates of IBS in African American boys and autism spectrum disorders in general but remained silent.

In 2013 Dr. Wakefield got an unexpected reprieve from a CDC whistleblower. The scientist, Dr. William Thompson, confessed that the CDC had intentionally omitted crucial data in their final report revealing a relationship between the MMR vaccine and autism. Dr. Thompson and Dr. Hooker provided the collaborative evidence to Dr. Wakefield, revealing the confidential data that was ordered to be destroyed by their colleagues at the CDC. Dr. Thompson had made copies of the actual data before destroying the studies data.

Dr. Hooker was compelled to speak up, since he has a son with autism. If there were indeed a link between autism and the MMR, Congress needed the evidence to bring to the public's attention. In September of 2014, Dr. Thompson turned over thousands of pages of CDC documents to Congress via Rep. Bill Posey of Florida. The documents revealed the lies told to the public by the CDC regarding the link between thimerosal-containing vaccines and neurodevelopmental disorders (including autism), as well as the links between the MMR vaccine and autism in African American males. CDC scientists colluded to cover up a relationship between the timing of the MMR vaccine and autism that was first discovered in November of 2001. Rather than reporting the results to the public, all data regarding this relationship was destroyed at a secret meeting held sometime in August/September of 2002.[74]

Vaxxed, the movie,[75] and the documentary "The Truth About Vaccines" examine the evidence behind the appalling coverup committed by the CDC, the government agency charged with protecting the health of American citizens. In the documentary, Dr. Wakefield explains how his original research was altered by omitting crucial data that led to his conclusion that the MMR shot had significant potential for a skyrocketing increase in autism. This was a coverup of the most catastrophic epidemic of our lifetime.

Since the intentional revelation of the CDC coverup of the potential MMR/autism connection, over 300 research scientists from around the world have duplicated Dr. Wakefield's results and conclusions in 28 independent studies. Incredibly, as of this writing, searching for the relationship between the MMR shot and autism will yield only that there have been no studies demonstrating even a causal relationship between the MMR vaccine and autism. To ensure no possible chance that the US might follow the lead of Japan in administering the MMR as separate vaccines, the CDC has taken away the right to obtain the MMR vaccine components separately, stating that to do so would hinder compliance with the currently approved vaccine program. The globalists, this time with deep financial interests in vaccine manufacturing, dispense corruption with impunity at the highest levels of organized medicine.

Cancer

As mentioned, my purpose is not to disparage or discredit what has been accomplished in medicine over the years; I intend to expose what is rarely in public view. The most significant medical sacred cow is the cancer industry. With over a third of all medical, pharmaceutical, and research spending and income devoted to cancer, business is booming. Although started in 1913, with help and funding from the Rockefeller Foundation, it was not until the 1950s that the financial support to the American Cancer Society (ACS) skyrocketed. The society's allocation of funds for the fiscal year ending August 31, 2010, lists 72% of funds for running the massive organization, with about 28% going to patient support and research and 16% for prevention, detection, and treatment. In 1950, the cancer rate in the US was roughly 150 per 100,000 people. The 2008 statistics from the CDC show that the cancer rate increased to 543 per 100,000 people developing the disease. The CDC stated in 2011 that the risk of cancer is 1:3, meaning that roughly 33% of all citizens will get cancer in their lifetime—a grim statistic for the American Cancer Society indeed.

Do the math! How effective have the "war on cancer" and the ACS been? How successful are our cancer treatment protocols? The ACS listed cancer cure rates as high as 45% to 55%, yet the Centers for Disease Control states that the cure rate for conventional cancer treatment is less than 3%. How is this possible? The reason the ACS can claim such high rates is that they use a "5-year survival" rate rule. The five-year survival rule is the ability to live for at least five years after diagnosis and treatment. Conventional cancer treatment consisting of chemotherapy or radiation poisoning does kill cancer cells; it also kills healthy cells, while destroying one's immune system or killing the host. This is caused by toxic treatments that leave the patient vulnerable to bacterial and viral infections leading to pneumonia, immune failure, and death. If you survive the cancer treatments and live for five years, but die one day after the five years, even from the same or a different cancer, you are considered successfully "cured" of cancer by conventional treatment, and your number is added to the cure rate roster. This is totally unacceptable and a manipulation of cancer statistics to deceive the general public.

Of course, the motive behind this is the profiteering of the billions of dollars the medical and pharmaceutical industries receive from existing and potential cancer patients. Cancer treatment centers are popping up all over the country, with incredibly sophisticated and expensive technologies, to meet the needs of an ever-growing cancer population. It is difficult to speak of cancer in terms of supply and demand, but the troubling question this brings up is the elephant in the room: With all the technologies and treatment protocols developed to meet the cancer challenges, where is the equivalent effort to find ways to prevent its cause? My family, like most, has been affected by cancer. Having a working knowledge of human physiology, family members made attempts to investigate nontraditional approaches to cancer treatment, including the working factors toward its prevention. My father developed stage 3 prostate cancer with a six- to twelve-month survival expectancy. It was he who decided to investigate viable alternatives, knowing that his life was held in the balance. The result of those efforts was that within six months he was totally cancer free. His was not an isolated case. Reports like this are never touted by the American Cancer Society or the oncology community.

The most celebrated case of medical cancer under-reporting of alternative treatment protocols was demonstrated against Dr. Burzynski. He developed an alternative cancer treatment solely dependent upon natural therapies. His success rate was staggeringly effective but gained no notoriety by the FDA, CDC, or ACS.

In fact, in 2012 the FDA lost its thirteen-year lawsuit against Dr. Burzynski, who broke no laws but the use of nonconventional treatments as a medical doctor.

Dr. Burzynski owns the patent for this alternative treatment, and if it should actually gain FDA approval, not only would it threaten conventional chemotherapy and radiation, but it would also result in billions of dollars of cancer research funds being funneled over to the one single scientist who has exclusive patent rights. Dr. Burzynski is now doing the unthinkable: he is "the first and only scientist in United States history to enter the federal drug approval process for a proprietary [non-conventional] cancer therapy without any financial support from the American government, the pharmaceutical industry, or the cancer establishment."[76]

My purpose is to point out that marketing, profits, and an unholy alliance among the makers of synthetic pharmaceuticals, advanced technologies, and the doctors who prescribe them, is not an arm's length relationship from the vast financial profits but is intimately connected to "regulations and legislations" designed to link cancer treatments to insurance coverages. The cost of an orally administered cancer drug can be up to $11,325 per month. The machine used to close the wound from breast cancer removal can cost the individual $9,000, with an additional $9,000 in chemotherapy treatment for the first year. Some cancer treatments include surgery, chemotherapy, and radiation, which can cost the individual $115,000, not including post-cancer treatments. Who can afford such medical expenses without insurance? The 2015 total estimated healthcare costs of cancer treatment were $87.7 billion, with 2022 estimated costs reaching $158 billion.[77]

Profit always play a part in any industry, with direction favoring the most profitable venues. The cost of alternative healthcare, in general, is 1.6% of our total healthcare industry expenditures. From a pure profit initiative, why would our healthcare system entertain any alternative healthcare protocols? People need to understand that whether or not an alternative treatment protocol works has little to no bearing on the medical establishment. Alternative protocols are not synthetic and therefore return no "patent" profits, rendering them of little value to the medical industry, let alone the insurance industry.

Alternative cancer treatments require affordable "out of pocket" expenses, with little or no counsel from medical experts. My father, who was part of "America's Greatest Generation," lived twelve years longer than his six-month terminal cancer prognosis at the cost of a nice vacation. I am not advocating abandoning traditional medical cancer treatments; this is a personal choice available to a free society. Any government-run healthcare system that mandates one direction of treatment in order to comply with insurance guidelines or other government entitlement programs, under penalty of fines, is socialism. Any doubt as to the dangers of modern drugs, cancer treatments, or vaccines can be seen within the "adverse effects" dialogue of the one-third of all TV advertising that consists of drug commercials. The choice is yours, . . . while we still have a choice.

Obamacare

The pharmaceutical industry is not the only "fibber" in our healthcare system. One must take the time to study and understand that "Patient Protection" and the "Affordable Care Act" of 2010 (Obamacare) are riddled with disinformation and outright lies. The language is so confusing that congressional approval did not come from reading the two-thousand-plus page document but from an outrageous statement by the Speaker of the House, Nancy Pelosi: "We have to pass the bill so that you can find out what is in it."[78] Instead of exercising their constitutional duty to digest the bill and decide whether it was in the best interest of the citizens they represent, Congress passed the bill sight unseen. President Obama stated in 2009 that the Affordable Care Act would reduce the cost of general healthcare to the public from 27% to 2%. Forbes magazine in a May 2013 article stated, "Rate Shock: In California, Obamacare to Increase Individual Health Insurance Premiums by 64–146%."[79] Other source estimates go as high as 169%, depending on the non-medical spending attached to the legislation. Along with this incredible but not-so-surprising fact is that there are mandates for insurance carriers who wish to participate that will force them out of the marketplace should they chose not to comply.

There were once some 153 independent healthcare insurers; after Obamacare only 5 insurance carriers remain. In my opinion, this was the plan all along: force people into a situation where there are no affordable choices, along with required penalty taxes for nonparticipation, setting the stage for the eventual public acceptance of a "single payer government healthcare system" that few want. This forces the alliance between the Medicine Men, the pharmaceutical industry, and a government willing to fundamentally change our founding principles via "entitlements" resulting in a country ripe for a socialized takeover or revolt.

In a quote incorrectly attributed to Donald Trump long before his presidency that covers the salient points that make the Affordable Care Act a "master progressive debacle":

Let me get this straight . . .
We're going to be "gifted" with a health care Plan we are forced to purchase and fined if we don't,
which purportedly covers at least ten million more people, without adding a single new doctor,
but provides for 16,000 new IRS agents,
written by a committee whose chairman says he doesn't understand it,
passed by a Congress that didn't read it but exempted themselves from it,
and signed by a President who smokes,
with funding administered by a treasury chief who didn't pay his taxes,
for which we'll be taxed for four years before any benefits take effect,
by a government which has already bankrupted Social Security and Medicare,
all to be overseen by a surgeon general who is obese, and financed by a country that's broke!!!!!
What the hell could possibly go wrong?[80]

Members of Congress applied for and got a special dispensation from Obamacare, the very law they had approved. Congress, therefore, does not participate in Obamacare but retains its private healthcare coverage, paid for by the American taxpayer. As of the time of this writing, the rest of the population must choose from one of the Obamacare exchanges or be fined by the IRS. Is it just me, or is there something fundamentally wrong with this arrangement? Of course, we know that over ninety percent of Congress never read the bill but signed on anyway. Congressional salaries are paid by taxpayer money; why not get the best for their money? Jimmy Hoffa Jr., who represents "Big Union," stated that he "wants nothing to do with Obamacare since it will fundamentally devastate the traditional 40-hour work week of the middle class." Former Speaker of the House John Boehner, in a press conference on July 9, 2013, stated, "If businesses can get relief from Obamacare the rest of America should, too."[81]

We have *big* government, big unions, and big corporations opting out of Obamacare mandates, yet the rest of America must comply. This incredibly illogical rationale fits into the socialist agenda perfectly, yet few even know it exists. Obamacare will collapse under its own weight if it does not enroll the youth and blue-collar working class. It will be their money that will prop up the initial funding of Obamacare and the additional rider federal programs. However, as with Medicare, the money will be sucked out of the system long before its mandatory financial supporters ever receive benefits.

Obamacare is a sham with nearly seventy percent of Americans disapproving the bill. With the threat of a government shutdown, combined with the raising of the debt ceiling, all tied together with the funding of Obamacare, the House of Representatives had one opportunity left to defund Obamacare. US House of Representatives Speaker John Boehner, struggling to ease Republican divisions over how to fight Obamacare, vowed to try to erode the healthcare law but stopped short of weighing in on a push to deny its funding.[82] In short, Speaker Boehner shamefully and secretly backed away from statements he had made on July 9, 2013, to stop Obamacare. He did this by reverting to the argument that Republicans would be blamed for the possible shutdown of the American government and the inevitable Democratic backlash, even though the vast majority of Americans were for defunding Obamacare. The "fix" was in!

It is the opinion of this author that the overwhelming evidence that Obamacare will be a failure is *intentional*. So shameful is the charade of the government being able to administer and control nearly twenty percent of our total economy via the healthcare system that few have paid attention to its basic shortcomings.

The Obama administration allotted three years to develop the vast web resources necessary to run such a system at an estimate of some 60 million dollars to fully develop the website. Upon its opening day, the website failed miserably to allow any activity. Holding the taxpayers hostage, the administration has actually spent 164 million (of taxpayer money) on this failed website, a fact that boggles the mind.

Obamacare became the talking point for the first real test of the Republican Congress and presidency. The Trump administration entered office with its own promise of "repealing and replacing" Obamacare. Little did Trump realize that he did not have the combined support of the landslide Republican Congress. Oddly, those members of Congress, some of whom had run on the platform of "repeal and replace" Obamacare, suddenly found themselves faced with reconditioning people away from several years of healthcare chaos and warming up to yet another healthcare change that had not been fully thought out. With the progressives essentially out of power, a full court press took place in the media to upset Trump's initial "repeal and replace" promise. The congressional vote to approve the initial Republican version of the American Healthcare Act was pulled because the new bill was poorly written and did not represent input from the Republican Congress. Further, the non-vote represented a deep schism within the Republican Party over ideology. The Conservative Freedom Caucus believed that the bill keeps too much of Obamacare intact, while the Republican moderates worried that they would pay an electoral price if millions of Americans were to lose their health insurance. Not a single Democrat supported the bill or wanted anything other than a no vote, thus maintaining Obamacare government controls.

On May 4, 2017, the US House of Representatives voted to pass the revised American Healthcare Act (and thereby repeal most of the Affordable Care Act) by a narrow margin of 217 to 213, sending the bill to the Senate for deliberation. The Senate had indicated that they would write their own version of the bill instead of voting on the House version. Conservative members of the Republican Party wanted a complete repeal of Obamacare, but as the history of the progressive movement has demonstrated, once entitlements are in force, even if they hurt the very people they are supposed to help, they are nearly impossible to repeal. By design, entitlements soon become human rights issues that deliberately imply "rights" where no such rights exist. Once again, politics overrides commitment.

The Democratic position, insisting that 20 million otherwise uninsured citizens now had health coverage, was difficult to overcome. The actual *paid* number of new enrollees was not 20 million but 9.8 million, half the Congressional Budget Office estimates, representing half the profit margins for medical providers. The reality is that some of those now covered under Obamacare are faced with staggering yearly deductibles ($5,000 or more) that they can't possibly afford, effectively nullifying their coverage—but hey, why sweat the details?

Keep in mind the radical agenda of Saul Alinsky's Rule #1: "Power is not only what you have, but what the enemy thinks you have. Power is derived from 2 main sources—money and people. "Have-Nots" must build power from the flesh and blood of those who have."[83] The executive branch of our federal government did not have the constitutional authority to implement Obamacare, disguised as a healthcare bill, yet the most vulnerable in our population, including the middle class, are being coerced into believing that it did. Article I, Section 1 of the Tenth Amendment states, "Congress has sole power to create law and does not possess any authority to delegate this power to other actors within the government, including the president."[84] This has become the intentional byproduct of the progressive movement to circumvent our Constitution.

President Obama instituted the Affordable Healthcare Act via executive order. President Trump had the legal authority to rescind the previous president's executive order because it did not represent congressional law. However, doing so, would have furthered the bastardization of constitutional law, leaving Congress and the electorate out of the equation. This deliberate, devious act by the progressives set the stage for the perfect storm between the president, Congress, the people, and the rule of law, ultimately undermining American due process. The Supreme Court has ruled that "Obamacare is the functional equivalent of a tax and is an exercise of the taxing power of Congress,"[85] accounting for almost twenty percent of the US economy. How difficult is it to understand that if the federal government imposed perceived constitutional powers (that do not exist) in order to implement Obamacare, the government essentially owns twenty percent of our economy (Alinsky's Rule #1, "perceived power").

The signature proposal for Obamacare was that everyone would be covered. Unfortunately, in this case "will be covered" was equivalent to "must be covered." I say it again: words have meaning! The problem was that "we the people" were also told that we could keep our present health plan, leaving many confused. Those who chose to wait for further clarification found out that the IRS was given the authority to impose an Individual Mandate penalty tax for nonparticipation. Chief Justice John Roberts ruled that the penalty was an allowable use of the taxing power granted to Congress by the Constitution. The penalty tax for that year started at $395, or 1% of that person's income, increasing to $695, or 2.5% of income, by 2016, where it would remain in effect forever. Some six million healthy Americans decided to pay the tax rather than join one of the exchanges.[86] Now that President Trump rescinded the Individual Mandate tax, a major bite has been taken out of Obamacare; however, no one yet knows what has happened to the taxes collected from those Americans while the Individual Mandate was in effect.

After a few years of economic agony, bickering between political parties, induced class warfare, and the inequalities bestowed on those who can vote themselves amnesty, the time will arrive for the very same federal government to again blame the shortcomings of the healthcare bill on Congress, the opposing political party, and/or the greed of the people. The federal government can then step in to rescue the population by instituting its original hidden agenda plan for a single payer healthcare plan. The people would welcome the relief, ignore sound opposition, and accept the government's solution willingly.

Accepting a single payer healthcare plan would seal the ownership of healthcare. Since all checks would be written by the federal government, the government would decide who, what, when, and whether payment would be made. Those dependent on government subsidies would be rewarded, while those still in control over expendable income would be punished, thus fulfilling the balance of Alinsky's Rule #1.

The year 2014 brought a second wave of healthcare losses to the American people, only this time through the loss of employer-initiated healthcare programs. In a study released by the American Enterprise Institute, up to 100 million Americans may not have had employer-provided healthcare coverage by the fall of 2014 because the plans did not meet Obamacare's standards.[87] In 2010, when Obamacare was introduced, it was clearly stated that those citizens covered by employer health insurance plans would not be affected. President Obama wanted us to believe what we now know was another progressive attempt at circumventing the truth. It is ultimately more difficult to rescind and replace a flawed healthcare system in which truth; fiction; and, yes, lies, complicate the decision process. Politics moves with intentional slowness, making immediate changes nearly impossible to implement.

One of the more troubling hidden aspects of Obamacare was that HealthCare.gov would be administered, in part, by "Solo Health Stations" containing scanner technology that would read National Healthcare RFID chips (radio frequency identification chips), to be embedded in the hands or shoulders of citizens and containing all their personal information. Radio frequency scanners are surveillance devices. RFID chips may sound innocent enough and be super convenient in cases of emergency, but since RFID chips can possibly contain personally linked information that can be retrieved without consent, serious privacy concerns must be considered. Even though the chip readers are set for a specific short distance, no one knows for certain whether other devices can be programmed to read the chips. Tracking devices for any reason reek of "Big Brother." Traffic cameras, for example, were sold to the public as public safety tools to monitor traffic. Have you watched any police shows on TV lately where these same cameras are now surveillance tools that track people and monitor them 24/7? Although the RDIF microchip is still a "rumored" device, the Affordable Care Act is the perfect venue to make the rumor a reality.[88]

Data mining and intrusion into our private lives have become center stage, in all areas of life, with the revelations of Google's patented technology to track one's every movement via GPS technology within an individual's cellphone, even if one's smartphone is turned off and without a SIM card. Facebook can activate a person's microphone and camera on their computer to develop facial recognition technology, even if the computer is turned off. Just as with your laptop, your smart television also has a microphone, and some have a camera. When Samsung released its new smart television, it warned customers not to discuss sensitive information in front of it. Most late model automobiles come with "On Star" capabilities and tracking devices, to be used in emergency situations. Unfortunately, these devices, being essentially two-way communicators, can be activated by a command center at any time. Even your smart watch that monitors your footsteps can be used by the CIA to collect data on your personal habits.[89]

The irony of the healthcare debacle is that none of it would be necessary if the democratic process of free market capitalism were left to the private sector. With competitive insurance pricing that crosses state lines, the marketplace would level the pricing playing field. Without mandated government drug insurance, pharmaceutical companies would be less likely to attain insane profits and would have to compete with generic alternatives. No one objects to developing insurance coverage for those with minimal income; in fact, this would be a profitable niche market for a communal health insurance conglomerate. People are swayed by the emotional, progressive rhetoric that healthcare is a right. If it is accepted that healthcare is a right, the next step is to regulate it. The emotional healthcare argument that makes no sense in a democracy is the notion that everyone is responsible to share the cost of healthcare. If we are truly free to choose in a democracy, then we are also free to choose not to participate. Progressive ideology is so pervasive in Obamacare that people were, at the time of this writing, willing to accept financial punishment, via IRS withholdings, for not purchasing mandated healthcare options from the Obamacare exchanges.

During the 2017 Miss USA pageant, Miss District of Columbia, Kara McCullough, won the title, but here, too, the politics of healthcare was on full display. Miss McCullough stunned the feminist and mostly liberal audience with her politically conservative answer to the question posed to her by the co-host, Jullianne Hough: "Do you think affordable healthcare for all US citizens is a right or a privilege, and why?" Miss McCullough responded, "I'm definitely going to say it's a privilege. As a government employee, I am granted healthcare, and I see firsthand that for one to have healthcare, you need to have a job. Therefore, we need to continue to cultivate this environment that we're given the opportunities to have healthcare, as well as jobs, to all the American citizens worldwide." By the mere setup for such a question, the co-host was pretty certain that the answer to a nationwide audience would be consistent with the liberal mantra that healthcare is a human right; but not so in this case![90]

The pursuit of "smaller government" is not just a catchy phrase; it is a founding principle under our Constitution. The incremental erosion of our democratic process is an act of war on "we the people." The only recourse to retain our democratic principles is the ballot box. Voting for representatives who are best suited to answer to their constituency is only part of the process; demanding accountability when our representatives are swayed by political forces should be swift and relentless. Those citizens who accept complacency are destined to compromise their principles. If you do not stand for something, you stand for nothing.

For Further Reading

Centers for Disease Control and Prevention. http://www.cdc.gov/vaccines/default.htm (accessed June 17, 2014).

Child Health Safety. "30 Years of Secret Official Transcripts Show UK Government Experts Cover Up Vaccine Hazards." http://childhealthsafety.wordpress.com/2012/03/14/government-experts-cover-up-vaccine-hazards/ (accessed June 17, 2014).

Food Freedom News. http://foodfreedomgroup.com (accessed June 17, 2014).

Miller, Neil Z. *Immunization theory vs. reality: exposé on vaccinations.* Santa Fe, NM: New Atlantean Press, 1996.

Wikimedia Foundation. "Patient Protection and Affordable Care Act." Wikipedia. http://en.wikipedia.org/wiki/Patient_Protection_and_Affordable_Care_Act (accessed June 17, 2014).

Chapter 3

Constitution vs. Executive Order

American history, as was taught in our schools, required students to understand the essence of our country's founding. Great detail was taken to ensure familiarity with our Constitution and the resulting Bill of Rights (the first ten amendments of the Constitution) to demonstrate how dramatically different it is from that of all other countries. However, as our country passed the two-hundred-year mark, the teaching of American history and historical events was wallowing in unchartered territory. Rarely have democracies survived beyond two hundred years. Why do democracies fail? Two major reasons are:

1. Democracies generally progress through an initial period from bondage to spiritual faith, escalating to the point at which the citizens become so totally dependent on the government that they eventually revert back to bondage.
2. When the democracy begins to prosper, the people vote to allow the public treasury to benefit them generously, which then allows the majority to vote for the candidates who promise the most benefits from the public treasury.

Does this sound familiar? Entitlements, anyone?

It is important to establish just what our Constitution is and what is happening to it as we venture past two hundred years. The Constitution of the United States is the supreme law of the United States of America. The first three articles of the Constitution establish the separation of powers of the three branches of the federal government: the legislature (Congress); the executive branch, led by the president; and the federal judiciary, headed by the Supreme Court.

Unlike some other constitutions, the US Constitution cannot be changed; instead, constitutional amendments are added to it, altering its effect. It has been amended on numerous occasions to meet the needs of the time. However, recently there have been attempts at altering constitutional law for the purpose of balancing the federal budget. In 2013, the federal deficit was $300 billion, with the federal government borrowing forty-six cents of every dollar spent.[91] The Congressional Budget Office projects a federal budget deficit of $3.3 trillion, more than triple the 2019 shortfall, mostly due to the economic disruption caused by the 2020 corona virus pandemic.[92] That compares with 79% of the 2019 Gross National Product.[93] This is an obvious threat to our financial stability as a nation.

The greatest fear the founders of this nation had was the establishment of a strong central government and a strong political leader at the center of that government. They no longer wanted kings, monarchs, or czars; they wanted an association of states in which the power originated from the states and not from the central government. There is no greater threat to state power than that found in the form of the presidential executive order. The process totally bypasses congressional and legislative authority and places almost unlimited power in the president's hands. The executive order has been used many times. Presidents have used the executive order in times of emergency (such as wartime) to override the Constitution of the United States and the Congress.[94] President Ronald Reagan said it best: "As government expands, liberty contracts."[95]

The purpose of this discussion is to demonstrate that our Constitution no longer has the universal authority it once had because of the very reasons our founding fathers feared: the untethered growth of the federal government. Article I, Section 1 of our Constitution is concise in its language: "All legislative powers herein granted shall be vested in a Congress of the United States, which shall consist of a Senate and House of Representatives." That is no longer true. The Bill of Rights protected Americans against loss of freedoms. That is no longer true. The Constitution provided for a balanced separation of powers. That is also being challenged by a "socialized progressive democracy."

Presidents Lincoln, Roosevelt, and Wilson used executive orders during wartime, when the very life of the United States was threatened. The president, in essence, has dictatorial powers never provided to him under the Constitution. The president has the power to suspend the Constitution and the Bill of Rights in a real or perceived emergency and can single-handedly declare martial law, which effectively suspends constitutional law, if he so chooses. Does the present federal deficit meet the requirement of national security, or how about the disarming of the citizens by executive order?

Perhaps the situation can be summarized in the words of the conservative economist Howard J. Ruff: "Since the enactment of Executive Order 11490, the only thing standing between us and dictatorship is the good character of the president, and the lack of a crisis severe enough that the public would stand still for it." Executive Order 11490, of October 28, 1969, calls for federal agencies to prepare plans for a state of emergency that would require "over-all civilian manpower mobilization programs" and related emergency measures.

To summarize: presidents, by executive order, can rise above constitutional law. The president has the power to seize property (gold, as with FDR[96]), organize and control the means of industrial production (steel mills, as with Harry Truman[97]), assign military forces abroad, call reserve forces amounting to 2.5 million men to duty, institute martial law,[98] seize and control all means of transportation, regulate all private enterprise, restrict travel, and in a plethora of particular ways control the lives of all Americans.[99]

Now, I ask, does this sound like the Constitution our founding fathers envisioned? It is my fear that our present debt crisis will be resolved not through congressional action but by executive order to raise the debt ceiling without limit. If that occurs, freedoms as we know them will be a footnote in some American history book decades from now, if they still exist at all.

Depending on the rationale for the use of the presidential executive order, freedom hangs in the balance. When looking at how many executive orders have been issued by past presidents, one will find that President Obama issued 168 executive orders as of January 14, 2014, and that by election day 2020 President Trump had signed 176. However, a list of a few past presidential executive orders shows that Theodore Roosevelt issued 1,081, Calvin Coolidge issued 1,203, Woodrow Wilson issued 1,803, and Franklin Roosevelt issued a whopping 3,522. The issue is not that the executive orders were written but the purpose for which they were used.[100]

An executive order is a type of written instruction that presidents use to work their will through the executive branch of government. Congress and Federal courts can strike down executive orders that exceed the scope of the president's authority.[101] The Constitution itself does not address executive orders but Article II vests the executive power in the president, which gives him the power to oversee and direct the various aspects of executive branch of government. Executive orders do not affect the legislative or judicial branches of government, nor do they directly affect "we the people." However, executive orders can eventually trickle down to the average citizen[102]. In recent years, presidents have wielded executive orders as political weapons to push through controversial policies or regulations without Congressional or judicial oversight. Congress's gridlock and increased polarization have pushed executive actions more and more as substitutes for legislation[103]. The most recent example of the misuse of executive orders took place within the first few days of Biden's presidency, where he used executive orders to dismantle former president Trump's actions without congressional oversight.

President Obama openly defied Congress by taunting compliance . . . or else. Obama had illegally declared Congress out of session for the purpose of enacting important legislation. Obama defied Congress by altering existing laws to suit his agenda, like that which took place with regard to selective noncompliance to sections of Obamacare. The most egregious threat in the use of the executive order is the deliberate dismantling of congressional due process. It is the job of Congress to buffer attempted presidential bullying by debate. President Obama openly stated on national TV that his programs would be enacted, either by congressional action or by the use of his pen. President Obama represented the epitome of what our founding fathers attempted to protect this nation from: a tyrannical misuse of power. Presidents have the right to issue executive orders for national security reasons and minimum wage issues, but other signature pet projects of presidents hardly meet those standards and must be stopped by immediate review of the Supreme Court.

The Syrian Crisis
The most dangerous example of the executive order is during a time of war. On April 14, 2018, President Trump (by executive order), joined France and Great Britain in strategic air strikes on Syria. The reason for the air strikes was evidence from international sources that pointed to the deaths of hundreds due to the inhalation

of poison gas, under the direction of President Bashar al-Assad's government.[104] However, just days after the horrific event, evidence came to light from numerous news and foreign embassy sources that the Syrian rebels and not Assad's forces were responsible for the gassing of Syrian civilians.[105] With a breach of international law in the balance, plans were made for a limited air strike on key targets within the Assad government as "punishment" for a violation of *moral* conduct against Assad's civilians, without alluding to the possibility of the rebels being responsible.

The point is that our Constitution absolutely forbids a president from committing the US to an act of war without the expressed consent of Congress. In this case, Theresa May of Great Britain and Emmanuel Macron of France shared responsibility for the attack. Our founders knew that a tyrannical president could someday bring irreparable damage to our country, acting as a rogue monarch rather than an agent sworn to uphold the constitutional laws of our land. The president can act as commander-in-chief when and if a war is declared but cannot act apart from or in spite of Congress. This would be an impeachable act.

It is Congress that must investigate every aspect of a war scenario. In this case, the facts were not clear about who actually used poison gas, so why was the president about to bypass Congress and commit this country to an act of war? If it had been the rebels and not Assad's government, then where did the rebels get the chemical weapons from, and were they intentionally provoking a tactical US response to gain a military advantage over Assad's regime? If that had been the scenario, the US would have been complicit in an unjustified act of war—the very reason our founders wanted the collective minds of 435 members of Congress, rather than just one man, to investigate and decide.

In 2013, President Obama was faced with a similar crisis in Syria, where it was reported that hundreds of civilians were being killed by poisonous gas under the Assad regime. A Mint Press News article by Associated Press reporter Dale Gavlak states that the Syrian rebels, not the Assad regime, were responsible for the chemical attack and that the chemicals were supplied by Saudi agents.[106] This challenges Secretary of State John Kerry's claim that the Assad regime was responsible. It was interesting to watch the Obama administration's struggle for political dominance, pushing the lie as far as public acceptance would allow. When, or if, caught, the Obama administration would have resorted to congressional statesmanship. This is not new to the political arena of executive orders but is an example of why our founding fathers insisted on severe limitations of presidential executive orders.

Speaking to the nation, Obama said that he was "mindful that I'm the president of the world's oldest constitutional democracy. I've long believed that our power is rooted not just in our military might, but in our example as a government of the people, by the people and for the people." One week prior, Obama had stated that he had the authority (via executive order) and would do what he felt to be necessary, apparently without concern about "government for and by the people." After the Syrian crisis became a near embarrassment, President Obama stated to the nation that he would take action against the Syrian government, but not without congressional approval. Obama also noted, "While I believe I have the authority to carry out this military action without specific congressional authorization, I know that the country will be stronger if we take this course, and our actions will be even more effective."[107] In short, Obama was saving face even with his proverbial hand caught in the cookie jar.

Forty years ago, when faced with a similar potential war scenario, Congress passed the War Powers Resolution in 1973 over President Richard Nixon's veto. Its intent was to rein in Nixon, who had used military force in Cambodia without notifying Congress— and to curb future presidents who might wage unauthorized wars. However, prior to Obama's public announcement to temper his Syrian bombing agenda, he maneuvered his political machine to do "an end around" the War Powers Resolution, claiming that Assad has used chemical weapons before and would most likely use them again against our allies and possibly the US. This wording represents the basis for sidestepping the War Powers Resolution but does nothing to check the actions of a possible tyrannical act by a sitting president.

The Obama administration found itself in a political conundrum. Without a clear objective or benefit to the US for his retaliatory action, with or without congressional support, what would the potential air strikes have accomplished now that military targets had had time to relocate? What possible justification could be given for taking action at that point, when poison gas was being used to kill, as opposed to when 100,000 had died under the same regime when bullets were the method of choice? Who made the US the policeman for the world, and where is the physical support from other "denouncing" nations?

For Further Reading

Hoppe, Hans-Hermann. *Democracy--the god that failed: the economics and politics of monarchy, democracy and natural order.* New Brunswick [NJ]: Transaction Publishers, 2001.

Chapter 4

The Presidents:
White House Leaders or Residents?

The formation of a sovereign country does not come with instructions; ours is no exception. There have been forty-six presidents of the United States and, despite perception, some have been less than stellar. Keep in mind that until our twenty-fifth President, William McKinley's, assassination and the subsequent presidency of Theodore Roosevelt in 1901 (approximately 126 years after our founding), most of our population had never had the ability to hear or see who their president was. They voted based on what they read about and what was happening in the country. President McKinley, for example, was faced with the Spanish American War and a devastated economy. McKinley was also the last president who firmly believed that the nation must adhere to the fundamental principles on which it was founded. It isn't that subsequent presidents didn't speak the appropriate words, but presidents like Theodore Roosevelt, William Taft, and Woodrow Wilson began to move the country from its limited government into a "progressive" government, in which the size of the federal government grew exponentially. It was President Woodrow Wilson who became the leader of the progressive movement, destined to change the course of this nation.

World War I moved this nation from neutrality to the status of a world industrial power. Ever since then, politics trumps (no pun intended) the essence of our founding. President Wilson drastically pushed a socialist agenda, which included the Federal Reserve Act of 1913 that created the Federal Reserve central banking system, granting the legal authority to issue federal reserve notes known as US dollars. Originally the dollar was backed by gold, but it is now backed by nothing other than trust in the US government. Going off the gold standard allowed the federal government to print fiat money, which is essentially modern-day Monopoly money. If all agree that this fiat money has value, all is well. However, try to exchange your paper fiat money for its equivalent face value in gold or silver—good luck!

The Federal Trade Commission Act of 1914 gave the federal government the power to control private corporations and what they can or cannot do. The Clayton Antitrust Act of 1914 further restricted private competition (something well described in Ayn Rand's *Atlas Shrugged*). Income tax was designed to help fund the social programs of the federal government and the war effort. The problem was that *only* the federal government can decide tax rates, leaving the country at the mercy of an ever-growing government.

Numerous pieces of legislation between 1913 and 1918 were drafted to control business practices. They are actually the subtle but deliberate mechanism of an ever-expanding presence of government in private enterprise, allowing free market competition to be controlled by government.

The socialized agenda became more evident when Wilson instituted a mandated seventy percent income tax to pay for the war debt. Soon Wilson, by executive order, took control over food supplies, farming, fuel, railroads, and the banking system. Before long the federal government rose to a staggering 80,000 employees, funded through the newly established Federal Reserve Bank, which, of course, is not what its name suggests but instead consists of private corporate entities acting as a "depository" for confiscated private wealth. Understanding the details of our history and the men who served as president is crucial to our present-day economics and political structure.

At the end of World War 1, the US was deeply in debt. Social entitlement programs and inflated business gave the appearance of prosperity, but on October 29, 1929, reality set in with the stock market crashing. Unparalleled growth had spurred investing, but behind the scenes the true value of those investments was highly inflated (fiat money), and the massive market correction created a panic, leading to a selling spree that quickly put the country into the Great Depression. Coupled with President Wilson's formation of the League of Nations (the precursor to the United Nations), American sovereignty was now given to a global body, further crippling the confidence of the American people.

Continued government interference in the individual affairs of the people resulted in the start of the Welfare State known as Social Security. It is commonly thought that FDR brought the US out of the Great Depression. By instituting massive government programs that led to out-of-control government spending, partially paid for by the "legal Ponzi Scheme" known as Social Security and borrowing against future generations, FDR actually fostered an entire dependency on the federal government. The government acted as a "bank" to take a percentage of a citizen's salary, matched by their employer, and "save" it as guaranteed retirement income. According to the Social Security Administration, with over eighty million Baby Boomers entering Social Security, the program is essentially bankrupt, saved only by printing fiat currency and stealing from future generations. Added to the Medicare/Medicaid socialized program of healthcare, the entitlement programs of the past sixty years are unsustainable. In essence, FDR's New Deal prolonged the depression while giving the appearance of an artificial recovery. It must be obvious that in present time, without a federal budget, as with the last four years of the Obama administration and trillions in federal deficit, we are governed by the same deception as before the Great Depression and are destined to repeat it because of new entitlement programs designed to increase dependence on the federal government. It is true that under President Trump's 2018 budget, some 66 federal programs were scheduled to be eliminated, saving taxpayers some $26.7 billion but hardly a drop in the bucket against trillions in federal debt.

By the end of FDR's presidency, the size of the federal government swelled to 190,000 employees; this is hardly a limited government. Following the presidencies of JFK, Johnson, Nixon, Ford, and Carter, some Democrat and some Republican, our government grew to unprecedented proportions with an ever more socialist agenda. The significance of our two-party system has become essentially "one party posing as two," with little or no attempt at changing direction toward our constitutional founding. President Reagan and President Trump were flukes, unexpected blips in the agenda that our previous twelve presidents adhered to. Reagan was a conservative, balancing the federal budget in each of his years in office. He was also a constitutionalist. If our next four presidents had acted similarly, our country might have been redefined as a true democracy. Trump is a converted Republican but, more importantly, a consummate businessman who understands money apart from the baggage of political bondage. He is hated by the establishment because he is owned by no one and has caused havoc within the federal bureaucracy.

As previously mentioned, no other democracy has ever lasted for more than two hundred years. The reasons are many, but the pattern is clear. Democracy requires diligence and public involvement. How easy is it for complacency to dominate, when the promise of entitlements results in the loss of personal responsibility? A strong country requires a strong leader. Time has shown that when a president is more concerned about reelection than about doing what is required, there is no need for a president at all. Very few of our former presidents were true leaders. Try to name just ten of our forty-five presidents, after the commonly known founding presidents Washington, Adams, Jefferson, Madison, Monroe, and Lincoln. Most presidents were mere residents of the White House, making few or no constitutional contributions.

However, presidents have understood that the people they surround themselves with must have skill and the business sense to make sound decisions for the country. The percentage of past presidential Cabinets that actually knew the private sector, with real-life business experience prior to their appointment to the Cabinet (as opposed to a government job), would astound you when compared to the recent Obama Cabinet. Past presidential Cabinets averaged 43.5% with former business experience; some Cabinets were as high as 57%. The Obama Cabinet's average was just 8%. It is absolutely incredible that Obama's administration was trying to tell our big corporations, the private business sector, and the healthcare industry how to run their businesses. How could the president of a major nation that had the most successful economic system in world history talk about business when he had never worked for one? How could he talk about jobs when his only salaried position had been that of a part-time professor and community organizer? Worst of all, 92% of the Obama Cabinet had spent most of their adult life in academia, government, and nonprofit jobs, rarely, if ever, involved in the lives of everyday working citizens.

It is my opinion that President Obama mastered socialized democracy. His rhetoric resonated with those eager and naïve enough to think that borrowing forty-six cents of every dollar spent, without a budget to monitor spending, is somehow good business practice and easily fixable by increasing taxes to unrealistic levels. The extent of this lunacy is defined as quantitative easing (QE). Wikipedia offers a simple explanation: "A central bank [the Federal Reserve] implements quantitative easing by buying financial assets [printing fiat money; money backed by thin air] from commercial banks and other private institutions [debts], thus creating [inflated] money and injecting a pre-determined quantity of money into the economy."[108] The problem with QE is that the money it injects into the economy has no real value. Furthermore, any countries that have used this system of artificially stimulating their respective economies have caused those economy to collapse, destroying their monetary systems (recently Greece and Japan). Doing a QE once goes against any sound business theory; doing it twice is madness, but attempting QE a third time, as the Obama administration proposed, is insane. It's no wonder that a Cabinet with only 8% of its members having business experience would try this. *A Wall Street Journal* poll in July 2013 revealed that a staggering 83% of those polled felt disapproval for Congress and would have fired most of its members had they been given the chance. It's just a matter of time before public patience wears thin.

Increasing taxes removes individual financial resources, stifles free enterprise, and gives untethered power to an already inflated federal government. This can occur because of the efforts of FDR, who effectively changed the republic of the United States of America to the corporation of the United States of America. However, this is not the forum for that discussion. Simply put, the federal government is no longer a servant of the people but will soon take ownership over them.

We are told that we have a choice; either fight the evil Democrats or fight the evil Republicans. The truth is that what we actually have, based on the performance of our last eight rotating presidential parties, is "one party posing as two," keeping us busy in political fisticuffs while the real transformation of the country takes place. Until a viable third party arises, not controlled by the political elitists of today, freedom in this country is an illusion. Our Constitution depends on the integrity of our president, who was given special power called the executive order, to be used in times of war and national crises. Within the first week of President Obama's second term, he signed thirteen executive orders, bypassing congressional debate. More astounding was the insane flurry of thirty executive orders signed by President Joe Biden in his first three days in office, ten of which were executive orders to directly reverse President Trup's policies[109]. The difference between a despot and a president lies in his intent. The untethered use of executive orders for purposes of avoiding constitutional responsibilities is the equivalent of soft despotism. Political agendas are achieved by eliminating the constitutional safeguards against such government behaviors.[110]

The present Democratic Party is not in the political business to fix government practices or to correct social injustices as their media campaigns try to portray. Clearly the rise of extreme left socialist agendas in today's America is a fulfillment of Obama's 2008 presidential campaign that he and his party wanted "to change society and create a new social order," which they referred to as social justice. The campaign slogan of "yes we can, yes we can" was about their goal of "fundamentally transforming" the United States of America into a progressive, dependent society and not about uplifting the seemingly independent entrepreneurial spirit that most voters thought was Obama's intent. The progressive strategy of over-promising and under-delivering worked to perfection by deceiving the public, allowing emotions to override their intellect. The public has yet to grasp the concept that the further loss of freedoms, higher debt, and increasing dependence on entitlements will destroy free enterprise. It is my fear that the American people will never really understand that social justice in the progressive lexicon means justice by the few over the many. It would serve the American people well to better understand world history to truly understand the game plan for the demise of one's sovereignty, which is socialism. In 1917 the Russian people, under the continued promise of a better life by the social engineering of a progressive political party, redirected the power that had always been in their hands by sheer numbers, fighting back in what became known as the Bolshevik Revolution in Russia. It had taken seventy years for the people to understand that the promise was all an illusion.[111]

Chapter 5

Media Deception

Since the beginning of time, information has been the key to development, science, and communication. In 1690, the first newspaper was published in America; it was named *The Publick Occurrences*. By 1870, the number of newspapers published in the US skyrocketed to 5,091. The age of information and news became vital to any civilized nation. Journalism became a profession created out of the rise of media. Those who chose to seek out and report news to society at large were revered as dedicated public servants not bound to any political party or faction. In fact, if one did not learn to befriend the news media or gave the impression of hiding from the public's eye, their days were numbered as a public figure. Many of our presidents learned to respect the journalist media; if they did not, their longevity as a leader was in jeopardy. The early days of newspapers and what later became the media were truly the essence of democracy, in which the will of the people played heavily in the checks and balances of politics.

With increased technology, especially television, the visual component of the news was born. The media quickly learned that the power to sway a country was within its control. In just eighty years the power of the press in reporting the news lost its luster, and the number of daily newspapers in the US declined dramatically over the past half-century, according to *Editor & Publisher*, the trade journal of American newspapers. In 1950, there were just 1,772 daily newspapers, and by 2008 that number had dropped to 1,422 daily papers. Historically, with three quarters of all US newspapers out of business, the print media of the day was becoming irrelevant. The day of the independent journalist was slipping away. It was time to take a long, hard look at reporting the news.

By the early 2000s the transformation of the media had taken itself from news reporter to newsmaker. Journalists quickly learned that they had to make reporting the news more visual and more like Hollywood, often creating news rather than reporting it. Gone are the days of Walter Cronkite's timeless reporting of the world's most influential events, including the real-time assassination of JFK. Gone is the quality reporting done by Edward R. Murrow, Chet Huntley, and David Brinkley and their reporting of the Russian Sputnik. Instead of Huntley and Brinkley, we got Ken and Barbie. Turn to any TV news channel; sex appeal dominates news broadcasting. News broadcasting has become more agenda driven than it is a reporting of raw news. Reporting the news and commenting on the news are quite different. One needs only to look at present day politics to witness the fawning taking place between the media and the liberal Democratic party.

To the unengaged population, the visual impact of what these new media "talking heads" have to say often overrides the truth. News channels now are carbon copies of each other, with key words being scripted and repeated over and over. Gone are the hard-hitting questions; even the timeless Larry King faithfully followed the present agenda of the news, often asking "softball" questions with pre-scripted answers, if this met the agenda of the topic material. There are six corporations that presently own almost all media outlets. In essence, these corporations are controlling what we see and hear. The corporations are National Amusements, Disney, Time Warner, Comcast, News Corp., and Sony. Between them they own and operate some 456 television, film, and video companies, investing some $430 billion dollars—so much for an independent media.

The senseless shootings at schools and theaters have left the anti-constitutionalists, presently in power, frothing at the mouth to rid this nation of its Second Amendment. Gun control became the talking point for every news station. Nearly every news channel now begins with "an agenda" story or two of a shooting somewhere in the country, mostly void of any balanced reporting from the media. Fast forward to present-day news reporting from Australia, which enacted the strictest gun confiscation laws in the world several years ago. The first-year results are now in: Australia-wide, homicides are up 3.2 percent, assaults are up 8.6 percent, and armed robberies are up 44 percent (yes, 44 percent!). In the state of Victoria alone, homicides with firearms are now up 300 percent.[112] Note that while the law-abiding citizens turned in their firearms, the criminals did not, and criminals still possess their guns! Loss of liberty equals loss of life. If the media in this country continues to push administrative agendas rather than reporting unbiased accounts of the news, journalism is dead.

Keep in mind that the media in general is big business requiring sponsors. The media can be bought and sold to the highest bidder. The events in Benghazi, Libya, on September 11, 2012, demonstrated incredible media bias. At the "hearings" where the truth was to be revealed, not a single news channel asked the hard questions of how this attack could have happened, nor did they ask why five days of misinformation was spewed daily, while just one day after the event Libya's president had confirmed that the attack was not spontaneous but an Al-Qaeda terrorist attack. Later testimony from the then CIA deputy director Mike Morell revealed that he was briefed on what was about to happen the day before the attack in Benghazi from firsthand reports from within the Libyan embassy itself but chose to rely on his CIA advisors in Langley, Virginia.[113] More important was the cover-up when Mr. Morell admitted to changing the storyline to the press, supposedly in an attempt not to inflame any further attacks, by leaving out key phrases (like the fact that the attack was initiated by Islamic terrorists). Instead, he continued the spontaneous protest storyline sparked by an obscure YouTube movie.[114]

Similarly, media bias changed the course of history by simply putting out false information on whomever the media did not support. Examples of media bias are the destruction of Governor Sarah Palin by false accusations, climate-gate, the claim that guns in themselves are evil, Senator Edward Kennedy's Chappaquiddick (where a young woman's death literally got swept under the media's rug), and the media's apparent indifference toward reporting all that was known about President Obama prior to his election, as required by the Constitution. Strikingly different is the media coverage of Donald Trump, where absolutely nothing positive has been reported. The public is aware of the media bias and has latched on to the "fake news" narrative espoused by Trump during public appearances.

So strong has the influence of the media been that it can shape political outcomes. Presently, with a split Congress, the progressive Democratic agenda is on full display with a complicit media seeing to it that the public sees only what the media deems it necessary to them to see and hear; the Republican Party has gone into shock mode. How can the media, disguised as unbiased journalism, have such power of persuasion? It is as though the media has become an actual third political party, while giving the appearance of neutrality.

Politics is power, whereas the media must maintain an apolitical stance. Presently the media has demonstrated anything but an apolitical stance. Presidential elections are won or lost in the court of public opinion. However, there have been four presidential elections where the candidate has won the popular vote but lost the election.[115] Public opinion is shaped by what people hear and see. Before modern media, people often never saw the presidential candidates, depending only on word of mouth and newsprint. Today, candidates raise millions of dollars to be seen and heard in the media, leading to coverage on the highest bidder. The visual appeal of a candidate can be destroyed by scandal, whether the scandal is real or contrived.

In 2013, Republican Governor Chris Christie of New Jersey was the target of a media frenzy over alleged political maneuvering. Christie was alleged to have intentionally shut down one lane of the George Washington Bridge in Ft. Lee, New Jersey, for four days as retribution against the town's mayor for declining to endorse Christie in the most recent reelection. As a result, a special committee was created by the New Jersey Assembly and was given subpoena powers, appointing former federal prosecutor Reid Schar to serve as special counsel.[116] In the Christie case, media coverage was enormous. Every news channel, newspaper, and media personality covered the airwaves over this relatively insignificant event. A closer look at this event finds cause to question the media's intent. Republican Chris Christie was a leading presidential candidate for the Republican Party. The leading candidate for the Democratic Party was former Secretary of State and former first lady Hillary Clinton.

The irony is that the media is Democratically biased. For Hillary Clinton to gain a presidential status, her Benghazi mishandling without any federal special committee, resolution, or meaningful investigation had to be kept out of public view. The disproportionate media coverage of a lane closure on a busy bridge vs. the killing of the American ambassador to Libya and three others clearly demonstrates media's willingness to demonstrate bias. Sadly, the public is being led to believe that the killing of American diplomats on foreign soil, as well as the subsequent lies told by the executive government officials as a cover-up, is of little consequence when compared to a traffic jam on a bridge in a local city in New Jersey. The American public then misses the political implications of this type of coverage.

The time to take a stand has long passed. The Republican Party, specifically the conservative minds of this country, has absolutely nothing to lose by standing on principles instead of acting like school children being sent to the principal's office for misbehaving. My point is not about political parties; it is about exposing the journalistic fraud. Pretty faces and universal talking points rather than neutral reporting and unbiased journalism of the news have successfully convinced the low-information citizens that the progressive movement is in their best interest—something akin to journalistic malpractice.

"We have nothing to fear but fear itself." These famous words of FDR in 1932 were intended to remind Americans that the nation's common difficulties concerned only material things. Media bias has become a driving force that should never be. "False Evidence Appearing Real" is an acronym for "fear"; only those with vision and experience can fight off the paralyzing effect of fear. It is my hope that we do not allow actors reporting so-called news on national TV to be seen as experts, let alone to control a nation's identity.

Historical Media Reference
Keep in mind that media outlets are supported by advertising dollars and by elite controlling foundations like the Rockefeller Foundation, who set the news agenda behind the scenes.[117] This presents a unique challenge for both the news outlets and the public. TV and newspaper outlets used to have a monopoly on news coverage; however, differing opinions brought to the public's attention via social media have challenged the status quo. As a result, TV news outlets have gone to Hollywood style production sets and slick marketing to overcome the social media presence and hold the viewers' attention. Similarities can be drawn to the taxicab industry's challenge with Uber. Uber has set the taxi industry reeling with better, personalized service at a price far less than

traditional taxi service. No longer is there a monopoly or need for expensive state-government-controlled taxi medallions (up to a million dollars each), allowing taxi medallion prices to plummet to all-time lows.[118] In the process, some independent Uber drivers are on the receiving end of violent acts of car sabotage. Social media and Uber have changed the way business is conducted, in ways that favor the public, to the chagrin of the formerly unchallenged elites.

The news media is focused on creative ways of making the news rather than on reporting it. Controversy is what keeps the public engaged. The public is now faced with the prospect of deciding what is fake, agenda-driven news and what is genuine. Thanks to the candidacy of a nonpolitical presidential candidate who would not "go along to get along," the influence of the media on public opinion was severely challenged. It's no secret that the news media appears to have an overwhelmingly liberal bias, but what does that actually mean? When taking a critical look at news outlets, it's important to understand historical perspective. There is a major difference between opinionated and agenda-driven news, as it relates to liberal vs. conservative views. The premise of this book is that "words have meaning"; without understanding the political, social, and economic terminology, it's very easy to get lost in the hype rather than the content.[119]

To put this discussion into perspective, let's understand that all is not what it appears to be. There is a hierarchy or chain of command in every corporation; no surprise, therefore, that the news media is owned by multiple layers of corporations. Things tend to get murky, as they relate to the media, when names like the Bilderberg Group, the Council on Foreign Relations, or the Trilateral Commission enter the conversation. Either people will simply ignore the reference or experience a gut-wrenching tremor, since "conspiracy theory" is readily associated with these organizations. The fact is that the Bilderberg Group, for example, meets every year in private, with its 120 or so powerful and influential heads of state, corporations, and banking members to discuss world policy, including how the media is to put out its message. George Soros is a long-standing member, so it's also no surprise that we hear his name bandied about in present day media and politics.[120]

To be more specific, media outlets back in the 1980s were owned by some fifty media companies/corporations. Today, thanks to mergers and outright takeovers, the entire news media is controlled by six major media giants (GE, News Corp, Disney, Viacom, Time Warner, and CBS), which control ninety percent of what we read, watch, or listen to, all designed to give the illusion of choice. To the astute observer, this consolidation and control over news media coverage is readily seen on TV news outlets like CNN, CNBC, ABC, NBC, MSNBC, and others, in that they all have similar attractive "talking heads," appearing on similar sets with similar colored, moving graphics, that essentially report the same news. To be honest, modern news coverage has come a long way from the days of Walter Cronkite's monotone voice or the dry presentations of the Huntley-Brinkley Report, with nothing more than a bland backdrop and a clock, but, nonetheless, we must separate marketing from news reporting.

There are well over two hundred media executives who literally control all the content of the news we see every day. Information overload is part of the plan, since most people tend to shut down, shut up, and become complacent when faced with conflicting stories presented in rapid succession. Media now dominates one of every five hours of television. Print media is dominated by the *Wall Street Journal* in America, the *Sun* in Europe, and the *Australian* in the land down under. Newspapers have disappeared exponentially with the rise of social media outlets like Google, MSN, and the multitude of privately-owned web news outlets. Corporate media control of radio is no different. Eighty percent of all radio station programming has matching playlists, from music to news. The result of all these mergers, corporate control over news content, and the ever-growing challenges of visual marketing appeal, has led to a polarization toward liberal Democratic ideologies.[121] Over the past one hundred years the Democratic liberal wing of both the US Senate and the House has held power nearly twice as long as the more conservative wing of the Republican Party, including the White House.[122]

In May 1985, Australian publisher Rupert Murdoch announced that he and American industrialist Marvin Davis intended to develop "a network of independent stations" to compete directly with CBS, NBC, and ABC. Around the same time, the political voice of "conservative talk radio" was being heard in Sacramento, California, with the Rush Limbaugh show. By 1988, it was clear that conservative talk radio, under Limbaugh, had finally come of age, as a counterbalance to the liberally dominated TV news media. It was only a matter of time before other conservative voices like Sean Hannity, Herman Cain, Glen Beck, Mark Levin, and others joined in spreading the conservative voice in America.

In 1996, Murdoch asked former Republican Party political strategist Roger Ailes to start the Fox News Channel, and a new chapter in competitive news media reporting was born. Combined with the growing listenership of Conservative Talk Radio, the Fox News Channel presented the first real challenge to liberal-dominated national news corporations. The silent millions of people, stymied by a lack of ideological diversity, suddenly had a voice, and the ideological "war" had begun. The Fox News Channel made no pretense of promoting conservative political positions. Critics of the Fox News Channel have stated, "Fox News has a bias favoring the political right and the Republican Party." Fox News host Chris Wallace joined the conversation in saying, "I think we are the counter-weight to NBC News . . . They have a liberal agenda, and we tell the other side of the story."[123]

The Effects of Shrinking News Outlets

Aside from the obvious superior marketing appeal TV news now has, key news factors are being lost. Net Neutrality is at stake when media mergers occur. Net neutrality involves a lack of restrictions on content on the internet; however, with big businesses supporting campaigns financially, they tend to have influence over political news issues. These big businesses that also have control over internet usage or the airwaves could possibly make the content biased from their political standpoint, or they could restrict usage for conflicting political views, therefore eliminating net neutrality.

An oligopoly is a situation in which a few corporate firms dominate a marketplace. When large-scale media companies buy out the smaller-scaled media companies, they become more powerful within that market. As large media firms continue to eliminate their business competition through buyouts or forcing them out (because they lack the resources or finances), the remaining companies dominate the media industry and create a media oligopoly.[124]

Diversity of Viewpoints

It is important to elaborate upon the issue of media consolidation and its effect upon the diversity of information reaching the public. Critics of consolidation raise the issue of whether monopolistic or oligopolistic control of a local media market can be fully accountable and dependable in serving unbiased information to the public. Depending on one's political slant, one can make the case for media bias. The most widely watched channel these days is Fox News, which has amassed a larger volume of viewers than NBC, CBS, or ABC News. So, it's hard to make the argument that network news or "mainstream media" is mostly liberal when the network leader is a news source that leans to the right of the political spectrum. The argument, therefore, should not be about media bias favoring one political ideology or another but rather what "elite" agenda is appropriate at the time.

During the Obama administration, media coverage favored the liberal agenda, since the foreseeable future was another Democrat-dominated administration. Hillary Clinton was to be the next media darling, which suited the status quo of mainstream media. The Republicans were on the defensive and resorted to the same media tactics as the Democrats. Fox News was ablaze, pointing out the agenda of the Clinton Foundation, which was pouring huge sums of donations into the Clinton campaign in what appeared to be a "pay for play" opportunity for supportive corporate interests. The mainstream media remained generally silent. When the plane of the then attorney Loretta Lynch met with Bill Clinton on the tarmac in Phoenix, to discuss "golf and the grandchildren," just prior to Hillary's congressional hearing on her email scandal, the mainstream media, except for Fox News, again remained generally silent. Conservative outrage erupted when days later FBI director James Comey announced that Clinton's indiscretions over top secret government emails residing on her private server did not meet prosecutorial standards. Mainstream media is still nursing its black eye for that one, depending as it did on "plausible deniability" rather than factual news reporting.

The Conservative Daily Post is the counterbalance to *Politico*. Both publications specialize in creating "fake news," whether intentionally or otherwise. Both publications rely on bloggers who hyperventilate political stories that favor their readers' political views. Both publications have the right to speak (or write) what they want under First Amendment protection, but both are guilty of promulgating fake news. *Politico* partners with mainstream news organizations like CBS and NBC, while the *Conservative Daily Post* takes in content from many sources but focuses on stories that invoke visceral responses.[125] Surely, political slants are part of the equation for all media outlets; that's why we have choices in America. If you do not like what you see on TV, change the channel. The motives of mainstream news media coverage are readership, viewership, and advertising dollars.

Freedom of the Press and Editorial Independence

Very often network heads refuse to print or air stories that run contrary to their base's views and opinions. Past examples would be the repeated refusal of networks to air ads from anti-war advocates to liberal groups like MoveOn.org or religious groups like the United Church of Christ, regardless of factual basis. Journalists may be directly sponsored by parties for whom they write, slanting the subject of their journalism to favor their sponsors' opinions. If the companies dominating a media market choose to suppress stories that do not serve their interests, the public suffers.

The First Amendment to the US Constitution was intended to encourage a free press. It was Thomas Jefferson who said, "The only security of all is in a free press. The force of public opinion cannot be resisted when permitted freely to be expressed. The agitation it produces must be submitted to. It is necessary, to keep the waters pure."[126] Freedom of the press has become a contentious issue, since "freedom" doesn't necessarily imply truth.

A few years ago the Obama-friendly news media carried on the traditions of selective news reporting by minimizing the 2010 FBI's seizure of the personal emails of the journalist James Rosen without a warrant,[127] as well as the National Security Administration's spying on millions of unsuspecting American citizens[128] and the many blocked attempts by journalists to investigate controversial stories via requests, under the Freedom of Information Act, by the Obama administration.[129] Media is at war over words, not substance. Media reports civil disobedience as our First Amendment right—no dialogue involved, just relentless organized civil disobedience disguised as the right to protest.

So strong has the influence of the media been that it can shape political outcomes. The progressive Democratic agenda, along with a complicit media, ensures that the public views only what they want it to see and hear. The inauguration of Obama's second term left the Republican Party with an approval rating of only sixteen percent, partially because of media bias. They became the party of lying low and cajoling the Democrats for fear of further bad press. How can the media, disguised as unbiased journalism, have such power of persuasion? It is as though the media has become an actual third political party, while giving the appearance of neutrality.

Politics is power, whereas the media has to maintain, at least overtly, an apolitical stance. The media has in fact demonstrated anything but an apolitical stance. Presidential elections are won or lost in the court of public opinion. However, there have been four presidential elections in which the candidate has won the popular vote but lost the election.[130] Public opinion is shaped by what people hear and see. Before modern media, people often never saw their presidential candidates, depending only on word of mouth and newsprint. Today, candidates raise millions of dollars to be seen and heard in the media, leading to coverage of the highest bidder. The visual appeal of a candidate can be destroyed by scandal, whether real or contrived.

Hilary Clinton was caught with a private email server in her house containing classified documents, verified to have been hacked due to lack of any government security measures. The media played the incident down as an oversight having little or no consequence to American security. Donald Trump was accused of coercion with the Russians to disrupt the presidential elections, plus having diplomatic discussions with Russian officials, with the intent of furthering his business empire. The media used a document from unnamed sources to make the case for Trump's guilt, even though government officials stated that there was absolutely no proof of any collusion.

The intent of this discussion is not to report the "he said, she said" aspect of media coverage but to point out the hypocrisy that "all is not what it appears to be." Further, with respect to the Trump/Russian connection, perhaps the media was duped by the Democrats as well. Clear photographic evidence exists demonstrating that top Kremlin officials like the Russian ambassador Sergey Kislyak met with Democrats Chuck Schumer and Nancy Pelosi numerous times before the 2016 presidential campaign. The Obama White House was sponsor to other Russian dignitaries and lobbyists more than twenty times during his administration. Perhaps the initial document leaked to the press by the Democrats was designed to blame Trump for the exact deeds committed by the Democrats, thus allowing fake news to become the focus of public attention.[131]

Politics has become an exercise in military tactics. The military of all countries rely on stealth and deception to win conflicts. There are thirty-two news media outlets (armies) in the US, all but six of a liberal mindset. To win political wars, oftentimes several fake plans are leaked intentionally, in the hope that the opposing forces fall for the deception, while the real plan is initiated behind the scenes. The mainstream media has become the whipping post for both political parties, depending on which is in power. Fake news becomes the deception tactic, while the controllers (corporations) of the media exercise their real plan. The population of the US, and the power granted to the people under the Constitution, are the spoils of political warfare. Politicians are no longer the employees of the people but instead the ranking officers of political warfare, taking their marching orders from the corporate and elite generals who oversee the political landscape for power and wealth.

Despite the best efforts of the media and the political elites, there is an occasional disruption of plans. History has shown that the power of the media and the resources of political parties eventually encompass all individuals (politicians) who enter politics. Strategic alliances abound, delicately intertwined so that no politician need ever stand alone. It has been said, once again, that we have one political party posing as two; this is for the purpose of allowing the public a sense of authority and control. History is replete with examples of alternate political parties gaining control over the country with similar rhetoric year after year, while accomplishing little of their intended goals. The reason may be that a politician's first allegiance is to fulfill the objectives of his ideology (corporate sponsor) and not the will of the people he represents. Politicians who defy their obligations to those seeking payback for their support soon find themselves embellished in scandal or facing the wrath of a compliant news media.

The election of Donald Trump set politics and the news industry reeling. "Swamp" politicians find themselves with no alliances to Trump. How could this outsider, this TV personality, slip past their defenses? The very best efforts of the corporate elites, the dutiful efforts by a compliant media, and the lack of insider political support . . . yet every political poll in American got it wrong. The reason for Trump's victory over the establishment, including the massive Clinton political machine, was the fact that Trump touched the inner soul of a formerly compliant citizenry. The people realized that Trump had no political ties or alliances with Washington. Trump was a consummate businessman with a no-nonsense attitude toward success. Trump was not intimidated by empty suits who speak with eloquence but proceed with agendas. Despite eighteen legitimate Republican candidates speaking party rhetoric, Trump touched the souls of voters yearning for common sense. The population was energized by a massive surge of realism that they had not seen in their lifetime.

It made no difference that Trump did not have any real political experience; for that matter, neither did Obama. For the first time in memory, a presidential candidate was speaking the language people understood, which made mainstream media coverage less relevant. People realized that the media was not happy with Trump's popularity based on their continual attacks on everything Trump did, some of which became humorous. Courage and the ability to stand on one's principles is not a strong point in politics. One can compromise within one's principles but should never compromise on one's principles. Obvious media bias broke the rules on principles every day, only managing to raise the courage of the silent masses who yearned for the return of common-sense principles. In the end, it is this author's opinion that the mainstream media did more to help Trump than to hurt him, despite the appearance of attacking him. The lessons to be learned are not to underestimate the will of the people and that media bias is a double-edged sword.

This is the time to make a stand. The Republican Party, specifically the conservative minds of this country, has absolutely nothing to lose by standing on principles. The proverbial media bully had met its match under the Trump administration. It was time to man up and level the political playing field. Pretty faces and universal talking points, rather than neutral reporting and unbiased journalism, had successfully convinced the less informed citizens that the progressive movement was in their best interest—something akin to journalistic malpractice. My point is not about political parties; it is about exposing the journalistic fraud.

For Further Reading

Answers Corporation. "How Many US Senators and Congressmen Are Convicted Felons?" WikiAnswers. http://wiki.answers.com/Q/How_many_US_senators_and_congressmen_are_convicted_felons (accessed July 17, 2014).

Benson, Bill, and M. J. Beckman. *The law that never was: the fraud of the 16th Amendment and personal income tax.* South Holland, IL (Box 550, South Holland 60473): Constitutional Research Assoc., 1985.

"COMMON CORE." COMMON CORE. http://whatiscommoncore.wordpress.com/ (accessed July 16, 2014).

Sothern, Marci. "Responsibilities of the Federal Government." eHow. http://www.ehow.com/list_7654222_responsibilities-federal-government.html (accessed July 16, 2014).

Wikimedia Foundation. "Patriot Act." Wikipedia. http://en.wikipedia.org/wiki/Patriot_Act (accessed July 16, 2014).

YouTube. "Gun Myths Gone in Five Minutes: ABC News 20/20." YouTube. https://www.youtube.com/watch?v=682JLrsUmEM (accessed July 17, 2014).

Zieve, Sher. "Behind Common Core: Forcing Marxism/Nazism on America's Children." GulagBoundcom. http://gulagbound.com/38714/common-core-forcing-marxismnazism-on-americas-children/ (accessed July 16, 2014).

Chapter 6

Global Warming

The United States distinguishes itself from all other countries in that its power base resides with the people and the states that make up this great country. As framed by our founding fathers, the Constitution of the United States intentionally limits the power of the federal government to that of an overseer: it is charged with providing a military defense and granted the powers to declare war, to levy and collect taxes, to coin money and regulate its value, to establish post offices and roads, and to exercise exclusive legislation in the District of Columbia.

There have been countless attempts to circumvent our unique Constitution, usually resulting in constitutional conventions in which potential amendments are proposed. However, the real power still resides in the sleeping giant known as the citizens of the United States of America, who, because of increased media outreach, are more attuned to media influence than to government politics. Politicians and government special interest groups have taken notice and have begun a campaign of influencing the citizens of the US through media talking heads rather than their respective elected officials.

One of the most influential attempts at controlling citizen behaviors is the concept of "man-made global warming," which is a generation apart yet akin to the 1960's "Earth Day" rallies. Both were designed to limit citizen freedoms by the presumption that "our species" is destroying life on earth. The global warming advocates, headed by Al Gore, CEO of his Climate Reality Project, have used the media to great advantage. As noble as the cause may be, behind the intent dwells the planning of a global economy looking for the next great economic expansion to capitalize. For example, the rhetoric of the global warming gurus is to convince humanity that the use of aerosol spray, plastic bottles, and the burning of fossil fuels is the cause of greenhouse gasses that build in the atmosphere, somehow destroying the protective ozone layer, leading to increased warming of our planet and the eventual destruction of life as we know it.

The movement is centered around placing guilt on humanity. As convincing as the narrative is to the less informed citizen, the facts being used as scientific proof are turning out to be a step above *"junk science."* There is a difference between actual scientific proof and the use of computer-generated models of potential catastrophic events initiated by data supplied by climate predictions substituting as scientific proof. In 2013, "a group of 50 international scientists released a comprehensive report on the science of climate change that concluded that evidence now leans against global warming resulting from human-related greenhouse gas emissions."[132]

With the arrival of each summer, the global warming minions and their partners in the media ramp up their airwaves with images of drought, famine, and the destruction of the ice fields at the poles, which are so vital to nature's balance and our environmental stability. It is true that images are powerful tools in the media, but questions that have always come up yet never been addressed by either Al Gore or the media include these: Since science has proven the existence of recurring cycles of ice ages and severe droughts, long before man ever set foot on this planet, what should the temperature of this planet actually be? Since man is the most recent inhabitant of this planet, who said that the planet's temperature is fixed to our species' liking?

To understand the agenda of the man-made global warming movement is to understand how conveniently this movement takes a vacation during the winter months, when year after year we get stories of record cold temperatures. In January of 2014, all-time record cold temperatures swept across the mid-North American continent, leaving global warming enthusiasts miffed at nature's inability to back them up. It appears that facts do not seem to matter. Similar events have occurred in 2017 and 2019. In an interview by the Media Research Center, German Climatologist Hans von Storch was asked to reveal his findings on a fifteen-year study. Storch stated that "temperature data for the past 15 years shows an increase of 0.06, or very close to zero." Storch was asked why the Earth's temperature has not risen significantly in the past 15 years despite 400 billion metric tons of carbon dioxide (CO_2) being emitted into the atmosphere from human activities. His response was, "According to most climate models, we should have seen temperatures rise by around 0.25 degrees Celsius (0.45 degrees Fahrenheit) over the past 10 years, but it didn't happen."[133]

The media is now left with a dilemma: How can it spin these new research findings to save face? A partial answer came from the *National Journal,* an American weekly magazine that reports on the current political environment and emerging political and policy trends.[134] Their conclusion, along with that of the US Geological Survey, was that the reason global warming has taken a hiatus has been the counter effect of numerous volcanoes spewing sulfur dioxide into the atmosphere, in effect blocking the sun's rays from penetrating to the earth's surface.[135]

There are presently only seventy active volcanoes on the planet today, spewing sulfur dioxide into the atmosphere, just as they have since the birth of this planet. Why is it that global warming is on hiatus only at the present time? Earth is a vibrant, adaptable speck of dust in the universe. Its resilience is based on billions of years of cosmic calamity and adaptability. Numerous ice ages followed by eons of drought are known to have occurred. Asteroids have hit the planet with the power to alter Earth's axis, yet it has adapted and flourished. Continents have shifted across the seas to form new continents, each with its own unique ecosystem. When the time was appropriate, the oceans spawned the planet's first microorganisms. Land creatures developed to enormous proportions, limited only by what the environment could maintain. In mere cosmic minutes, all life on Earth was obliterated by intergalactic pebbles, only to find its equilibrium and begin anew.

Global warming has less to do with climate change; it is about the transfer of political power from the people to the United Nations and other independent agencies working autonomously to achieve a global agenda. The global warming agenda is a convoluted maze of half-truths, scientific malpractice, and governmental attempts at controlling world economies. It is therefore prudent to review the events that have shaped the movement.

It is so important to understand that claims of climate change and global warming are just part of a master plan, begun in the early 1900s, to reduce the sovereignty of independent nations into a New World System of government. This master plan was exposed in 1969 by Dr. Lawrence Dunegan's reporting of Dr. Richard Day's description of the New World Systems in a paper titled *New World Order Plans Exposed by Insider.* This paper detailed more than fifty goals that must be understood to intelligently discuss what is happening in this country today. One of those goals was referred to as "weather control."[136]

In 1979, the First World Climate Conference took place, outlining humanity's role in climate change and providing the basis for the United Nations to study the issue. Carbon dioxide was the focus of attention. In 1988, the UN officially formed its panels on climate change: the UN Environment Program and the World Meteorological Organization. These became the Intergovernmental Panel on Climate Change (IPCC). In 1997 The Kyoto Protocol was adopted, requiring thirty-seven industrialized nations, including the US, to reduce greenhouse gas emissions. In 1998, developed nations formed the Global Warming Skeptics Plan (later known as the Oregon Petition). For the first time the science of global warming was being questioned, on the realization that much of the impetus was to create an atmosphere of uncertainty against conventional wisdom. In 2001, the US and Russia withdrew from the Kyoto Protocol because the treaty puts an excessive burden on developed nations, and by 2005, when the Kyoto Protocols actually took effect, they essentially became a symbolic gesture among the remaining 141 nations.

To keep the US in the global warming arena, former Vice President Al Gore became the face for climate change and man-made global warming, both in the US and in the international community. Mr. Gore's 2006 documentary *An Inconvenient Truth* won him the international community (IPCC) Nobel Peace prize.[137] Since then, Mr. Gore has refused to answer any questions or appear in any public forum on climate change or man-made global warming. It's important to understand that a global enemy like "global warming" can unite a nation. People often respond emotionally before considering the facts. Mr. Gore has absolutely no credentials as a scientist, let alone an expert on climate change, yet his movie was quickly adopted as fact and was shown in most schools.

The Earth has not warmed in seventeen years. Computer models created by global warming scientists were based on hypothetical data—not fact—and have constituted a massive exaggeration, if not a total falsity. The Arctic ice cap has not melted by 2013, as Mr. Gore suggested in 2007; instead, the Antarctic ice cap has actually grown. Despite all of this, the UN has doubled down on its extremist global warming/climate change theories to the point that to deny global warming has become nearly tantamount to criminal activity. Adam Weinstein, a prominent progressive spokesperson, in his article "Truth Above All," expresses a desire to imprison climate change deniers.[138]

Free speech and open debates are the basis of a free society and the enemy of global governance. Dr. Henry Kissinger, in a 1991 speech before the Bilderberg Conference in France, stated, "The one thing every man fears is the unknown. When presented with this scenario, individual rights will be willingly relinquished for the guarantee of their well-being granted to them by the World Government."[139] Former president of the Czech Republic Vaclav Klaus, an expert on climate change and economics, stated that the climate change debate is a throwback to the tactics of the Communist and Fascists regimes that he experienced. Under those regimes the objective was to have people choose between climate change mandates and freedom. Agenda 21, under the control of the UN, has become the new fascism of an emerging World Government where, under the guise of global warming mandates, property rights and individual freedoms could vanish.[140] For a complete summary of Klaus's words on the subject, refer to the "For Further Reading" section following this chapter and see the video *Lord Al Gore: The Global Warming Fascist.*

In 2009, President Obama called for a "Cap and Trade" bill, whereby a tax on the amount of carbon emissions would be imposed, essentially beginning the deindustrialization of US businesses and increased governmental intervention in private business. Later that same year the Non-governmental International Panel on Climate Change (NIPCC) stated that the Earth *may* be warming but that the cause is primarily natural.[141] In 2013, the International Panel on Climate Change made its findings known to policymakers: "Human influence has been detected in warming of the atmosphere and the ocean, in changes in the global water cycle, in reductions in snow and ice, in global mean sea level rise, and in changes in some climate extremes. This evidence for human influence has grown since its 4th assessment report. It is extremely likely (95–100%) that human influence has been the dominant cause of the observed warming since the mid-20th century."[142]

The formation of the Environmental Protection Agency (EPA) by executive order of President Richard Nixon in 1970 set the stage for future man-made global warming agendas. The EPA is an agency of the US federal government that was created for the purpose of protecting human health and the environment by writing and enforcing regulations based on laws passed by Congress.[143] The EPA was signed into law by executive order and was ratified by Congress, not as a Cabinet department, but its administrator is considered to hold a Cabinet rank position, the Cabinet being the highest body of leadership in the government. The EPA is essentially autonomous, answering only to the president and Congress, if its members so desire.

In 2005 the EPA revealed that Philip Cooney, former chief of staff for the Bush White House Council on Environmental Quality, had personally edited EPA documents summarizing government research on climate change before their release. In December of 2007, EPA administrator Stephen Johnson approved the edited documents, declaring that climate change imperiled the public welfare. This single statement triggered the first of many national mandatory global warming regulations. Under intense scrutiny over the lack of substantive scientific research (other than computer models) to back up the global warming statement, Johnson rescinded the document in 2008, issuing a new statement that global warming was not a danger to the public welfare.[144]

Presently, the EPA has police powers to enforce its regulations, leading to incredible acts of unconstitutional behavior and to sanctions by the federal government. An example of out-of-control EPA behavior was the August 19, 2013, raid on Chicken, Alaska, a small gold-mining town with seventeen total inhabitants. Ten heavily armed EPA agents, accompanied by helicopters and all-terrain vehicles, raided the mining operations unannounced to investigate whether the mining families were violating the Clean Water Act. The mining operation consisted of basically sifting through riverbeds for leftover gold. The event constituted a clear case of overkill by federal authorities seeking violations of environmental regulations.[145]

A sinister, if not humorous, example of intentional government intervention in the private sector was the announcement that the EPA would attempt to regulate cow flatulence as part of the climate change agenda. Methane gas is considered to be a greenhouse gas and, as such, can be regulated under the global warming agenda, if not the Clean Air Act. The lunacy of this assault on dairy and cattle farmers is that since 1990, levels of methane emissions have dropped. Even though methane gas accounts for less than 9% of greenhouse gases, the EPA wanted a 25% additional reduction by 2020.[146] The EPA is not suggesting the ingestion of Gas-X or Beano by their herds but the physical reduction of herd sizes by 25%. Keeping in mind the economic value of meat and dairy to our economy, the reduction of meat and dairy inventories would drive up supply and demand prices, draining more money from the population and into the hands of respective corporate giants.

The political ideology for man-made global warming began with "a group of world citizens, sharing a common concern for the future of humanity." In 1968 they formed The Club of Rome, which is "a think tank or discussion group that represents the interests of the establishment or, more specifically, the interests of the elites who control the establishment."[147] The man-made global warming fraud is clearly all about the influence of some of the wealthiest people in the world seeking to maintain and increase both their wealth and their political power, using fear of global warming consequences as a tool for gaining global political control.

In 1992, the Club of Rome produced a report called the First Global Revolution, which stated, "The Common Enemy of Humanity is Man." The report included the following:

> In searching for a new enemy to unite us, we came up with the idea that pollution, the threat of global warming, water shortages, famine and the like would fit the bill. In their totality and in their interactions these phenomena do constitute a common threat which demands the solidarity of all peoples. But in designating them as the enemy, we fall into the trap about which we have already warned, namely mistaking systems for causes. All these dangers are caused by human intervention, and it is only through changed attitudes and behavior that they can be overcome. The real enemy, then, is humanity itself.[148]

The First Earth Summit in 1992 was part of the global warming agenda for transition to sustainability in the twenty-first century (Agenda 21), under the direction of the UN. Part of the extensive transition program included the assumed "fact" that human beings are responsible for a large amount of global warming.[149] The purpose was to intentionally insert this idea into the consciousness of the people as being important if they truly loved the environment and nature.

To hope to alter the thinking of a complacent society, one must alter their belief system. Few people actually understand the biochemistry of life, let alone how the elements in the periodic table interrelate in our atmosphere.

CO_2 Is Not a Pollutant

CO_2 is not a pollutant, as Mr. Al Gore infers. It is, in fact, essential to life on the planet. Without it there would be no plants, and therefore no oxygen and no life. "To suddenly label CO_2 as a pollutant is a disservice to a gas that played an enormous role in the development and sustainability of all life on Earth. The earth has clearly demonstrated over the eons that CO_2 is not a pollutant."[150]

We commonly think of pollutants as contaminants that make the environment dirty or impure. A vivid example is sulfur dioxide, a byproduct of industrial activity. High levels of sulfur dioxide cause breathing problems, and too much causes acid rain. Sulfur dioxide has a direct effect on health and the environment. Carbon dioxide, on the other hand, is a naturally occurring gas that existed in the atmosphere long before humans. Plants need it to survive. The CO_2 greenhouse effect keeps our climate from freezing over.[151] How can CO_2 be considered a pollutant?

Over the past 10,000 years, the level of atmospheric carbon dioxide has remained at relatively stable levels. However, over the past few centuries human CO_2 emissions have upset this balance. The increase in CO_2 has some direct effects on the environment. Rising CO_2 levels cause an enhanced greenhouse effect. This leads to warmer temperatures, which have many consequences. Some effects are beneficial, such as improved agriculture at high latitudes and increased vegetation growth in some circumstances. However, the negative can far outweigh the positives—it is here that the global warming minions begin to blur the lines of scientific fact. The media is quick to point out that coast-bound communities are threatened by rising sea levels and that melting glaciers threaten wildlife habitat. Species like the polar bear can become extinct.

The scientific facts are that, while the major greenhouse gas is actually H_2O, which substantially warms the Earth, minor greenhouse gases such as CO_2 have little effect. The sixfold increase in fossil fuel burning (internal combustion engines of automobiles) since 1940, leading to increased CO_2 in the atmosphere, has no noticeable effect on atmospheric temperature. It is here that the media demonstrates its hidden agenda. The media simply reports the news and then investigates to ensure correctness in an unbiased fashion. Does it seem unusual that the media continually leaves out important findings like the facts that ocean temperatures have not risen, the ice fields are not melting, and polar bears are not endangered but flourishing? To the untrained mind, watching ice walls breaking away from huge glacier fields, while impressive, is a normal occurrence each and every year.[152]

A recent media event that has damaged the man-made global warming agenda is the trapping of the Russian ship Akademik Shokalskiy in Antarctica. On board this ship were fifty-two research scientists who were on a mission to study the effects of global warming on the destruction of the Antarctic ice fields. The ship is itself an ice breaker with sophisticated equipment that estimated its position as being just two nautical miles from open water at the time of its trapping. The enormous miscalculation was not only an embarrassment but turned up the heat on the global warming agenda.

Changing weather conditions occur all over the planet, and this reality was used as the excuse for the mishap. What the media failed to mention was that this was not a weather bleep but a total miscalculation of actual conditions in Antarctica. All reports from the National Geological Society state that the Antarctic polar ice fields are thicker and more widespread than ever due to the natural "wobble" in the earth's orbit and the effect of the sun on the oceans of the southern hemisphere. Shockingly, these fifty-two expert climate researchers simply ignored these facts. Within four days of the ship's being trapped, the distance to open water had risen to sixteen nautical miles, leaving it ensnared indefinitely. Instead, the media concentrated its reporting of the incident on interviewing the scientists by phone as to what they were eating and how they would pass the time until rescued—but not a word about the expedition's intent.[153]

There is a truism that applies to the global warming agenda: *words have meaning.* Often, word meanings are deliberately changed, the nuances going almost unnoticed, giving faulty science an escape. It took less than three years to quietly change the concept of man-made global warming to a more subjective "climate change." The scientific community became so vocal in its pursuit of the documentation that it initiated a peer reviewed climate change study by the Non-governmental International Panel on Climate Change. The results of the study found the threat of man-made global warming to be not only greatly exaggerated but so small as to be "embedded within the background variability of the natural climate system" and not dangerous.[154] Undaunted by the shift in scientific thinking, the global warming advocates altered their mantra from man-made global warming to climate change, not changing the rhetoric to any degree. At no point has the media admitted that man-made global warming is not what they originally stated; they have instead continued their pursuit under the guise that humans are altering the climate, totally ignoring any scientific evidence to the contrary.

In 2006, when Mr. Gore presented his documentary, *An Inconvenient Truth,* he did so to make the issue of global warming a recognized problem worldwide. His most important message was that global warming is a man-made phenomenon. His intent was to shame the populations of the world into believing that the earth is being influenced by what humans are doing to the planet. The first assault came by alarming people into believing that the use of aerosol cans is contributing to the destruction of the ozone layer, leading to global warming. He also declares that the use of fossil fuels is increasing greenhouse gasses and that petroleum is a limited resource that humanity is exploiting and that will soon be in limited supply. Mr. Gore is trying to redefine global warming as a moral and spiritual issue. But doing so takes the science out of global warming and replaces it with whatever he defines as moral.

Since the 2006 release of *An Inconvenient Truth,* Mr. Gore has remained hidden from the debate. He refuses all interviews to debate any of his critics since the heat has turned up (no pun intended) on the global warming agenda. It appears that by positioning the alleged global warming crisis as a moral issue with spiritual implications, Mr. Gore has no more need to debate global warming than one would have when debating a religious belief.

On June 29, 1993, President Clinton signed Executive Order 12852, establishing the President's Council on Sustainable Development.[155] Appropriately Gore, as vice president, was given authority over the council and would aid in selecting its twenty-five ultraist members. Gore's council was cleverly convened to push a plan inconsistent with the constitutional principles of life, liberty, and the pursuit of happiness, once again cleverly insulating himself from scrutiny:

> The Council should not debate the science of global warming but should instead focus on the implementation of national and local greenhouse gas reduction policies and activities, and adaptations in the US economy and society that maximize environmental and social benefits, minimize economic impacts, and are consistent with US international agreements.[156]

Mr. Gore often talks about the carbon footprint that humans are leaving on the planet. Humans, he insists, should be ashamed that they are using resources faster that the earth can sustain. We all should live more modestly, using less fossil fuel, electricity, water, and the other necessities of life in order to save the planet. One would think that the leader of the man-made global warming movement would set the example for others to follow. With little or no research effort, it was found that Mr. Gore's mansion, located in the posh Belle Meade area of Nashville, Tennessee, uses more electricity in one month than the average home uses in one year. At 221,000 kWh, Mr. Gore proved himself to be a worthy hypocrite for the cause of global warming. Virtually no part of Mr. Gore's personal life reflects his global warming rhetoric.[157]

True to form, when agendas are being legislated into the public domain, especially by executive order, with little or no validity other than as a moral or spiritual issue, one has to raise suspicion by the tried-and-true method of following the money trail. Simply ask yourself who wins and who loses by this agenda. In the case of Mr. Gore, his "Inconvenient Truth" was certainly not inconvenient to his personal life and wealth; he never mentioned that he had applied for and received a $529 million US-backed loan for building hybrid cars in Finland before becoming the spokesperson for the global warming agenda.[158]

Mr. Gore is certainly free to be as entrepreneurial as he chooses, but the salient point to be remembered is that, based on his declaring fossil fuels to be the key reason for man-made global warming, he essentially is guilty of "insider trading," i.e., intentionally destroying an industry while profiting from its alternative. Under the guise that electric-powered cars will save the planet from greenhouse gasses, Mr. Gore's new company is producing hybrid cars by using sophisticated Tesla battery technology targeted to the wealthiest individuals, while depending on the US taxpayer to fund his company.

In Dr. Jerome R. Corsi's *The Great Oil Conspiracy*, Dr. Corsi proves that the earth produces oil in abundance deep within its mantel (*in ways that have nothing to do with dead dinosaurs*) and gives no indication of ever stopping this natural process. Further, the use of oil for fuel and for thousands of other applications, not the least of which is plastics, is one of the great blessings of modern technology and life. Dr. Corsi proposes that the attack on fossil fuels is intended to stimulate an economic revolution into newer fuel technologies for the purpose of economic control over world societies. What better way to control the economics of the world than to legislate alternative fuels as the "new" standard to save the planet?[159]

Knowing all along that there really is no oil shortage or scientific proof of damage to our planet due to fossil fuels, how sinister are the political powers that be? The signs have always been there. The nonsensical legislation, proposed by the autonomous Environmental Protection Agency, to not drill for oil within our borders due to the impact on the environment is, once again, depending on moral issues that circumvent scientific validity. Having us believe that the OPEC nations produce and sell oil because they have no regard for the environment is an incredible stretch of the imagination. As mentioned earlier in Corsi's book, restraints on free enterprise are always about money. Henry Kissinger, in the 1970s under President Richard Nixon, signed a deal with the emerging OPEC nations (specifically Saudi Arabia) to purchase oil from OPEC in return for their financing half the US debt. If the US had decided to drill for oil within its own borders, bypassing the Arab agreement, the Kissinger deal would have been void.[160]

For Further Reading

Corsi, Jerome R. *The great oil conspiracy: how the US government hid the Nazi discovery of abiotic oil from the American people.* New York, NY: Skyhorse Pub., 2012.

Jasper, William F. "EPA Water Police Coming to Your Farm, Business—and Back Yard." EPA Water Police Coming to Your Farm, Business—and Back Yard. *http://www.thenewamerican.com/tech/environment/item/17164-tna-online-epa-water-regulators-coming-to-your-farm-business-and-back-yard* (accessed July 13, 2014).

King, Alexander, and Bertrand Schneider. "The First Global Revolution." http://www.geoengineeringwatch.org/documents/TheFirstGlobalRevolution_text.pdf (accessed July 13, 2014).

"Lord Al Gore: The Global Warming Fascist." YouTube. http://youtu.be/i9WFDcZxT0s (accessed July 13, 2014).

Wikimedia Foundation. "Agenda 21." Wikipedia. http://en.wikipedia.org/wiki/Agenda_21 (accessed July 13, 2014).

Wikimedia Foundation. "Club of Rome." Wikipedia. http://en.wikipedia.org/wiki/Club_of_Rome (accessed July 13, 2014).

Wikimedia Foundation. "Federal government of the United States." Wikipedia. http://en.wikipedia.org/wiki/Federal_government_of_the_United_States (accessed June 24, 2014).

Chapter 7

Government Deception and the Fourth Branch of the Federal Government

Government Deception

Toward the end of Obama's presidency, it appeared that political deception was on the rise. The US population was just beginning to get a glimpse of the realities of a progressive government. Words have meaning, and the interpretations of words change over time, either by intention or by cultural conditioning; the key is knowing when deception is occurring. It must be clearly understood that "liberalism" and "progressivism," as economic mindsets, are not synonymous. Liberalism focuses on using taxpayer money to help better society. Progressivism focuses on using government power to make large institutions play by a set of rules. A progressive government, therefore, exists for the purpose of redefining the fulfillment of human capacities as the primary task of the state.[161]

The 2016 election cycle stunned the progressive movement. Hillary Clinton's loss to Donald Trump gave America a unique glimpse of the dark side of progressivism. The slow, relatively peaceful and relentless process of making bigger government an essential requirement for the US citizenry was faced with a new leader capable of dismantling decades of progressive planning. As a result, the progressive movement went into panic mode, no longer capable of hiding its intentions. The pressure was on to destroy Trump's presidency at all costs. America got a rare glimpse at how ruthless politics can be. At the time of writing, there had been thirty-seven attempts to destroy Trump's presidency, from the Russian collusion story to win the election to having the "deep state" take Trump out by invoking the 25th Amendment.[162] All attempts failed.

Just in time for the 2020 election cycle, the Covid-19 pandemic appeared. The progressives wasted no time in invoking draconian measures never before witnessed in any pandemic. The intent was to maintain a pandemic atmosphere to keep people contained and compliant, while destroying our economy and allowing outside organizations to terrorize the country under the protection of our First Amendment.

The progressive movement began in America in the twentieth century, in cities where settlement workers and reformers, who were interested in helping those facing harsh conditions at home and at work, needed protection from oppression. Progressivism was embraced by American presidents like Theodore Roosevelt, Woodrow Wilson, Franklin Roosevelt, Lyndon Johnson, and others. As the industrial revolution fundamentally transformed migrant workers into corporate employees, the progressive movement transitioned from helping the oppressed to initiating social oppression. In general, the progressive philosophy is synonymous with advocating gradual social, political, and economic reform—moving society away from democratic principles.

Historically, as mentioned earlier, no previous democracy has survived for more than two hundred years. The reasons are many, but there is only one cause. Democracy requires continued diligence and responsibility to founding principles. With each generation, responsibility wanes in favor of political or social groups acting on their own behalf. The result is that eventually all responsibilities (dictated by founding principles) are deferred to others who are willing to take responsibility.[163] Sooner or later those political or social groups get infiltrated by the default government. This is socialism, euphemistically renamed progressivism. The US population never experiences social change until it once again becomes oppressive. By that time, it's usually too late to recover.

The classic modern example is a group called Democracy for America. This sounds like a group to get behind, for sure. Keep in mind, though, yet again, that words have meaning! Democracy for America has been redefined by the Democratic Party as a "progressive political action committee," the result of which became the basis for the then candidate Barack Obama's platform slogan, "Change we can believe in."[164] What Americans actually voted for and gave their approval to was to fundamentally move America from a democracy to socialism, under the guise of progressivism.

It is at this point that one must ask the question: Did most Americans who voted for Obama understand that progressivism is not a better form of democracy? Did they really understand that the word "progress" in progressivism does not mean a better way to enhance democracy, but that progressivism is, instead, an ideology that moves a population toward socialism? There are only two possibilities: perhaps they did understand, in which case our country is in for a rude awakening, or they have been duped into an emotional, "adolescent" desire to rid the country of what they might believe to be constitutional restrictions on their lives. Either possibility ends up in the same place: America loses its identity.

One must clearly understand that government mandates are euphemisms for *law*. The incremental abuse of constitutional power, seemingly approved by Congress, empowers the federal government. It is my opinion that our government is rapidly approaching a point in its progressive agenda at which it has minimal need for congressional oversight. The main functions of the federal government are to create and enforce laws to ensure order and stability within society; to coin money and regulate its value, ensuring a stable economy; and to raise and maintain our armed forces for our national defense. The executive branch of government also has a specific degree of constitutional interpretation through use of the executive order in times of national emergencies; the executive order must have a constitutional basis.

The progressive method of over-promising and under-delivering became evident when Americans in general realized that virtually none of the tenets of "The Healthcare Affordability Act" (Obamacare) were true and that they really had no choice whether or not to participate. Those who failed to join the "exchange" would be penalized the cost of the exchange policy on their tax return. The IRS became the enforcement arm for Obamacare. The Trump administration's promise to repeal or replace Obamacare faced the progressive talking point of "How can the Republicans even consider rescinding the healthcare of twenty million Americans now covered by Obamacare?" The reality that the twenty million Americans were forced to join the exchange is of little consequence. Deception is a wonderful tool in controlling a population.

Most citizens are not familiar with the specifics of the Constitution and are dependent on their elected congressional representatives to ensure that their interests are being well protected. To an unsuspecting public, rogue government officials or policies can easily be implemented. The Constitution was designed to limit the ability of the federal government to act autonomously but cannot stop this from occurring. Months into Obama's second term, the lies and hidden agendas within progressivism began to emerge, including scandals of enormous significance to the economic security of this country, i.e., expanded government control (regulation), de-privatization of our healthcare system (one-fifth of our gross national product), open borders, lax immigration policies, sanctuary cities for undocumented immigrants, NAFTA, and the Iranian Nuclear Deal, to name just a few.

The North American Free Trade Agreement (NAFTA), for example, is a progressive movement attempting to redistribute the wealth in America between Canada and Mexico. Just the tone of what was just stated has probably "tuned out" many of you who are reading this. But bear with me by considering the following realities of NAFTA:

John is an American worker who earns $22.50/hour making chrome-plated widgets for a major corporation that has 5,500 other employees also making the same widgets. John has great healthcare benefits and a partially paid retirement plan with a company matched 401K plan, owns a house in the suburbs of New York, has two cars, and is married with 2.5 children. The board of directors and CEO of John's company were looking into ways of boosting their profits. The company tried to reduce company benefits and freeze salaries, but the company's union, who fought hard for these benefits (now seen as entitlements), threatened to strike.

The CEO, being aware of NAFTA, decided that it was time to investigate the possibility of farming out the production of the widgets to Mexico, where they found a company that manufactures the identical chrome-plated widgets for far less money than in the US. John's company struck a deal with the Mexican company, bypassing American government regulations due to NAFTA. Soon John's company had doubled its profit margins by making its widgets in Mexico and shipping them back to the US without tariffs (taxes on imports), thanks to NAFTA.

One day John's company sent a "dear John letter" (no pun intended) to half of its employees, informing them that they were being laid off. John, fortunately, was not one of them, at least for the time being. The laid-off workers immediately applied for State- and company-funded unemployment benefits, as approved by the US Secretary of Labor.[165] Six months later John's company decided to merge with their counterpart in Mexico and close their plant in New York. After eighteen years of service, John was unemployed, along with thousands of other employees from different such companies around the country because of NAFTA guidelines. John's and his family's lifestyle was in shambles, dependent on an ever-growing demand for government subsidies (entitlements).

Although the story is fictitious, it demonstrates the actual result of NAFTA on the American worker and our economy. The salient message hidden within NAFTA, which caused President Trump to openly condemn the agreement as a disaster for the American economy, is that without tariffs on goods and services produced outside the US, American workers are doomed.

Keep in mind that tariffs on products are paid for by the consumer, not by the country of origin. In 2019, President Trump actually used the power of the tariff on Mexican goods, not to balance fair trade with Mexico, as with the fictitious NAFTA example above, but to force Mexico to enact its immigration laws to stop the flow of illegal immigrant caravans from using Mexico as a free-passage route to the US/Mexican border. The progressives in Congress realized that their desire for open borders was doomed if Trump succeeded in doing an end around Congress via tariffs, and they attempted to whip the American people into a frenzy over increased prices because of the tariffs. Fortunately, the economic consequences of tariffs on Mexican goods were enough for Mexico to sign a deal with the US to stop the caravans before the tariff deadline.

So, who wins by having "free trade"? The answer, once again, lies within the progressive mindset of over-promising and under-delivering. Mega corporations (who represent the rich), enjoying the benefits from NAFTA, hire lobbyists and donate heavily to political parties and candidates to win political favor. This is not the forum for Progressivism 101, but understand that when capitalism is replaced by progressivism, society changes dramatically. Progressivism requires a greater, more powerful central government intrusion. Capitalism enhances the wealth of the middle class, while progressivism tends to eliminate the middle class, increasing government entitlement programs (ask John) and reducing our country's standard of living.

Progressives want the population to demonize the rich as the reason "the people" are poor; however, the progressives are the rich, and once in control they will have the power to perpetuate the myth while reaping the benefits. Posing popular emotional questions like "What's wrong with making the rich pay their fair share?" or "What's wrong with redistributing the wealth of our nation among the poor?" is the progressives' way of dividing the nation.

With no disrespect intended toward any particular group, consider the following facts before buying the myth:

- The rich supply most of the jobs. If progressivism replaces capitalism, the middle-class entrepreneur disappears. If the rich move their companies out of the country for higher profits (NAFTA), who will you work for? The government will become your de facto employer.
- In 1964 (the Johnson administration), our country declared a war on poverty.[166] Some fifty years later and with trillions of dollars poured into the effort, 15% of the US population is still in poverty, slightly more than it was in 1964.
- NAFTA has cost the US economy 700,000 jobs and huge trade deficits.

In fact, pick any government-funded program designed as a war on drugs, crime, cancer, or education equality and see how successful it has been. Government-funded programs spend taxpayer money with little or no accountability. The justification is always that at least we tried![167]

Free trade has been the signature agenda platform of giant corporations, political donors, and the progressive agenda. For a sitting president to openly rebuke free trade agreements is political suicide. President Trump was the first president to actually explain to the people why, economically, NAFTA and other World Trade Organization agreements were potential disasters for the American economy. President Trump is first and foremost a consummate businessman, who understands that the US cannot remain solvent with ever-increasing trade deficits. He also understands that if the US government wants to dabble in business, it must show a profit. What company in the history of the world can remain solvent without a strong profit and loss statement? There is no accountability with socialism because the money one receives and spends is not their own. As Margaret Thatcher once put it, "The trouble with Socialism is that eventually you run out of other people's money."[168]

One of the most profitable and successful private business corporations in America is Walmart. Few of us can remember that Walmart began in 1962, embracing its "Made in America" pledge that all product on its shelves would be produced, manufactured, and assembled in America. Walmart (like the example of John's fictitious widget company) found, however, that its board of directors and CEO could buy and sell products for less, while increasing their profits, if they partnered with Mexico, China, and other countries. I dare say that a quick look on any Walmart shelf will turn up "Made in China" or "Made in Mexico" labels on many, if not most, products. The Federal Trade Commission recently forced Walmart to scrub the "Made in America" slogan from its website, another example of why NAFTA was bad for America.[169]

Free Market vs Capitalism
To truly understand economics, one must understand that wealth, goods and services, profits, and job creation all depend largely on supply and demand," using a universally accepted rate of exchange. For the purpose of this discussion, I will address only government involvement in economics, not the sovereign rights of individuals to do business apart from government regulation.

- Due to social and cultural factors, the realities of economic "free trade" go well beyond textbook definitions.
- A capitalist system and a free-market system are economic environments in which the dictates of supply and demand are the main factors determining price and production of goods and services. Although the two economic systems are both based on the law of supply and demand, they are different.
- Capitalism is an economic system based on ownership of the factors of production. Some key features of capitalism are competition between companies and owners, private ownership, and motivation to generate a profit. The production and pricing of goods and services are determined by the free market, or supply and demand.

- A free-market system is based solely on supply and demand in world markets, without intervention from outside government forces, tariffs, or regulations. In a free-market system, a buyer and a seller transact freely only when they voluntarily agree on the price of a good or a service.[170]
- Capitalism is focused on the creation of wealth and ownership of capital, as well as factors of production, whereas a free-market system is focused on the exchange of wealth or goods and services. Due to an ever-growing presence of governmental regulations, the progressives have seized the opportunity of using greater government control ("for the country's own good") as a cover to move the country toward socialism.

Examples of Government and Executive Overreach

Common Core

One must clearly understand that government mandates are euphemisms for law. The incremental abuse of constitutional power, seemingly approved by Congress, empowers the federal government. It is my opinion that our government is rapidly approaching a point in its progressive agenda that has minimal need for congressional oversight, as witnessed by the numerous scandals against our Constitution and the public at large.

The Obama administration increased national control over our schools via the Common Core Curriculum initiative. Common Core is a new curriculum developed by a panel of so-called education (government) experts. The administration tried to turn Common Core into a national curriculum by offering states increased federal educational funding if they were to impose Common Core's curriculum on their public schools. In short, the government was using taxpayer money to fundamentally alter what students would learn about this country. This is yet another example of the government using tax money from the people to bribe states into obeying federal mandates.

Education is the responsibility of individual states. The federal government, under the Obama administration, really did not put the Common Core curriculum together; rather, it was the National Governors' Association that discussed the creation of Common Core state standards in 2007, a year before Obama's first term.[171] Obama incorporated Common Core principles into his "Race to the Top" educational initiative[172] by developing a four-billion-dollar grant program to provide incentives for states to implement Common Core. Federal funding rather than debate became the driving force.

Common Core curriculum fit perfectly into Obama's progressive ideology of "Hope and Change." For Obama, it was all about controlling the progressive narrative for his upcoming presidential election. One must recognize the pattern of the progressive agenda; it's all about urgency: no time to waste—our country's future is at stake. By using emotional hooks rather than constitutional debate, agendas get implemented. Remember that Obamacare was passed without congressional debate. One-fifth of the American economy got redirected to a "new" healthcare system, the details of which no one even read. As noted earlier, Nancy Pelosi put it best to Congress: "We have to pass the bill so that you can find out what's in it."[173] Hardly a democratic process, unless agenda driven. Once compromises are made for political and not for educational reasons, the intent becomes murky.

Critics of the Common Core say that it dumbs down education by replacing traditional English literature and history with informational texts, replacing actual facts with designer history.[174] Traditionally, education is a state-controlled responsibility. Having a centralized federal educational platform is tantamount to educational suicide, and with this change goes diversity of opinions (freedom of speech), which is a clever way to circumvent the First Amendment of our Constitution. As an aside, the Common Core curriculum also separates the parent from educating their child. Think this can't happen? Historically, this is exactly what the Nazis did with the youth of Germany: indoctrinate and separate.[175]

It is not enough that the federal government has granted itself legislative and implied powers never designated by the Constitution; the federal government is now expanding its "ownership" conquests into private enterprise. Along with the "corporate" auto, banking, mortgages, airlines, and other industries, the government has set its sights on extending federal monies to colleges.

On a bus tour through New York and Pennsylvania that began on August 22, 2013, Obama gave a series of poll-boosting speeches to university campuses as part of his "Foundation for the Middle Class" to reform higher education's increased tuition costs.[176] President Obama used the federal government's increased control over student loans to push for greater federal control over college administration, graduation rates, and tuition costs.[177] Obama told these young minds that he had "saved" GM from bankruptcy (implying that he could do the same for higher education), while neglecting to tell the students that, should GM fail to meets its reorganization obligations, the government would essentially own the company.

The government has no authority or mechanism to own a private industry. Obama did not save the auto industry, as he would have had the inexperienced college minds believe; he used "quantitative easing" funds to save the union in return for its loyalty and for ownership. Government assistance in higher education comes from taxpayer money and, as such, allows government a degree of control over the industry of higher education.

The real purpose of this meaningless bus tour was to rally the upcoming young workforce into accepting government assistance as part of their financial portfolio. These young minds lack life experience and are easily taught to embrace financial support from wherever it is offered. These young minds and pocketbooks were also necessary to initially prop up Obama's Healthcare Affordability Act. As a point of entry into the private sector, the government attempted to rig the outcome to ensure that it's only a matter of time before complete government compliance becomes the norm.

IRS

This is not the forum for a full IRS discussion or disclosure, but certain facts need to be known before one can understand the significance of the IRS scandals. Suffice it to say, the IRS has been given undue powers, based not on constitutional law but on federal government edicts. The IRS was technically set up by President Lincoln to fund the costs of the Civil War in the Act of 1862, which established the office of commissioner of the IRS. All that did was create the office of the commissioner, who is just the figurehead of a private corporation, just as the commissioner of the

Federal Reserve is the head of the private corporation but has no legal or constitutional connection to the US government.

Not only is the collection of taxes a questionable function of the IRS, but the situation was further scandalized by the government giving the IRS power to administer the financial implementation of the Affordable Care Act (Obamacare) of 2010, for which there was no legal precedent whatsoever. To implement this new responsibility, the IRS is merely a private corporation hired by the US government as a collection agency. The IRS has been given illegal and unconstitutional "police" power to bypass almost any constitutional amendment without congressional approval, and it answers only to the Department of the Treasury, which is under the control of the executive branch of our government. Translation: The IRS answers to the president and not to Congress. Hence the ease and secrecy with which it is able to perpetrate its Gestapo-like tactics, as well as its freedom to spend taxpayer money (some fifty-plus million dollars) on lavish hotels, baseball games, entertainment, inappropriate (IRS) parties, etc.—none of which could occur under the watch of a diligent and responsible president or Congress.

If a government agency has autonomy, it can act independently of any of the conflicts of interest or moralities faced by the rest of the population. Jaimie Dupree, a Washington, DC insider watchdog, reported that "A new report shows the Internal Revenue Service routinely gave bonuses and time off awards to tax agency workers who had been disciplined internally for job-related misconduct, which included fraud, misuse of government credit cards and the failure to properly pay their federal taxes to Uncle Sam." In short, the Treasury Inspector General found that 1,146 performance awards, averaging over $1,000 of taxpayer money, were issued to IRS workers despite misconduct that would likely have resulted in firing or jail time for nongovernment employees.

This scandal is a national eye-opener. More recently, the IRS was given the unconstitutional power to monitor "healthcare" decisions under Obamacare. An additional 16,000 IRS agents were put on the government payroll to ensure that all citizens complied with the purchasing of healthcare coverage or faced penalties inclusive of garnishing tax returns, while providing cover for the illegal distribution of all medical and personal records to any government or law enforcement agency, on demand and without a warrant.

The IRS is a "corporation" that administers the collection of taxes within the US; however, the Constitution of the US does not empower Congress to delegate any function to the IRS, nor does it have any jurisdiction in the fifty states. The Sixteenth Amendment of 1913, supposedly giving Congress the power to collect income taxes, was never ratified. Compelling evidence and documentation can be found in the book *The Law That Never Was*.[178][179] The definition of "income tax," as written in a proposed amendment never ratified, is a tax, not on wages or salaries but on the profit made from the investment of wages and salaries. Direct governmental lying about the passage of the 16th Amendment have placed fear into the minds of people. Regardless of the circumstances, the IRS has been "bestowed" powers, making it the most brutal collection agency in the nation, answerable to only the president.

The IRS was caught targeting organizations, specifically conservative organizations that applied for 501(c) (4) status. This targeting was based on political leanings. The IRS decided, by filtering organizations that used the words "tea party" or "patriot" (NSA spying), that they could slow down or stop altogether any opposition to the progressive movement (remember who is their boss). By not approving the same nonprofit status for these as for other political organizations, the IRS perpetuated its reign of tyranny. The White House claimed that it had no knowledge of this practice; the federal government lied. The acting IRS Commissioner, Steven Miller (the CEO of the "private" IRS Corporation), took the heat but was able to disclose to Congress that he had not been in charge during the time the IRS was given the green light to blatantly discriminate; instead, we find that senior White House officials knew of the IRS activity all along. The IRS official who oversaw the division that targeted conservative nonprofit groups was Lois Lerner.

At the House Oversight and Government Reform Committee hearings, charged with investigating the unethical and possibly criminal activity of the IRS, Lerner took the Fifth Amendment, protecting her (and the IRS) from possible self-incrimination. It appears that politics once again trumps truth.

Keeping in mind the arm's-length relationship the IRS has with the government; it is easy to understand why the Obama administration stated that it had nothing to do with the IRS targeting conservative groups. Simply put, the IRS was hired by the US government but is not a part of or directly accountable to the constitutional government of the US. The scam has perpetuated for over a century, with the secret well maintained to keep the population unaware of the truth and in constant fear of IRS reprisals. Any attempt to expose the openly available truth about the IRS is shut down with military-type efficiency, bypassing traditional due process. US government history textbooks have expunged any reference to the fraud that is the IRS.

The Department of Justice

The Department of Justice, during the Obama administration, was found to have seized the work and personal phone line messages of Associated Press (AP) reporters. This DOJ investigation came about because of an AP article on a foiled CIA terror plot in which the AP disclosed specifics of the operation. These phone records were seized as part of an ongoing investigation into the AP's practices and which government officials they had used as sources.

Then Attorney General Eric Holder claimed that he did not know the specifics because he had recused himself from the investigation. In a letter of protest sent to Eric Holder, the AP President and CEO said,

> There can be no possible justification for such an overbroad collection of the telephone communications of The Associated Press and its reporters. These records potentially reveal communications with confidential sources across all of the newsgathering activities undertaken by the AP during a two-month period, providing a road map to AP's newsgathering operations and disclosing information about AP's activities and operations that the government has no conceivable right to know.

He demanded the return of the phone records and the destruction of all copies.

The scandal resides in the fact that the federal government literally bypassed the constitutional rights of the free press because it was annoyed that government employees had perhaps provided the leaks to the AP. It did so by strong-arming the AP to release all phone and sensitive, privileged records to DOJ agents. No one is above the law, and allowing such untethered access without court order amounts to tyranny.

It appears that the DOJ could care less about the constitutional protocols with which they have been sworn to abide. It should be clearly noted that every US official of the Department of Justice must sign an affidavit Oath of Office that legally binds each officer to the Constitutional constructs appropriate to their position. *"I will support and defend the Constitution of the United States against all enemies, foreign and domestic; that I will bear true faith and allegiance to the same; that I take this obligation freely, without any mental reservation or purpose of evasion; and that I will well and faithfully discharge the duties of the office on which I am about to enter. So help me God."*[180] Failure to abide by the Oath of Office is subject to "perjury" statutes, which under federal law classifies as a "felony." **Federal Criminal Penalty for Violation of Oath of Office:** "Federal criminal law is explicit and direct regarding a violation of oath of office by federal officials. The law requires the removal of the office holder as well as a prison term of up to five years and a fine of up to $10,000."[181]

In 2018 the DOJ, in conjunction with then FBI Director James Comey, colluded in securing the now infamous, unverified Christopher Steele dossier to secure a FISA (Foreign Intelligence Surveillance Act) warrant to spy on the Trump campaign advisor Carter Page. The FBI withheld until months later the vital information from the FISA court, the American public, and Congress that Steele had been paid to find dirt on Trump by a firm doing political opposition research for the Democratic Party and for Democratic presidential candidate, Hillary Clinton.[182]

Is it any wonder that government intelligence agencies can and often do participate in illegal activities like seizing secret intelligence, not reporting the truth, or prying into the private files of future administration officials? Spying and espionage are common techniques used by all intelligence agencies or political parties, but outright lying and coverups for political reasons constitute tyranny.

Secrecy is the key to the success of intelligence gathering, but for every spy there is a counter spy. In 1961 Mad Magazine launched a parody about the intelligence-gathering community with a comic strip called "Spy vs. Spy." It featured two birdlike agents involved in espionage activities; one is dressed in white and the other in black, with identical features. The two are constantly at war with each other, each using a variety of booby traps to inflict harm on the other. The spies usually alternate between victory and defeat. The strip was created to depict the activities of the Cold War, but the reality is that, comic strip or otherwise, the storyline of illegal spying, wiretapping, and the seizing of public records for intelligence gathering goes on within all intelligence agencies and governments. The public becomes aware of this only when they get caught.[183]

James Rosen of Fox News

James Rosen was a journalist and television correspondent in Washington, DC for Fox News. On May 17, 2013, the *Washington Post* reported that the United States Department of Justice had monitored Rosen's activities by tracking his visits to the State Department through phone traces, the timing of calls, and his personal emails. This case is a quintessential scandal involving infringement on First Amendment rights. As a journalist, Rosen was working on a story about North Korea. An article appearing in the *New Yorker* states, "The search warrant for Rosen's e-mail account is the most troubling aspect of the scandal because in the search warrant application, prosecutors alleged that there was probable cause to believe that Rosen violated the Espionage Act of 1917."[184] United States Attorney General Eric Holder blatantly lied to Congress and overstepped his legal authority to go shopping for a federal judge willing to set aside a hundred years of constitutional privacy rights of citizens. In short, the federal government decided to pry into the private life of a news correspondent, naming him a criminal coconspirator for simply doing his job as a journalist. At stake here is defending the right to operate as a member of the free press.

Since when is the federal government above the law? Since when can a federal official manipulate the judiciary branch of government with impunity? Eric Holder not only lied to Congress (punishable as perjury on a federal level and carrying a possible sentence of five years in prison) in claiming that he knew nothing about the unconstitutional privacy invasion, but he was initially turned down by two federal judges before finding a third who was willing to comply, perhaps by making a bogus case of a possible national security breach.

Recent statements by the National Security Administration (NSA) and the Department of Justice (DOJ), designed to quell public concern over privacy rights, were that "these agencies do not have the right, nor can ever get the right, to read personal emails or tap into cellphone communications." This begs the question Why collect all this communication data in the first place? The fact is that the NSA, DOJ, and FBI, as seen in the James Rosen case, can void privacy rights at will. The Democratic chairman of the Senate Judiciary Committee Patrick Leahy authored a Senate bill to rewrite laws to allow federal officials to read personal email without warrants.[185] Within days, public outcry for upholding First Amendment rights forced Leahy to rescind his warrantless email surveillance bill, demonstrating that there is power in public opinion.[186]

The point is that our system of justice and constitutional law hangs in the balance. We must never forget how the Nazi party took over the stable German government, essentially establishing its precedent of untethered and illegal information gathering under the guise of national security, all of this spearheaded by the promises of a single man—Adolf Hitler.

FBI Seizing Personal Records

Google, this nation's largest and most comprehensive information search engine, is also a gold mine for data collection. Under the guise of national security, the FBI petitioned a federal judge to order Google to release customer data records to the FBI without justification. In short, this is a blatant invasion of privacy. After an initial rejection, US district Court Judge Susan Illston approved the order.[187] The scandal lies in the reason a federal judge would approve such an ill-advised action. Could it be that the present executive administration illegally uses the FBI to do its dirty work of collecting personal data on every citizen in the US, under the guise of potential terrorism prevention? This would seem plausible, since the same has occurred with the huge wireless phone company Verizon, where federal authorities secured the personal data of every single user on its vast network.

Information has arisen showing that the National Security Agency (NSA) has been, for years, spying on every American by gaining access to not only phone records but also to credit card accounts, health records,[188] life insurance policies, Facebook contacts, Twitter accounts, and just about any other collectible data they want, without reason or warrant. The administration defends the NSA's actions as part of the mandate of the Patriot Act to thwart terrorism. Amazing how phone numbers and credit card accounts help thwart terrorism, while having wide open borders, no immigration policy, and no program to deport foreign felons is somehow okay. The scandal is an obliteration of the First Amendment, as well as an overreach of authority.

The Patriot Act was an Act of the US Congress that was signed into law by President George W. Bush on October 26, 2001, in response to the 9/11 terrorist attacks on American soil. The act was hastily put together but received nearly unanimous support by both houses of Congress, giving great latitude to circumvent constitutional restraints on the invasion of privacy. After closer review, it was found that the act gave the progressive movement the needed precedence to bridge constitutional law. Some of the shortcomings of the Patriot Act are:

- giving authorization of indefinite detentions of immigrants
- searches through which law enforcement officers search a home or business without the owner's or the occupant's permission or knowledge
- the expanded use of National Security Letters, which allow the Federal Bureau of Investigation (FBI) to search telephone, email, and financial records without a court order
- the expanded access of law enforcement agencies to business records, including library and financial records, and the president's new ability to wiretap Americans' phone calls without a warrant, on the suspicion that the person might be a terrorist.

This single piece of legislation raises the question of trading security for freedom and can be argued as the justification for the scandals mentioned in this section.

In October 2015, the Inspector General of Homeland Security found and disciplined forty-one Secret Service agents who had illegally dug into the confidential personal files of Utah Republican Jason Chaffetz, who chaired the House Committee on Oversight and Government Reform. Chaffetz had applied for a job with the Secret Service years before he was elected to the House, and agents were looking for something that might embarrass him, according to the Inspector General's report.[189] Does this act by government officials rise to the level of suspected terrorism, or is it a bastardization of the Patriot Act for sinister purposes?

Benghazi Investigation

The actual events of September 11, 2012, in Benghazi, Libya, remain a mystery. The magnitude of the breach in international security, coupled with the nondisclosure of critical facts by responsible government officials to congressional review, is unprecedented, and is making it difficult to assume that there was no government liability. Suggestions that the White House, the Department of State, and former Secretary of State Hillary Clinton are all hiding something in the death of Ambassador Chris Stevens and three other Foreign Service officers are impossible to ignore. The White House released hundreds of emails related to Benghazi. The talking points delivered after the attack changed dramatically, leaving the public to believe this was a random act, whereas later revelations proved otherwise. Unprecedented are the outright and unpunished lies stated to the public.

Emails, obtained by conservative watchdog group Judicial Watch through a Freedom of Information Act request, include one in which a White House official, Ben Rhodes, presented the official narrative of the embassy attack as a spontaneous protest assault that never happened. The intent was to mislead the American people, while protecting the president from damaging criticism so close to the 2010 elections.[190] The then US Ambassador to the United Nations Susan Rice appeared on five TV news and commentary networks, stating that the entire event took place due to a video.[191]

Facts later revealed that this was a fabricated lie to hide the truth—a potential cover-up. The scandal resides in the cover-up and the extent to which the Obama administration was willing to go to keep it a secret. Although investigations are ongoing, President Obama's appointment of Susan Rice as his National Security Advisor demonstrates further that this was a scandal of monumental proportions. Susan Rice is now insulated from testimony in the Benghazi investigations by protection of executive power.

The fact remains that two ranking American ambassadors and two Navy seals were sacrificed for reasons yet to be discovered. Condemning the actions (or lack thereof) that the Obama administration took, allegedly to hide the real agenda, leads any American citizen to seriously question the depths of possible deception it was willing to take to uphold its agenda. Along with a complicit media, the best way to avoid public scrutiny and congressional action demanded by one's constituents is simply to not speak of the situation any longer. Not until the revealing new email evidence was released did the media break its deafening silence.[192]

Gun Control

This scandal is an affront to the Second Amendment of the Constitution. From the time Obama took office, disarming the public was part of his official progressive agenda. The attempts occurred following almost every instance of a mass shooting. This was an opportunistic attitude to push an agenda, playing on people's emotions. Taking guns from law-abiding citizens not only goes against our Second Amendment rights but also exposes the public to additional dangers in the eyes of a criminal mind. To assign gun control to an international body like the U.N. would be a clever way to circumvent the Second Amendment of the Constitution[193] Obama's reasoning was to limit US access to weapons to protect against potential terrorist activity under the Patriot Act. History shows that an unarmed population can offer little resistance. An example of this was the disarming of German citizens during the Nazi regime. Texas Attorney General Greg Abbott seized the moment, stating that if Obama were to have signed a UN agreement on gun control, the State of Texas would have sued the federal government for treason.[194]

On September 13, 2013, President Barack Obama addressed the four thousand in attendance at the Washington navy yard memorial services for the twelve victims of the mass shooting by former navy reservist Aaron Alexis. He called for a transformation in the nation's gun laws to address an epidemic of gun violence. He stated that "No other advanced nation endures the kind of gun violence seen in the United States" and blamed mass shootings in America on laws that fail "to keep guns out of the hands of criminals and dangerous people."[195] Having a national audience to speak to shouldn't give any president license to distort the truth. In a December 16, 2012 article in Newsmax, Daniel Greenfield notes that the media typically spins these mass shootings as a uniquely American phenomenon, suggesting that we ought to be more like Europe, with its strong gun control laws, to prevent these problems. However, if we look at the per capita rates of multiple-victim public shootings in Europe and the United States over the last several years, we will see that they have been fairly similar to each other.[196]

After every mass shooting that occurred during Obama's presidency, he pushed for stricter gun laws, as he did in the aftermath of the elementary school shooting in Newtown, Connecticut, that killed twenty first graders and six staff. The acts of violence in Newtown and the Washington, DC naval yard are tragic and may even point out laxity in basic security measures. But it is beyond comprehension that a US military naval base could be breached, leading to a violent massacre, because trained military personnel are unarmed. Closer scrutiny reveals that virtually every mass shooting, whether in the US or in Europe, has been perpetrated by individuals who have mental disorders, are on psychotropic drugs, or are just plain criminals. Not a single shooting is reported to have been committed by someone considered to be without mental aberrations. It is mind-boggling to think that disarming law-abiding citizens will keep guns out of the hands of criminals or the deranged. What possible questions, given stricter gun control, would identify a criminal or a mentally deranged person? I don't believe someone would openly identify themselves as mentally deranged, so their only option is to seek non legal means to obtain a gun? A criminal is a person who does not regard the law. Will a law stop a criminal from choosing to break the law and acquire a firearm?

The continual argument for stricter gun registration laws is, in my belief at least in part, for the purpose of disarming the law-abiding citizen, under the ruse that it will somehow keep guns from the criminal or mentally unbalanced individual. An armed citizenry can offer resistance to oppression, which is the very reason for the Second Amendment. The mentally unstable, and those hell-bent on violence or aggression, will seek out the weak and defenseless to achieve their ultimate goal. A total of one hundred-fifteen mass shooting murders have taken place since 1990,[197] all of them against the unarmed or the defenseless.

In a 2007 ABC 20/20 segment, John Stossel interviews Tom Palmer, who sued and won a favorable decision in the Federal Appeals Court for Washington, DC, reversing its ban on the private ownership of firearms.[198] Since the firearm ban took effect, murder and violent crimes with a weapon in Washington, DC have sky-rocketed, as they have in every other state with similar firearm bans. The court had no choice but to rescind the ban, dealing a serious blow to anti-gun legislators. This is not the forum for psychological analysis, but it can be safely stated that even criminals seek to avoid situations in which retaliation is a possibility. It may well be argued that the best deterrent against a criminal with a gun is a would-be victim unwilling to concede.

Another glaring example verifying the need to uphold our Second Amendment rights took place on June 16, 2016, when Omar Mateen swore allegiance to Abu Bakr al-Baghdadi before he opened fire at the Pulse Nightclub in Orlando, Florida, killing 49 and wounding 53 others.[199] After a three-hour standoff, police finally took Mateen down, but what if during the rampage a legally armed citizen, be it a patron or staff member, might have been in position to stop Mateen? This simple question sets the progressive's hair on fire. Their immediate progressive response would be that the armed citizen would be taking the law into their own hands. This would be a reasonable objection, but in the defense of one's life the law on self-defense is clear.

Proportional Response
"The use of self-defense must also match the level of the threat in question. In other words, a person can only employ as much force as required to remove the threat. If the threat involves deadly force, the person defending themselves can use deadly force to counteract the threat."[200] I would ask those who do not agree to ask themselves, if you were looking down the barrel of a rifle or other

gun pointed at your head by a madman, a terrorist, or a mentally disturbed individual, with the intent to end your life, would you object to your Second Amendment right to defend yourself?

The Department of Homeland Security

In August 2013, the Associated Press and other watchdog news organizations reported that the US Department of Homeland Security might in fact become the enemy of the people. In an August 7, 2013, article by Anthony Gucciardi of Global Research (an article that should have become front-page news), he stated, "The DHS has openly established extensive Constitution free zones in which your Fourth Amendment does not exist."[201] The Fourth Amendment to the United States Constitution is the part of the Bill of Rights that "prohibits unreasonable searches and seizures and requires any warrant to be judicially sanctioned and supported by probable cause."[202]

The Department of Homeland Security (DHS) and the Patriot Act were created in response to the September 11, 2001, attacks. The Department of Defense is responsible for military operations abroad, while the DHS is responsible for the activity of American citizens, whether inside or outside the borders of the US, with its stated goal "to prepare for, prevent, and respond to domestic emergencies, particularly terrorism." With more than 200,000 employees, the DHS is the third largest Cabinet department in the US government. DHS constitutes a diverse merger in terms of federal functions and responsibilities, incorporating 22 former government agencies into a single organization. DHS is headed by the Secretary of Homeland Security, who is appointed by the president of the United States with the consent of the United States Senate.[203] The secretary serves at the pleasure of the president, making the agency autonomous.

This discussion is not conspiratorial but is based in fact:

> The DHS has literally created an imaginary "border" that engulfs the entire United States, out 100 miles from every single end of the nation. Within this fabricated "border," the DHS can search your electronic belongings for no reason. We're talking about no suspicion; no reasonable cause whatsoever is required under their own regulations. The DHS is now above the Constitution and can operate under their own rules.[204]

The level of unreported pure tyranny going on here is unprecedented.

Ayo Kimathi was the weapons and ammunition purchaser for the DHS, specifically for the US Immigration and Customs Enforcement. As a DHS official, Kimathi's role at the agency was to procure guns and ammunition; the organization has purchased large quantities of both.[205]

In September of 2012, it appeared that government forces, specifically DHS, were attempting to dry up the market by purchasing nearly all of the ammo being produced and thereby causing panic buying in the private sector. The shortage was being blamed on panic purchasing by private citizens. However, the real reason was government hoarding and the closing of foreign ammo markets, which were setting the stage for the government to further its agenda for a gun control ban in conjunction with the UN. Does it surprise anyone that cargo ships from Russia and foreign countries that also supply ammo to US markets were being forced to return to their home ports?[206] Where was all the ammunition going?

Mr. Kimathi has been cited for running a personal website "War on the Horizon," specifically espousing a racial war against all whites.[207] His website criticizes whites, gays, those of mixed race, and blacks who integrate with whites. Despite the inflammatory rhetoric, Mr. Kimathi, who is black, was eventually placed on paid leave.[208] The Associated Press reported that US government officials were not immediately clear as to whether Kimathi had crossed the legal threshold into unprotected hate speech; his posts, the rationale went, might not violate DHS policies if he did not post them to the website at work or espouse the ideologies in the office. This kind of twisted, illogical application of government rules and regulations can occur only when there is an agenda to protect. That agenda appears to have been the perpetuation of racial tension in the US as a cover for the slow political, economic, and physical destruction of our American way of life into that of a totalitarian dictatorship.

Is history repeating itself? In the article Nazification of Germany vs. Nazification of America by Norman D. Livergood, a once stable (pre-1933) Germany became socially and emotionally enamored of a relatively unknown German WWI veteran, Adolph Hitler. Hitler's infamous oratory skills won the hearts and minds of the German people when he promised them a utopian society. Hitler convinced the German president Hindenburg to appoint the minority Nazi party as the dominant German political force and Hitler as chancellor. Hitler began immediately to orchestrate the complete takeover of all mechanisms of the governance and functions of state, to make Nazi Germany a totalitarian dictatorship. So similar are the situations between 1933 Germany and present-day America that a direct parallel may be considered almost predictable.[209]

Additional Evidence of Government Overreach

Every government scandal has the implied benefit of interpretation by the very people who wrote the law. However, when that agenda gets applied to an individual in the private sector and not a government entity, it typically results in the destruction of the individual's personal character and livelihood. An example of such political outreach is the Paula Deen story. Deen has been physically, economically, and emotionally destroyed by the "racist police" for alleged racially insensitive comments this southern Georgia girl made as far as thirty years earlier, during a time when the N word didn't carry the political death wish it does today. Deen may not be the role model for the ideal American image, but she is an example of an individual exercising her right to the American dream. Deen made millions consciously promoting morbid obesity. She was a Food Network star with corporate sponsorship from Target and Home Depot and even a spokesperson for a pharmaceutical company's diabetes drug that she herself was taking; her diabetes was very likely, at least in part, caused by her reckless consumption and promotion of foods that trigger or aggravate diabetes.

To understand the connection between this story and the progressive agenda, one has to look no further than Michelle Obama. The former first lady had taken on the mission (and legacy) of curbing morbid obesity, especially in children. Could the political agenda of having the internet and the media destroy Paula Deen be complicit with Michelle Obama's war on obesity? I dare say that Paula Deen was hardly a household name, but her success as an entrepreneur did go against the grain of the progressive agenda in terms of upholding the freedoms of the individual, let alone serve as an affront to the First Lady's future legacy.

Paula Deen had the constitutional right to buck Michelle Obama's agenda, but could the Obama administration's political machine have taken the opportunity of scoring a "two for one" victory by shutting down Deen's dynasty? When referring to the Saul Alinsky bible for a progressive, socialist takeover of a country, one could find an answer. Alinsky's Rule 5 states, "Ridicule is a man's most potent weapon, for which there is no defense." And Rule 12 invites, "Pick a target, cut off all support, and go after the person, not the institution."[210]

This story came to light when a complaint was made that this successful TV chef used the N word repeatedly in her past and thereby accusing Dean of being racist (Rule 5). Immediately following the racist story was the attack on what Dean did to gain her prominence and wealth: promote obesity. What was once Dean's right to freedom of expression gave way to an enemy of the people: obesity.

Perhaps this story was not about Deen's character as much as about the destruction of her character when the First Lady could not accomplish her agenda on its own merit (Rule 12). The agenda of the progressive movement is to move this country from its constitutional beginnings to a preplanned, government-controlled society. As we are witnessing in today's society, it is not a stretch for the progressives to use the race card to destroy its enemies.

These scandals occurred since January 1, 2013. The suggestion has been made that the idea is to push the public into information overload, whereby resistance and due diligence decline. As public scrutiny wanes, the progressive agenda advances, until it's too late to find any semblance of our once free nation.

Secondary nonfederal government scandals are arising at the same time. Just to name one, look at the red-light safety cameras, now part of every city in the US. The Chicago Tribune reported on March 3, 2013, that Chicago City Hall couldn't back up its claim of red-light cameras offering any beneficial safety enhancement.[211] Chicago voters were given nonexistent data to justify red-light safety cameras, supplied mostly by the camera's manufacturer. Illinois Inspector General Joe Ferguson had pointed out that the city had 389 red-light cameras at 190 intersections. The cameras cost $25,000 apiece, or $5.3 million, and the annual cost to maintain each camera was at the time $13,800. The scandal here lies in the reason for the cameras—they may not actually have been intended to promote safety. The city wrote 612,278 tickets based on camera images, generating seventy-two million dollars in revenue on a five-million-dollar investment. Money talks!

However, the scandal may lie in what these cameras provide for local officials and, eventually, for any governmental entity based on recent invasion-of-privacy scandals within the federal government. Besides providing a windfall revenue stream, these cameras function as public surveillance systems, providing license numbers; facial recognition technology; and, at minimum, an array of functions that invade privacy. Naturally, city officials state that no such data is collected; however, scandals abound, given such untethered opportunity. The pacifying argument is, "If you are doing nothing wrong, what does it matter?" The constitutional response is that our Bill of Rights and constitutional amendments were put in place to safeguard citizens from the potential for government intrusion. We must always remember that with safety comes risk. To have safety without risk is the sign of a totalitarian environment, in which the population is willing to trade freedom for the perception of safety.

Outright executive lying in congressional investigations has become the norm, with the escape clause being the use of executive privilege to circumvent prosecution. Such was the case involving the Fast & Furious scandal, where some 1,400 firearms were put into criminal hands to support rebel factions favorable to US policies. During Obama's administration, Attorney General Eric Holder signed the order but refused to hand over documentation for congressional investigation. As a result, the House of Representatives found Holder in contempt of Congress, making him the first Cabinet member in history to be so held. The White House simply dismissed the congressional charges by invoking executive privilege, thus legally sidestepping constitutional law.[212] This is not just government deception; it is government corruption.

Behind the scenes there is another deception taking place that will ultimately affect our two-party system of government. Our founding fathers were not interested in compromise to the point of single-mindedness when it came to setting policy for this country. Modern-day thinking is that our country is in trouble because Republicans and Democrats cannot agree on anything and that if they would only concede to a single-minded focus, this country could resolve its issues. The premise of a two-party system is to bring diversity of thinking, while minimizing the possibility of a tyrannical government takeover—a principle taught in every high school US government history 101 class. However, under Common Core guidelines, our historical reference to our founding principles will be lost.

If our two-party system of government essentially agrees on everything, then one party is expendable. A one-party system is comparable to types of government such as a monarchy, or at worst a dictatorship. Without our viable two-party systems, how long would it take for the next Hitler or Caligula to attain power? It took but six months for the Roman emperor Caligula to assume rule over the Roman Empire as a tyrant, perverting Roman civilization to utter chaos, with only his death by assassination saving the empire.

Without our educating our youth on the responsibilities associated with freedom and assigning historical significance to the genius of our founding fathers, our government officials will vie for personal power and wealth at the expense of the people. A good example of government officials vying for power presented itself within the Republican Party over the emergence of the Tea Party, which was formed by concerned citizens and government officials.

On October 7, 2013, Senate Republican Minority leader Mitch McConnell called a private meeting of all Republican senators behind closed doors. After the meeting, the senators were sworn to secrecy due to the sensitivity of the topic and its relevance to the future of the Republican Party. However, it was not long before the content of the meeting was leaked to key conservative news agencies, oddly enough not by the conservative constitutionalist Tea Party advocates within the Republican Party but by the more progressive middle-of-the-road Republicans, more aligned with traditional Democratic progressive views. Senator Mitch McConnell was furious that the potential future rival for his Republican Kentucky Senate seat, businessman and entrepreneur conservative Mathew Bevin, had bought airtime to disclose backroom dealings with the progressive agenda; these included pressuring Republican senators not to join the effort to defund Obamacare.

Senator Mitch McConnell had utter distain for the conservative Tea Party Republicans who threatened his power base.

The meeting was simple and direct. McConnell announced that any Republican senator who disagreed with his decisions in moving the Republican party away from the conservative movement would be considered an enemy, both of McConnell and of the country. McConnell called out freshman senators like Ted Cruz, Marco Rubio, Mike Lee, and Rand Paul because of their opposition to his decisions and their constitutionalist opposition to the progressive movement.[213]

Politics can be a dirty game, but under the US Constitution the brilliance of the founding fathers must be admired. Our Constitution essentially protects the people from a potential tyrannical takeover of our government. It is the will of the people that sends representatives to the US government. It is in turn their job to represent the will of the citizens who elected them. It is no longer difficult to see that our government is operating according to its own agenda, and only recently have some of our elected US government officials expressed concern that "something is afoul." The birth of the Tea Party was being portrayed as the brainchild of the radical fringe, when in fact just the opposite was true. The Tea Party was never meant to be a rival third party to our system of government but was an attempt to secure a nonprogressive stronghold for either the Republican or the Democratic party.

Keeping in mind that the socialist progressive agenda of Saul Alinsky is at work within our own government, it is no wonder that such turmoil now exists. On the one hand, the constitutionalists (Tea Party) are not the radicals but the norm this country was founded upon. On the other hand, nearly one hundred years of continual subversive actions have occurred that have led to the incredible accomplishment of making both the Democratic and Republican parties essentially one party posing as two. It is impossible to ignore the facts any longer, no matter what one's political affiliation.

Has it occurred to anyone to question how our constitutional government can totally ignore some of the most incredible breaches of trust in US history? Have you noticed that absolutely nothing has been done to punish or rectify the IRS scandal whereby *only* conservative political groups and certain ordinary citizens were targeted for audit or denial of their nonprofit status without cause? Have you also noticed that nothing has been done about the lie perpetrated about the rogue Cincinnati IRS agent who was responsible for the IRS scandal? Where is the outrage over the Benghazi incident, in which a US ambassador and several other US staffers were killed in the US consulate under the false flag of an anti-Muslim video? Why has this event been allowed to slip from the purview of continued news coverage? Where are the ongoing investigations by either party?

As this country slowly slips into an unrecognizable entity, it is the hope of the progressive movement in Congress to induce a checkmate scenario on US citizens whereby, by the time they realize what constitutional freedoms have been lost, there will be no hope for recovering them. Fortunately, our democratic republic can self-correct every four years, as we witnessed under the Trump administration.

Compliance is the necessary tool of tyranny. Compliance at the end of a gun barrel is communism, compliance at the end of entitlement programs is socialism, compliance to political and social theories is Marxism, and compliance to customer satisfaction is capitalism. The reason capitalism works, and all other political and economic models are doomed to failure, is that capitalism removes the need for a big, centralized government, thus minimizing the possibility of tyrannical influence. The failure of capitalism will come only at the hands of ordinary citizens unwilling to maintain their constitutional rights of individual responsibility, as delineated by the Bill of Rights.

The US has the power to pick and choose its elected officials. There are 535 members of congress (100 senators and 435 members of the House of Representatives) charged with representing the ideology of the people. Senators are elected for a six-year term with one-third of the senior senators up for reelection every two years, whereas each member of the House of Representatives serves a two-year term in order to provide access to those best suited for the task and for the removal of congressional representatives who are not fulfilling their obligation. The question is how ineffective, agenda-driven, or outright unlawful members of Congress get elected and reelected despite their destructive and, at times, illegal activities.

The answer lies in the voting process itself. One citizen, one vote, is the way to give equal representation to all legal citizens

who have a stake in matters of country. Voting requires participation by all. When one chooses to not vote, he or she is in fact
"casting" a vote. Voting records in cities like New York, where
vast pockets of influential people reside, are notorious for their
"groupie" type voter behavior. Whether for self-interests or political pandering, once a large number of voters obtains the influence to convince other voters that it is futile to resist their will
at the ballot box, complacency tends to override constitutional
responsibility. Once complacency becomes the norm, the seeds
for tyranny have been sown.

Capitol Hill Blue, the oldest political news site on the internet, revealed on September 3, 1999, that 29 members of Congress
had been accused of spousal abuse, 7 had been arrested for fraud,
19 had been accused of writing bad checks, 117 had bankrupted at
least two businesses, 3 had been arrested for assault, 71 had credit
reports so bad they could not qualify for a credit card, 8 had been
arrested for shoplifting, and 21 were current defendants in lawsuits.
The Capitol Hill Blue also reported that, in 1998 alone, 84 were
stopped for drunk driving but released after they claimed congressional immunity, noting that some were serial offenders with extensive track records of fraud or violence.[214]

Former Representative Corrine Brown (Democrat from Florida) had a "long, consistent record of deceit," including tens of
thousands of dollars in unpaid bills, allegations of bribery, and numerous lawsuits against her. Perhaps such irresponsible behavior
by members of Congress provides a clue as to why our country is
carrying a national debt of 22 trillion dollars and why federal programs are always over budget and wasteful. Given the economic
incompetence of so many senators and representatives, one can
only wonder why voters trust them with a budget to run the country. It is interesting to note that one of the platforms the Trump administration espoused was "draining the swamp," a brilliant visual
for a political system in need of an overhaul.

Steve Dasbach, former national director of the Libertarian Party, asked, "Are these really the kind of economically illiterate people
we want to trust with our money?" Mr. Dasbach also stated, "If
nothing else, the Capitol Hill Blue investigation may help puncture
the myth that Senators and Representatives are somehow superi-
or to ordinary Americans, or better equipped to solve the nation's
problems. By its very nature, politics tends to attract venal people

who crave power, who want to control the lives of other people, and who think they are above the law."[215]

One of the most glaring examples of voter negligence is that of Representative Charles B. Rangel, who as of 2008 had been re-elected into office twenty consecutive times since 1973. The issue is not his time in office but his dismal record of accomplishments, as well as his extensive record of ethics and censure violations. The Wikipedia article on Rangel states, "In July 2008, The Washington Post reported that Rangel was soliciting donations to the Charles B. Rangel Center for Public Service at City College of New York from corporations with prior business interests in his "Ways and Means Committee" and did so using Congressional letterhead.[216] Rangel rented Harlem apartments he owned at below-market rates, illegally receiving thousands of dollars in campaign funds from landlord kickback while using one apartment as a clandestine campaign office. Rangel had been using a House of Representatives parking garage as free storage space for his Mercedes-Benz for years, in violation of congressional rules. He faced tax evasion for failing to report income from the $1,100/night rental beachside villa he owns in Punta Cana in the Dominican Republic, as well as from the sale of his $500,000 home in Washington, DC and income from investment fund reporting.

Rangel has blatantly ignored the rule of law by hiding behind congressional privilege, yet he is reelected at each election. The reason appears to be simple: his loyal voters and the benefactors of his mischievous behavior show up in mass at each election, while the rest of his district stays home, knowing they can't do anything to unseat him—a classic miscarriage of constitutional responsibilities. Rangle represented districts in New York from 1971 to 2016 when he was finally unseated by Adriano Espaillat in 2016[217] after Rangle was convicted on 11 counts of misconduct by a House ethics panel.[218]

In comparison, what is the penalty for an average citizen who steals one stamp from a post office? The "United States Post Office is a federal operation; it would be a federal crime which can result in incarceration in a federal prison for at least 1 year. Federal prisoners serve every day of their sentence; no time off for good behavior."[219]

The voting record and personal activities of congressional officials are public record. Under our Constitution, it is perfectly legal to be stupid or incompetent; however, do we need stupid or incompetent people running our government—or, worse, controlling the activities of our lives? Once in violation of congressional rules, one's tenure should be over; this senator or representative should be held to no higher or lower standard of ethics than an average citizen. In the US, congressional tenure is terminated at the ballot box. How unconscionable for an elected official to force their electorate into servitude when they themselves are guilty of electoral prostitution and illegal behavior. Only by complacency and the willingness of individual citizens to give up their right of freedom of choice, so vehemently secured for us by our founding fathers, can an out-of-control government continue to prosper.

For Further Reading

Answers Corporation. "How Many US Senators and Congressmen Are Convicted Felons?" WikiAnswers. http://wiki.answers.com/Q/How_many_US_senators_and_congressmen_are_convicted_felons (accessed July 17, 2014).

Benson, Bill, and M. J. Beckman. *The law that never was: the fraud of the 16th Amendment and personal income tax.* South Holland, IL (Box 550, South Holland 60473): Constitutional Research Assoc., 1985.

"COMMON CORE." COMMON CORE. http://whatiscommon-core.wordpress.com/ (accessed July 16, 2014).

Sothern, Marci. "Responsibilities of the Federal Government." eHow. http://www.ehow.com/list_7654222_responsibilities-federal-government.html (accessed July 16, 2014).

Wikimedia Foundation. "Patriot Act." Wikipedia. http://en.wikipedia.org/wiki/Patriot_Act (accessed July 16, 2014).

YouTube. "Gun Myths Gone in Five Minutes: ABC News 20/20." YouTube. https://www.youtube.com/watch?v=682JLrsUmEM (accessed July 17, 2014).

Zieve, Sher. "Behind Common Core: Forcing Marxism/Nazism on America's Children." GulagBoundcom. http://gulagbound. com/38714/common-core-forcing-marxismnazism-on-america's-children/ (accessed July 16, 2014).

Chapter 8

How's That Radical "Change" Working Out for You, America?

In the true scope of world history, America is but a fledgling adolescent at a mere two-hundred-plus years old. Approximately five generations have passed since its formation, yet so much has happened. We have become the envy of the world, with our technology and industrialization creating lifelong jobs and the entrepreneurial spirit. Our freedoms, which we often take for granted, are ideals never realized by other countries well into their "Medicare years," by comparison.

Adolescents are known for believing that they know everything; we were that age at one time, so we understand the validity of that statement. America is an adolescent, too, and as such America can be as petulant and sometimes as impulsive as an adolescent, when compared to other, much older and more established nations in the world. Our ignorance of the thinking and cultures of world regimes is not an excuse for losing our identity as a country. America fought for its freedom by challenging British rule, in favor of independence, in the War of 1812. British rule was by monarchs, desiring to tame these young adolescents. Yet the call to freedom surpassed incredible odds and the might of a superior military force. America earned its place in the world as a free society. But winning the battle for freedom does not end by winning a war; freedom must be sustained and nurtured for it to survive.

Monarchs dictate what freedoms are allowed, whereas a free society must remain diligent to any encroaching forces of tyranny. It is unfortunate that we have come to realize over the years that all one has to do is over-promise and under-deliver and that the American free spirit can be overtaken by radical factions. For decades, our population has been infiltrated by controlling factors (activists) whose mere existence is testament to a weakening America. The American spirit is still naïve, void of the seasoned wisdom that only age and experience bring to the point that some in this society are willing to trade freedom for an unknown entity. Freedom comes with a price, including diligence to maintain the tenets of our nation's founding and the resultant laws of the land. In the 2016 presidential election exit polling, sixty percent of those who voted did not know that the Constitution was the supreme law of the land. Freedom implies not only lack of restrictions but also the ability to stand alone, not sustained by anything else, and, most importantly, to recognize the difference between "change" and transformation.

Radicals are a persistent lot, gaining power from two main sources: people and money. Radicals win over people with simple strategies. Without the knowledge or the experience of what other cultures endure under nondemocratic regimes, it becomes easy to convince a population to doubt their principles. The socialist radical uses class envy to replace work ethics, suggests problems where there are none, and then repeats the rhetoric over and over again until the weak-minded accept that only a centralized government—not the individual—can provide personal security.[220] The Marxist radical creates irrational arguments that ridicule our most successful principles or people, thus forcing the majority (in a democracy) to compromise principles as an intermediary between capitalism and communism, in which ownership is dictated rather than earned.[221] Allowing sacred documents like our Constitution and Bill of Rights to become "living documents" that can be interpreted by sinister minds is the working model for radicalization. Ever wonder why older, established cultures controlled by a centralized governmental anarchy never become radicalized toward freedom? What would a dominated culture do with freedom, when their very existence over the centuries has depended on strict economic, social, and cultural divisions? The Obama administration promised "change," hiding behind activism as the way of encouraging change, without ever clarifying what that change would be. Creating straw man arguments over enforcement of our rights, as in gun control, freedom of speech, immigration, and healthcare, and even allowing Congress to pass legislation never read (the Affordable Healthcare Act), encouraged change where none was needed. All these things and more are happening every day in our country, with hardly a whisper of resistance.

The 2,700-page Obama healthcare bill, which was never read before passage, is a perfect example. The healthcare bill was sold to a gullible population by invoking an easily agreeable statement, without ever giving details, purporting that healthcare is a right and should therefore be free. After the fact, we find that the reality is that the IRS expects families of four and five to pay $20,000 per year for the economy coverage Bronze healthcare plan under Obamacare. Of course, doctors and healthcare workers will be demonized as making a profit on the sick and will gain a sympathetic nod of approval, exactly as the activists planned. Obama's secret plan was to destroy and then rescue our healthcare system.[222]

The first step takes place by eliminating all private competition (insurance companies), allowing all private medical organizations to die on the vine. The second step is to allow for panic and near revolt by the population. The program is to create a sense of lack in the population so that they become irrational, with self-preservation and greed as their sole motives. An example of this can be easily demonstrated. In 2012, the federal government created a scare to take away our Second Amendment right to bear arms (gun control). Law-abiding citizens went on an ammunition buying frenzy for fear this right it would be lost. The result was no ammunition to be found anywhere.[223] The third step in this destroy-and-rescue strategy for healthcare is for the federal government to come to the rescue with its single payer plan, in which there is no longer any competition or choice. The result is that the population will willingly comply out of fear. As an aside, for all those who continue to point to the European government-run healthcare systems, it is not that their system is superior; it's all that is available to them.

Any revolutionary change in thinking must be preceded by a passive, unquestioningly affirmative attitude toward change among the people. To implement that change, the people must become so frustrated, so defeated, so lost, so futureless with regard to the system we live by that they are willing to let go of the past and take a chance on the future. The strategy is to divide and conquer, which is a fundamental rule of warfare. Sun Tzu wrote in *The Art of War*, "Keep your friends close and your enemies closer." The modern equivalent is the bible for "radical activism," written by Saul Alinsky, who was an American community organizer and writer. He is generally considered to be the founder of modern community organizing—and he was a teacher for Obama. A summary of his twelve principles is found in his book *Rules for Radicals*. His principles were adopted in many of our major universities and major cities in the 1960s and, unfortunately, have been the bible worshiped by Obama and the progressive Democrats. Keep in mind that Obama got his start in Chicago as a community organizer.

Rules for Radicals by Saul Alinsky, written for the Have-Nots on how to take away from the Haves:

- RULE 1: "Power is not only what you have, but what the enemy thinks you have." Power is derived from two main sources—money and people. "Have-Nots" must build power from the flesh and blood of those who have.
- RULE 2: "Never go outside the expertise of your people." This results in confusion, fear, and retreat. Feeling secure adds to the backbone of anyone.
- RULE 3: "Whenever possible, go outside the expertise of the enemy." Look for ways to increase their insecurity, anxiety, and uncertainty.
- RULE 4: "Make the enemy live up to its own book of rules." If the rule is that every letter gets a reply, send 30,000 letters. You can kill them with this because no one can possibly obey all of their own rules.
- RULE 5: "Ridicule is man's most potent weapon." There is no defense. It's irrational. It's infuriating. It also works as a key pressure point to force the enemy into concessions.
- RULE 6: "A good tactic is one your people enjoy." They'll keep doing it without your urging and come back to do more. They're doing their thing and will even suggest better ideas.
- RULE 7: "A tactic that drags on too long becomes a drag." Don't become old news.
- RULE 8: "Keep the pressure on. Never let up." Keep trying new things to keep the opposition off balance. As the opposition masters one approach, hit them from the flank with something new.
- RULE 9: "The threat is usually more terrifying than the thing itself." Imagination and ego can dream up many more consequences than can any activist.

- RULE 10: "If you push a negative hard enough, it will push through and become a positive." Violence from the other side can win the public to your side because the public sympathizes with the underdog.
- RULE 11: "The price of a successful attack is a constructive alternative." Never let the enemy score points because you're caught without a solution to a problem.
- RULE 12: "Pick the target, freeze it, personalize it, and polarize it." Cut off the support network and isolate the target from sympathy. Go after people and not institutions; people hurt faster than institutions.[224]

The "change" most of us believed the 2008 election would bring, but which was never explained, captivated the population. Hiding the truth in broad daylight is easy when the words are manipulated. Words have meaning! It was promised that the 2008 election would fundamentally change this country. To our adolescent mindset, we assumed change would be positive, that it would be wholesome and would rid the US of all its ills. Reality has shown just the opposite on every level, yet the activist rhetoric continues to hold out hope and promise for a better America—again, never expressing the true meaning but convincing our inexperienced nation to practice the insanity of doing the same thing while expecting a different result.

President Trump destroyed the facade of false hope by producing the best economy this country has ever seen, yet he did not phase the radical movement one bit; in fact, this emboldened the movement to resort to impeachment and accusations of obstruction of justice. It was not about a better economy—it was about control over the economy.

In 2008, Obama had differentiated himself from his then fellow candidate Hillary Clinton by criticizing her plan to use a "mandate" as an "enforcement mechanism" to "charge people who don't have healthcare." He claimed that the use of a mandate for those purposes was something he could not go along with—a stance that demonstrated a "genuine difference" between himself and Clinton. However, on April 4, 2012, Obama urged the Supreme Court not to rule against the mandate in Obamacare because his healthcare reforms could not survive in the absence of an individual mandate.

Little do people know that even the promise of insurance for the thirty million uninsured is a lie. According to the Congressional Budget Office (CBO), there are actually fifty-three million uninsured persons in the United States, including uninsured illegal aliens. The CBO states that the court mandate also gives greater latitude for state-regulated Medicaid eligibility, thus allowing states to entirely force additional people into the Obamacare exchanges.

The CBO and JCT (Joint Committee on Taxation) estimated that the Affordable Care Act would reduce the number of nonelderly people without health insurance coverage; however, the CBO concluded that, despite all the new government regulations and bureaucracies, as well as taxes and subsidies created by Obamacare, there would still be thirty million uninsured people in the United States a decade later.[225]

It appears that no one escapes the convoluted and often unrecognizable effects of Obamacare. Thankfully, the elderly and Medicare beneficiaries are not subject to Obamacare, at least on the conscious level. However, as with all socialized programs, the government "giveth" and the government "taketh"; so it is with "the Great Social Security and Medicare Tax Scam." Trump's "repeal and replace" strategy for Obamacare, while not implemented, would have brought choice and strength back into the private sector, dealing a deathblow to the radical agenda.

During our working years, our employers, even if we are self-employed, must withhold a percentage of our salaries for Social Security and Medicare in the form of a tax from our payroll. Employers must then match this amount and deposit the amount monthly as payroll taxes. When you apply for Social Security benefits, you receive a monthly amount deposited into your account, minus your Medicare premium based on a scale developed by the IRS. At the beginning of the following year, you receive a benefit statement (Form SSA-1099) showing benefits paid to you that will be taxed with your annual income tax return.

Since few Social Security and Medicare beneficiaries understand the tax code, let alone the Social Security year-end statements, the following scam has gone virtually unnoticed: the income you received from Social Security is listed, but additionally, the amount deducted to pay your Medicare monthly premiums is also listed and added as total income you received, thereby creating additional tax debt! Even though your employer paid payroll tax on that amount during your income earning years, you are not getting the full benefits. You are actually being taxed on your money that you lent to the government. As children and well before our Medicare years, we were taught that this was called stealing!

Chapter 9

Food as Fuel: The Truth Revealed

We are the only country in modern history where food is used as fuel. Initially, the discussion of fuel itself must begin with a basic premise that fuels are any materials that store potential energy in forms that can be released and used as heat energy. For this discussion, chemical energy that could be released through combustion will be discussed. From our earliest days in grade school, we were taught that "if it weren't for the dinosaurs and all the ancient forests, we would not have all the oil we use as fuels for gasoline, heating oil, and lubricants." We were also told that fossil fuels are nonrenewable resources because they take millions of years to form, that reserves are being depleted much faster than new supplies can be accumulated, and that the production and use of fossil fuels raise environmental concerns. To the unquestioning mind of youth, this was an acceptable explanation, except for the part about the use of fossil fuels raising environmental concerns. The classic textbook definition of fossil fuels is that they "are organic hydrocarbons (substances containing only Hydrogen and Carbon atoms), formed from the fossilized remains of ancient plants and animals by exposure to high heat and pressure in the absence of oxygen in the Earth's crust over hundreds of millions of years."[226]

In my young, inquisitive mind, I wondered, *since fossil fuels are part of nature, why would their use raise environmental concerns?* The answer I received was that the burning of fossil fuels leads to the production of greenhouse gasses," one of which is carbon dioxide. Since I knew that carbon dioxide is also a byproduct of our breathing, I wondered whether breathing, too, is dangerous to the earth. Trees and other plants, I knew, survive on carbon dioxide in return for the oxygen they release for us to breathe. As my youthful ignorance gave way to further knowledge and experience, of science, politics, and world affairs, the riddle of fossil fuels came to an end. The sheer magnitude of the fossil fuel we use is mind-boggling. In 2010, for example, the amount of fossil fuel (oil) used worldwide was approximately 85 million barrels per day. One barrel is equal to 42 gallons, equating to 3.57 billion gallons per day, or a mind-numbing 1.4 trillion gallons per year. My epiphany moment came when I realized, *That's a lot of dead dinosaurs and trees!*

What we have been told, however, is simply untrue. In the eighteenth century, German and French scientists discovered that fossil fuels are not the product of decaying biological matter but the result of an abiotic[227] process that is natural to the earth's core; these fuels are constantly renewing themselves as they spread across the mantle layers of Earth's crust.[228] In fact, oil may be found under virtually every land mass and ocean.[229] So significant was this discovery that it ranks up there with the realization that the world is not flat; yet it has been stifled and kept from the public's eye for two centuries.

The fundamental difference between theories is the misconception that sedimentary rock is the originator rather than the depository of the hydrocarbons. Oil is constantly being created by abiotic (nonliving) forces deep within Earth's core, from which it seeps into vacated, formerly filled, oil caverns, creating a renewable source of energy; the very last thing Big Oil wants people to realize.[230]

Within fifty years of this discovery, German and French scientists were met with stiff resistance from the Rockefeller Corporate Oil Majors, who were hell-bent on maintaining the charade that oil and resulting oil prices are based on shortages, production capabilities, and perceived strategic petroleum locations, all well off the shores of the US. The truth is that there were never oil shortages or lack of production capabilities, but instead drops in production intended to give the illusion of supply and demand economics. With Big Oil's secret well hidden by corporate greed and the ability for governments to control populations by raising or lowering oil prices for political gain, one of the greatest scams of all time had been perpetrated. So secret is the oil story that it has never been revealed by the media, our schools, or even by science. To this day, the scam is played out in every country.

Cracks in oil's storyline have always been there but never recognized. In an article I read in *National Geographic* many years ago, it was revealed that some of the original oil wells that dotted the Texas landscape, long since abandoned because these wells had dried up, have been re-opened. The reason given was that with new drilling technologies and extraction techniques, these old wells still have potential. When taken at face value, the explanation sounds reasonable. Yet it has recently been revealed that the closing of oil wells often occurs while oil production is still strong. The reason is to give the illusion of oil shortages, which boosts oil demand and crude oil prices. Numerous articles largely ignored by the mainstream media have reported that old, dried-out oil wells have mysteriously refilled, making them once again viable. There is no mystery here, just sleight of hand economics and politics.

Foreign oil prices can soar at any time at the behest of the elite. Ever wonder why that has not happened? President Trump pulled the plug on the lie that the US is dependent on foreign oil by simply opening the already existing oil fields and allowing "free enterprise," not socialistic lies, to compete. For over a century, the United States defied logic by not becoming energy self-sufficient under the false flag argument of protecting the environment. Bucking environmental concerns has become the political death wish for politicians. Trump may have taken the environmentalists to task by maintaining concerns over a safe environment in exchange for agreeing to keep the fossil fuel secret and by not exposing Big Oil to embarrassment.

Drilling permits for oil companies within the US go through years of expensive environmental studies to expose any environmental hazards, such as the possibility of displacing snail darters, scrub jays, or caribou beetles, all falling under the protection of the Endangered Species Act, which was enacted by Congress in 1973. This essentially gave the federal government the sole responsibility for their protection. In all, there are presently 10,796 animals listed as endangered, leaving almost no chance to avoid federal environmental statutes; this seems to be an intentional smokescreen to hide the truth. Since the Endangered Species Act, our entire nation's natural resources development has been essentially neutered, leaving us beholden to those "nasty" other nations who produce oil at the expense of their environment. For the last forty years this soap opera has played out without much resistance, burying what would appear to be the true reason for this illogical behavior. Funny how lies can work in your favor, given the right incentive.

Historically, when oil was being discovered and monetized in the Middle East, Big Oil companies divided the Middle Eastern

Arab world into regions, with each country carving out its plunder. The oil cartels took these desolate countries and helped form the Organization of the Petroleum Exporting Countries (OPEC) in the early 1960s. By the 1970s OPEC came to international prominence, as member countries acquired a major say in the pricing of crude oil on the world markets, leading to the Arab oil embargo in 1973.[231]

In 1973, President Nixon's Secretary of State, Henry Kissinger, during the Arab oil embargo made deals with Arab nations that the US would buy Arab oil and not pump large US oil fields; in return, Arab nations would invest up to one-half the money they received to buy US treasury bills, which is the economic mechanism to fund the US debt. The deal also included that all OPEC oil purchases would be in US currency. In essence, Mr. Kissinger convinced the Arab nations to offset future US debt by insuring US oil purchases from OPEC. Every Arab nation agreed with this deal, except Iraq and Iran. The US debt spiral began at this time, enabled by Arab treasury bill purchases. Decades of US debt have been absorbed by OPEC member nations.[232] Is it any wonder America's oil fields would not be harvested? The environmental Endangered Species Act of 1973 was the cover story necessary to draw attention away from the Arab nations underwriting US debt. It is totally insane to realize the degree of treason perpetrated against the US by our own government.

With the enormity of the US debt reaching into the tens of trillions of dollars, it was only a matter of time before Arab countries pulled the plug on US debt. With an ever-increasing and out-of-control debt, the US dollar is doomed as an international currency. Without Arab funding, the fossil fuel charade will end, with the acknowledgement that, "Wow, oil really doesn't come from decayed organic matter after all but actually is a renewable product manufactured by the earth's core itself!" When President Trump removed the stranglehold on US produced oil, the cartel's grip on oil pricing based on "shortages" ended.

The oil price per barrel, before the oil embargo of 1973, was around $25.00. After the Kissinger deal with Arab nations (OPEC), this shot up to over $100/barrel. The cover story was that there was an oil shortage, and that the US was being punished for its 1973 overt military support for Israel. The reality was that OPEC needed to cover its losses from the Kissinger deal. By 2000, the oil shortages magically disappeared, and oil prices found their market comfort level around $55–$65/barrel, where they still are today.[233]

To better understand the complexity of diplomatic relations as related to energy, it is important to review historical events that would eventually lead to destabilization of Middle Eastern oil supplies and the push for alternative fuels. During the years 1970–1980 the US faced imminent and strategic consequences from growing Middle Eastern tensions created by the longstanding conflicts within Iran and Iraq. Iran and Iraq did not sign on to the US debt relief for oil agreement with the other Arab nations. Iraq instead signed a twenty-year Friendship and Cooperation Treaty with Moscow, in which they pledged to develop cooperation in the strengthening of Iraqi defense capacities against the growing alliances between the US, Israel, and Iran. With the overthrow of the Shah of Iran during the 1979 Iranian Revolution, Ayatollah Khomeini became the supreme leader. The US was heavily reliant on Saudi Arabian oil, which became increasingly more difficult to export due to Khomeini's continued widespread riots designed to institute strict Islamic fundamentalism in the region. The Carter administration was unsuccessful in overthrowing the Khomeini regime, which lead to the 1979 Iran hostage crisis, in which fifty-two US citizens were held captive for 444 days.

As of March 2020, OPEC and Russia agreed to reduce oil production by 1.5 million barrels/day in an attempt to raise oil prices (counter US exports of oil). Unfortunately, Russia cannot afford the financial loss, so once again we are witnessing the strategic insights of President Trump, without resorting to war drums.[234]

Biofuels

The movement into biofuels and the making of auto engines to run on biofuels like ethanol, as in the E-85 blend (85% ethanol), that are designed to "help" our environment, may actually be the next generation energy control scam. Biofuels have increased in popularity because of rising oil prices and the need for energy security. However, according to the European Environmental Agency, biofuels do not necessarily mitigate global warming.[235]

Bioethanol is an alcohol made by fermentation, mostly from carbohydrates produced in sugar or starch crops such as corn or sugarcane. Ethanol can be used as a fuel for vehicles, but it is usually used as a gasoline additive to increase octane and improve vehicle emissions, a fact that has been touted but proven to be untrue. The actual energy value of ethanol, when added to gasoline, is very small and does little to reduce either imported oil or the need for imported oil to produce the ethanol. With respect to oil not being a fossil fuel at all but a renewable energy source, the ethanol scam becomes more apparent. Ethanol is the mechanism to bury the truth about the oil cartels and their clever secret.[236]

Pure ethanol has a very high-octane rating but will not run in the standard internal combustion, piston-driven automobile engines due to its low flash point when vaporized. E-10 gas (10% ethanol) effectively drops the octane rating by two to four points when mixed with gasoline.[237] This leads to decreased gas mileage; loss of power; and expensive engine repairs due to pre-ignition (engine ping), clogged fuel injectors, or dissolved sediment in traditional carburetors. E-85 gas drops the fuel efficiency by 27% and cannot be used in standard gasoline engines. Traditional internal combustion engines release water vapor as part of the process of combustion, as witnessed by most automobile owners as water dripping from the exhaust pipe when the engine is first started. Ethanol is essentially alcohol, the product of fermentation, and as such attracts or absorbs water into the gas mixture, resulting in "phase separation" of the fuel (incomplete combustion) and "water in the gas." Water is the enemy of internal combustion engines, while alcohol tends to dissolve fiberglass and rubber hoses.

Ethanol has roughly one-third lower energy content than gasoline, resulting in fewer miles per gallon, requiring larger (and therefore heavier) fuel tanks to travel the same distance. From an economic standpoint, ethanol fuel currently costs more per distance traveled than gasoline in the United States.[238]

With respect to public awareness, let's consider some fact checks on the benefits vs. risks of biofuels like ethanol:

What are the benefits?
- Ethanol burns cleanly and pollutes slightly less.
- Ethanol can be considered a domestic fuel source.

What are the risks?
- Ethanol costs more to produce than gasoline.
- Ethanol lowers octane by two to four points in the E-10 blend, well below the requirements of traditional automobile engines, resulting in expensive engine repairs.
- Ethanol reduces gas mileage, lowers power, and corrodes fiberglass gas tanks and rubber hoses.
- Ethanol often lowers the cost of fuel at the pump but is offset by the poorer milage.
- Ethanol has around 67% of the energy value per gallon of gasoline, requiring three gallons of ethanol to equal two gallons of gasoline output.
- Ethanol retains water during combustion, which corrodes metal engine parts.
- The higher the ethanol content in fuel, the greater need for consumers to purchase hybrid or flex-fuel vehicles, an intended consequence when attempting to stimulate the auto industry.
- Ethanol has minimal effect on air pollution.
- Ethanol does little to reduce dependence on foreign oil, since it doesn't have the properties to sustain the needs of effective transportation.

What are the effects of biofuels on food supplies?
- Corn is the source for 98% of our ethanol.
- The percentage of our corn crop dedicated to ethanol reached 30% in 2009, accounting for only 3.5% of our gasoline energy supply.
- Biofuels require intensive agriculture (fertilizer and herbicides), and it required three gallons of petroleum fuel to produce two gallons of ethanol fuel.
- If all the automobiles in the United States were fueled with 100 percent ethanol, a total of about 97 percent of US land area would be needed to grow the corn—nearly the total land area of the United States.

Corn should not be considered a renewable resource for ethanol energy production, especially when human food is being converted into ethanol. The only reason I can see for the commercialization of ethanol is that it provides a way for the American government to subsidize farmers and claim to be helping to reduce our dependence on foreign oil.[239], [240]

Biofuels and Food Shortages
World Bank policy released in July 2008 concluded that "large increases in biofuels production in the United States and Europe are the main reason behind the steep rise in global food prices" and that "food prices have risen by 35 to 40 percent between 2002–2008, of which 70 to 75 percent is attributable to biofuels."[241]

France, Germany, the United Kingdom, and the United States governments have supported biofuels with tax breaks, mandated use, and subsidies. These policies have the unintended consequence of diverting resources from food production and leading to surging food prices. The US government policy of encouraging the use of ethanol from corn is one cause of food price increases. US Federal government ethanol subsidies total $7 billion per year, adding $1.90 to the cost of a gallon of gasoline while providing only 67% as much energy as gasoline per gallon. Ethanol subsidies raise the price of corn, used to feed chickens, cows, and pigs, which drastically increases consumer food costs for chicken, beef, pork, milk, cheese, etc. With the advent of Hybrid engine technology, there is less demand for Ethanol fuel since self-generating electric power provided by Hybrid engines increases milage substantially on the same cost per gallon of gasoline.

The BioFuels Security Act was passed in 2006. "It's time for Congress to realize what farmers in America's heartland have known all along—that we have the capacity and ingenuity to decrease our dependence on foreign oil by growing our own fuel," said then US Senator for Illinois Barack Obama.[242]

Two-thirds of US oil consumption is due to transportation needs. The Energy Independence and Security Act of 2006 has a significant impact on US energy policy. With the high profitability of growing corn, more and more farmers switch to growing corn until the profitability of other crops goes up to match that of corn. So the ethanol/corn subsidies drive up the prices of other farm crops. The US converted 18% of its grain output to ethanol in 2008. Across the US, 25% of the whole corn crop went to ethanol in 2007. To avoid overproduction and to prop up farmgate prices for agricultural commodities, the US has farm subsidy programs to encourage farmers to leave productive acres fallow.

Following is a summary of historical events and possible outcomes of the "food as fuel" scenario:

- 1901 marked the first gusher of oil in the US in Texas (no big oil companies before then).
- Large oil companies then led the Industrial Revolution and the booming economy.
- Oil was discovered in the Arab Middle East.
- Oil companies divided up the Middle Eastern Arab world for the pickings.
- Henry Kissinger made deals with Arab nations that the US would buy Arab oil (and not pump US oil fields); in return, Arab nations would buy US treasury bills (which fund US debt).
- Every Arab nation agreed with this deal, except Iraq and Iran.
- The US debt spiral began at this time, enabled by Arab T-Bill purchases.
- America's oil fields would not be utilized because the US needed the Arabs to buy US debt.
- Globalists are planning to out the US and to destroy the US dollar.
- Strategically created chaos in the Middle East, beginning with Egypt and Libya and now including Syria, will have a domino effect and trigger the fall of Arab nations into chaos.
- "Muslim Brotherhood" is staged and supported by elitists to bring about the Arab chaos, nation by nation.
- Crude oil could reach $150–$200 a barrel, increasing biofuel production and further crippling food supplies.
- US gasoline could reach $7.00/gallon, leading to economic chaos, skyrocketing prices, and a devalued dollar.
- China is entirely insulated from Middle Eastern oil because it buys 100% of its gas and oil from Russia and does not exchange in US dollars.
- If international markets decide to abandon the dollar, the US dollar will totally devalue within years.

- If the US defaults on Arab T-Bonds, US influence in the Middle East will evaporate, perhaps halting oil imports.
- China and Arab nations will translate worthless T-Bonds into hard assets.
- A new world currency will emerge, leaving a desperate people no choice but acceptance.

Much has been said about a possible coming crisis, not only in the US but around the world. At every step, the words *conspiracy theory* is thrown about to detract from basic facts that have already played out in countries around the world. I am of an opinion best expressed by Sun-Tzu's words: "Keep Your Friends Close and Your Enemies Closer." Nothing is lost when one is prepared. Life has always been predicated on the survival of the fittest, not always referring to the body but to the mind as well. An advance warning always provides an advantage, as in the adage that to be forewarned is to be forearmed. President Trump provided the needed mental attitude that being prepared without an action step is a futile exercise.

If any lessons may be learned from that historic meeting on Jekyll Island in 1913 and the writings of Ayn Rand, it's that change is on the horizon. Looking back on the 2008 presidential campaign, in which change was the focal point of Obama's platform, little did we know Obama was destined to make yesterday's conspiracy theories—i.e., change—into today's reality. Change can be good if exercised for the benefit of the country and not toward an agenda. Whether or not one likes him, Trump has demonstrated that, without political baggage, America can maintain free market capitalism.

The following brief exchange is offered as a timely explanation of recent events in the Middle East that threaten the stability of energy and food. It is consistent with numerous corroborative sources.

"How the Crisis in the Middle East Began" by Kenneth White, president of the Virginia Taxpayers Association:

> Lindsey Williams called me and explained what is going on in the Middle East . . . Now I understand why the regimes there are being removed.

Very briefly as background, Henry Kissinger made a deal with the Middle East some decades ago that we would make them wealthy beyond their expectations by buying their oil. In return, they were to take a portion of their income from oil sales and buy our debt by purchasing Treasury securities, T-Bills, etc. . . .

We would then produce but a pittance of oil in this country although we have literally enough oil in this country to last us 200+years. Now the elite are going to double cross the Middle East and OPEC.

The current crisis was initiated by the CIA using paid agitators in Egypt. The crisis will spread to the ENTIRE Middle East. Although they did not initiate current events, the Muslim Brotherhood is being supported by the elite in the crisis areas in the aftermath. Once Iran and Saudi Arabia fall, oil will soar.

Between the on-going crisis and the continued decline of the dollar, oil will go to $150–200 within nine months. When it gets close to the $200 level, the U.S. will cease to purchase Middle East oil. At that time, we will produce oil from Gull Island in Prudhoe Bay and ANWR (Arctic National Wildlife Refuge) in Alaska, the Bakken Formation in the Dakotas and the Rocky Mountain shale oil. (He said "Below the Rocky Mountains are two trillion barrels of oil.")

The elite will then sell OUR $200 oil to us at the gas pump for $6–7. This will further devastate the American economy as Americans will be hard pressed to drive long distances to work. Truckers and airlines will be hard pressed to operate. The military will be badly affected.

Once we cease to purchase oil from the Middle East, the Arab nations and Iran will go broke. The billions or trillions of Treasuries, dollars etc., held by the Arab Nations will become worthless when the dollar collapses next year.

China is not reliant on Middle East oil (much to my surprise). Russia has surpassed Saudi Arabia as the no. 1 oil producing country in the world. This was accomplished by Russia drilling mega-wells down to 40000 + feet and discovering essentially unlimited supplies of oil. Now Russia and China have entered into an agreement whereby Russia will supply

ALL of China's oil. The US will not be able to buy from Russia, forcing us to rely on our own oil production.

Again, there will be no food shortages in this country, but the decline of the dollar will create hyper-inflation, making food extremely expensive. He cited garlic as a recent example which doubled in price in one week. Have six to twelve months supply of emergency food (dehydrated) on hand. (As a side note to this, FEMA has been buying dehydrated foods for a couple of years. Now one of the largest dehydrated food producers in the country announced last week they will no longer sell to the public as FEMA is buying 90% of their production.)

Lindsey reminded me that Bush Sr., CFR, (Council on Foreign Relations) was ambassador to China when China was a closed society and a closed market. Subsequently, Bush opened China, and it is now destined to replace the U S as the world's superpower. As a side note to the nonbelievers, Bush's opening line in his speech after Desert Storm was "We now have a New World Order." China now produces 80% of all components for the US military. When Caterpillar and other US companies open plants in China, they must turn over all patent rights to China. That is but one of the costs of doing business in China. China is now using its excess dollars to quietly buy controlling interest in American corporations. Essentially, they own this country because money talks.

The end game is to bring the US into the New World Order. This has been accomplished by shipping jobs and factories overseas and destroying the dollar. China will replace the US as the world power. The Renminbi (Chinese currency) will no doubt replace the dollar in that regard. China will not dump the dollar or treasuries but is cooperating with the US to steadily depreciate the dollar.[243]

Pardon my political overtones, but for us as Americans this should not sit well. President Trump turned the ongoing socialist/liberal agenda on its ear and renewed the American spirit by his deeds, not his rhetoric. Freedom is a precious commodity that, once lost, will never return unless there is another New World hiding somewhere for humanity to start over.

For Further Reading

Harkin, James. "Middle East: The Rest of the Story."—Middle East: The Rest of the Story (FULL). http://www.lindseywilliams. net/lindsey-williams-middle-east-the-rest-of-the-story-full/ (accessed July 18, 2014).

Hiro, Dilip. *The longest war: the Iran-Iraq military conflict.* New York: Routledge, 1991.

Kay, Joseph. "World Socialist Web Site." The diplomacy of Imperialism: Iraq and US foreign policy. http://www.wsws.org/en/ articles/2004/03/iraq-m17.html (accessed July 17, 2014).

Chapter 10

Decoding Agenda 21

Agenda 21 was designed to anticipate the environmental concerns of the twenty-first century. The implementation of Agenda 21 was put under the control of the United Nations, with the support of 178 nations, including the US. The topics covered read like science fiction, and at first glance they almost appear to have the impact of a good comedy skit. However, the scope and breadth of the content evoke an immediate visceral response of shock and a recollection of the final product of a New World Order concept presented at the 1913 meeting on Jekyll Island. Agenda 21 is a nonbinding, voluntarily implemented action plan of the United Nations regarding sustainable development. *Sustainability* is the latest revisionist word for *environmentalism* because Americans have learned too many negative things about environmentalism. *Sustainable development* is a term that could regulate and restrict any parts of our lives. For example, when will the level of carbon emissions be low enough, or how much must we reduce our consumption of petroleum fuels?

The concept of sustainable development is a product of the UN Conference on Environment and Development (UNCED) held in Rio de Janeiro, Brazil. In 1992, Agenda 21 was introduced to the world as an action agenda for the UN and other multilateral organizations. It was designed to be executed by individual governments around the world at the local, national, and global levels. Since its inception, Agenda 21 has become the central component of the New World Order (NWO), and although touted as voluntary and nonbinding, member nations have put military type emphasis on its implementation.[244]

The New World Order began during the founding of our country. Adam Weishaupt, a professor of Canon law who was financed through international bankers, created a secret society on May 1, 1776, named the Order of the Illuminati. "The objectives of the Illuminati were the establishment of a New World Order, which sought:

- Abolition of all ordered governments
- Abolition of private property
- Abolition of inheritance
- Abolition of patriotism
- Abolition of family
- Abolition of religion
- Creation of a world government."[245]

Over the years, the term New World Order has been associated with conspiracy theories in an attempt to minimize its reality as a movement. However, the term has been spoken about openly on numerous occasions by high-profile political figures, such as in the 1990 George H. W. Bush speech "Toward a New World Order." Another example is the Winston Churchill speech about the principles of a world order. "Henry Kissinger used the term 'New World Order' in the advocacy for a comprehensive reform of the global financial system."[246]

In Pat Robertson's book *The New World Order,* he notes that recent American history is the stage on which groups such as the federal government, Wall Street, the Council on Foreign Relations, the Bilderberg Group, and the Trilateral Commission control events off stage. Their decisions quietly push society toward a central world government.

Although President Obama was not responsible for the program known as Agenda 21, he did comply with its mandates. Using an executive order, he expanded its scope within the US, designating new federal powers designed to map out areas intended for sustainable development, as well as areas off-limits to the US population. President Obama signed his eighty-sixth executive order (13575) on June 9, 2011, establishing the White House Rural Council.[247] The federal government will seemingly control every aspect of rural America's heartland.

The United States is a signatory country to Agenda 21. It is not a treaty, and the Senate is unable to hold a formal debate or vote on it. Agenda 21 is therefore not considered to be law under Article Six of the US Constitution. Several US officials, congressmen, and senators had spoken in Congress in support of Agenda 21; these include Representative Nancy Pelosi, former Secretary of State John Kerry, and Senator Harry Reid.[248]

With Agenda 21 to be implemented by the states, fierce debates have taken place in state legislatures as its true meaning. The state of Florida, for example, has repealed its thirty-year-old growth management law (also called "smart growth," UN Agenda 21, "compact development," and "livability"). Under the law, local jurisdictions were required to adopt comprehensive land use plans stipulating where development could and could not occur. These plans were subject to approval by the state Department of Community Affairs, an agency that would be abolished by the legislation.

If you are wondering why you keep hearing so much about sustainable development, smart growth, open spaces, environmental justice, social equity, population control, eminent domain, and redistribution of the wealth (which includes land, in addition to money), it is because the Obama administration infiltrated every aspect of our society via executive orders and agencies. Florida has realized what Agenda 21 would mean to its overall rural landscape and has exercised its right to not implement Obama's executive order 13575, which pushes Agenda 21 into every aspect of rural America. It cedes US agriculture to international guidelines under the authorship of the UN. Obama had in effect "signed" the Kyoto treaty without a physical signing. He ceded US agriculture to the UN and by doing so was destroying Florida's independent agricultural job market.[249]

As with most secret governmental programs that are based on agendas, as opposed to need, their identifying names are chosen with great care for maximum public acceptance. Such is the case with Agenda 21, which innocuously stands for "Sustainable Development for the Twenty-first Century." So impactful and sinister are the goals and objectives of Agenda 21 to world populations and the human rights of their citizens that they should have been front-page news in every media outlet. Since 1992, I dare say that no school, civic organization, or political party has even made mention of Agenda 21. Silence is the weapon of secret agendas; their accidental or intentional exposure is considered a conspiracy theory. It must be understood that secret agendas are enacted with military precision and stealth. Populations are controllable assets necessary to achieve the desired results of the agenda. The disadvantages populations have against sinister forces are that they rarely have forewarning and do not understand the impact until it's too late. The advantage that populations have against sinister forces is sheer numbers and the power of civil disobedience, something well documented by the historical events of Gandhi and Martin Luther King Jr.

What makes the exposure of the elements of Agenda 21 so dangerous is that it is promoted by the elites to "save the planet" and implemented by governments worldwide. In a TedX lecture, Bill Gates even shared his view about how to achieve this goal by vaccinations: "The world today has 7.7 billion people. That's heading up to about nine billion. Now if we do a really great job on new vaccines, health care & reproductive health services, we could lower that by perhaps 10 or 15 percent."[250]

Sustainable Development for the Twenty-first Century

Who would ever suspect planning for a better future to be sinister? The optimal word here is "better," a word never actually mentioned or defined as a byproduct of Agenda 21, but certainly implied. Humans are trusting by nature until taught otherwise. Show me a child who will not innately follow an adult with an offer of candy. Similarly, "locks" and "trust" carry the connotation of being for honest people. For the dishonest, a simple set of bolt cutters solves the lock issue; for those with an agenda, lying gets past most objections. The point is that nothing is as it appears to be, leaving no opportunity for interpretation or review.

Below is a summary of the salient points contained within Agenda 21:

- Develop a comprehensive plan of action, under the control of the United Nations, that will affect all nations.
- Change the rule of law to "guilty until proven innocent." Notice that our court systems are based on the constitutional premise of "innocent till proven guilty." However, take a look at IRS enforcement, in which you are assumed guilty until you can produce evidence of your innocence.
- The elimination of the sovereignty of all nations (President Bush Sr. pledged US compliance before the United Nations Council in 1993).
- President Clinton, by executive order, established the President's Council on Sustainable Development.[251]
- Confiscate all private property.

- Eliminate private ownership of cars.
- Restructure the family unit with the collective as surrogate parents.
- Sustainable Development of micro-living units. Populations would be "stacked and packed" in mammoth high-rise micro-housing units to maximize resources. Experimental testing of micro-living units is presently occurring in New York City.
- Restriction on individual travel and independent opportunity.
- Education would be geared to environmental concerns from UN initiatives like the United Nations Educational, Scientific and Cultural Organization (UNESCO), espousing "Education for All" based on the same ideas as Common Core.

Following is a partial list of the non-sustainable, according to Agenda 21: private property, fossil fuel (still hiding the truth), irrigation, paved roads, inalienable rights, commercial agriculture, golf courses, ski lodges, fishing camps, and all privately owned recreational facilities and farmlands, with more being added each year.

To accomplish the objectives of Agenda 21, without raising the suspicion of the populace, is to indoctrinate the youth by instituting Common Core school curricula with textbooks void of historical reference to this country's past. The concept of the Common Core education is not new and was successfully implemented (under a different name) by the Nazis from 1930 through 1945, as a way to separate the morals of the children from those of the parents in the occupied countries. Germany knew that it was the children of the captive countries who would become the slave labor for Germany. "Conquering their minds" was the objective. The Nazis took 250,000 children from their families, intent on Germanizing them through German re-education reflecting the values for their new reality.[252]

Common Core schools will teach that knowledge is not about facts but about values. Mathematics will be taught as arbitrary and man-made, and the notion will be promulgated that good solutions are arrived at by consensus among those who are considered experts. The rationale of the Agenda 21 program is that with higher education come increased incomes, leading to increased consumption, resulting in lower sustainability. The poor, with lower education and greater dependency of government programs, have lower incomes, less consumption, and are more suitable for sustainable development. The collective mentality is that higher education equates to a threat to sustainable development.

US Opposition

During the last decade, opposition to Agenda 21 has increased within the United States at the local, state, and federal levels. In January 2011, Commissioner Richard Rothschild of Carroll County, Maryland, became the first elected official in the United States to successfully remove a US jurisdiction from participation in Agenda 21. The Republican National Committee has adopted a resolution opposing Agenda 21, and the Republican Party platform stated that "We strongly reject the UN Agenda 21 as erosive of American sovereignty."[253]

Several state and local governments have considered or passed motions and legislation opposing Agenda 21. Alabama became the first state to prohibit government participation in Agenda 21. Many other states, including Arizona, drafted legislation to ban Agenda 21.

It must be crystal clear that the ultimate agenda of the New World Order is to reduce the populations of the world; contain individual freedoms; wield total control over the necessities of life; control all natural resources, including water; and control monetary exchanges, goods, services, education, and the individual's "inalienable" right (as declared in the US Constitution) of self-determination. Agenda 21 contains within it the means for making all of the goals of the New World Order come to fruition.

Activists, some of whom have been associated with the Tea Party movement, the *New York Times*, and the *Huffington Post,* have said that Agenda 21 is a conspiracy by the United Nations to deprive individuals of property rights.[254] Columnists in the *Atlantic* have linked opposition to Agenda 21 to the property rights movement in the United States.[255] A poll of 1,300 United States voters by the American Planning Association found that 9% supported Agenda 21, 6% opposed it, and 85% thought they didn't have enough information to form an opinion.

The United Nations issued a Declaration on the Rights of Indigenous Peoples to guide member-state national policies to the collective rights of indigenous peoples—such as culture; identity; language; and access to employment, health, education, and natural resources. Although no definition of indigenous peoples exists, estimates put the total population of post-colonial indigenous peoples who seek human rights and discrimination redress between 220 million and 350 million. This is akin to the Endangered Species Act, where definitions are made with a broad-brush stroke, technically encompassing everything affecting the desired legislation.

Greenhouse Gases / Climate Change
The terms used in the climate change movement are often intentionally misused so as to confuse the average American. It is imperative to understand that greenhouse gases are natural to our environment and do not pollute the air but that man-made air pollutants are unnatural to our atmosphere and tend to settle on our water, land, and polar ice fields. Greenhouse gases are essentially water vapor (99.999% of natural origin), carbon dioxide, methane, nitrous oxide, and miscellaneous other gases. Human activities contribute slightly to greenhouse gas concentrations through farming, manufacturing, power generation, and transportation.[256] However, these emissions are so dwarfed in comparison to emissions from natural sources we can do nothing about that even the costliest efforts to limit human emissions would have a very small—perhaps undetectable—effect on global climate. In other words, despite the UN's appearance of forced regulations aimed at stemming climate change, science and climate data have proved otherwise. The American Free Press states that:

> Global warming is phony science that was concocted to justify implementation of an international political agenda. The idea of using "man-caused global warming" as a "surrogate for war" and as a way to "destroy excess wealth" originated in American and UN-related think tanks such as the Club of Rome back in the 60's and 70's. This pseudo-science is the centerpiece of a phony environmental movement by which the UN hopes to redistribute wealth in the world (toward the super-rich and away from the people) to de-industrialize the industrialized countries (via the UN Kyoto Protocol-type carbon taxes, cap and trade schemes, etc.), and radically reduce the human population.[257]

Smog, on the other hand, is a mixture of pollutants that mix with the ozone in our atmosphere, producing a chemical reaction in the air that forms a dense haze. Burning of petroleum, like gasoline, or the manufacturing of paints and other chemical solvents are just some smog producers. Smog can harm health and damage the environment in areas that have little access to natural air currents like the lower-level jet stream; examples are Los Angeles and Beijing. What is never mentioned in these discussions, however, is that the earth is self-cleansing and continually redefining itself—surely an honest oversight!

The eruption of Mount St. Helens in 1980 was the most economically destructive volcanic event in the history of the US. The volcano released over 540 million tons of ash and pollutants into the atmosphere, laying waste to 200 square miles of terrain. However, only forty years later nature has reclaimed the land into a flourishing new landscape. Similarly, the underwater devastation of the Gulf oil spill in 2010 leaked 39 million gallons of crude into the Gulf of Mexico, making this disaster more widespread than the Exxon Valdez Alaskan spill and the worst in American history.[258] National Geographic conducted a study of the remnants of the Gulf oil spill just three years later and concluded that, despite the enormity and consequences of the spill, nature is already reclaiming the environment and may soon restore its delicate balance. These are just two examples of natural disasters and how nature rebounds from these events.

The significance of natural disasters is that they dwarf those influenced by humans. One cannot obtain a patent on naturally occurring phenomena, but one can capitalize on the theories. So it has been with the Sustainable Development theories of the UN's Agenda 21 program. Theories are just that—unproven facts. The greenhouse theory of global warming is factual, but the data leading to its conclusions that the United Nations can somehow control natural events by controlling the activities of the populations of the world is intentionally flawed. Not deterred by facts and the false premise that our present energy reserves are limited and nonrenewable, many of our educational institutions are offering degreed programs in Sustainable Management, perpetuating the myth while fulfilling the primary objective of the NWO of training the youth as a means toward political and economic control.

Sustainability
New and retooled environmental degree programs are placing fresh emphasis on practical problem solving. The University of Tennessee offers a solution-oriented curriculum that spans law, business, science, resource management, and ethics. Sustainability managers in all sorts of companies and organizations look for ways to make the "institution more efficient and produce less waste and pollution."[259] In 2012, at least 17 schools added sustainability majors, including the University of South Dakota, Cornell University, and Oregon State University—Cascades.

Left wing Billionaire George Soros's "Open Society" has provided $2,147,415 to the ILCEI (International Council for Local Environmental Initiatives) . . . Van Jones' "Green for All" and the "Tides Foundations" Apollo Alliance are also reportedly ICLEI contributors.[260][261]

Global warming is the whipping post for most environmental agendas. It is no surprise that the environmental push for global warming awareness was adopted by the UN after the "Global Warming Convention" and the Kyoto protocols were established in 2015, realizing that such a mission can have global significance toward forwarding the Agenda 21 initiatives. Here was the opportunity to control almost every aspect of world cultures and economies by making predictions of gloom and doom, followed by self-appointed regulations spanning all aspects of natural global behaviors. The idea is to separate this initiative from the tree hugger's movement of the 1960s (adherents of which were more interested in environmentally communing with nature), then direct people to a movement aimed at blaming humanity for man-made global warming. This has become the holy grail of the Agenda 21 movement. Great opportunities have been presented to develop legislation, taxes, and a general overhaul of the economic structure of the US, all in the name of saving the icebergs; the real intent is to control and contain every aspect of human behavior.

However, it wasn't long before basic high school science debunked much of the man-made global warming theory. There are more greenhouse gasses released into the atmosphere every year by natural sources than by all the auto emissions since the inception of the internal combustion engine.[262] Undaunted, however, the movement quickly and silently changed from man-made global warming to climate change, moving the blame for alleged global warming away from humanity and toward nature itself. This makes solutions less likely to find. The Agenda 21 environmentalists now have science on their side. Virtually all people know about the changing climate cycles of warming to ice ages over the eons; however, this does not imply that humanity can alter nature's cycles simply by altering human activities. This creates the perfect scenario for a never-ending attempt at controlling human activities.

By definition, global warming has been on the rise in the average temperature of Earth's atmosphere and oceans since the late nineteenth century. Since the early twentieth century, Earth's mean surface temperature, according to UN reports, has increased by about (1.4°F), with about two-thirds of the increase occurring since 1980. However, the actual climate data demonstrates a fluctuation of only .02 degrees Fahrenheit, mostly accountable to seasonal shifts in the jet stream and the abundance of atmospheric water vapor.[263] The UN data is fraudulent.

Homo sapiens has been on this planet for approximately 200,000 years; however, the earliest record of an industrious man capable of exploiting nature's resources is from around 10,000 years ago. The last ice age lasted for around 40,000 years, with shifts from global warming to global cooling occurring every 130,000 years. It is a deliberate misuse of climate data to imply that humanity has much to do with climate change, other than the usefulness of a UN agenda to attempt to control the populations of the world.

Obama, as indicated earlier, signed Executive Order 13575 in 2011, establishing a White House Rural Council prescribed by Agenda 21.[264] The amount of government resources Obama directed to administer this council is staggering. This president committed thousands of federal employees in twenty-five federal agencies to promote sustainability in rural areas, completely bypassing congressional approval. Some of these agencies are totally unrelated to rural areas. Agenda 21 is the action plan to inventory and control all land, water, minerals, plants, animals, construction, means of production, information, energy, and human beings in the world.

The United Nations Educational, Scientific and Cultural Organization (UNESCO) has a program called Education for All that includes the same people and ideas as Common Core. The UN-

ESCO goals and objectives for education are very similar to the Agenda 21 and Common Core goals and objectives. Continually creating new terms and euphemisms to ensure concepts with easily acceptable phrasing and wording ensures that the public will never grasp the true significance of Agenda 21 and the continual dissolution of our freedoms without our realizing the constitutional losses being allowed.

President Trump weighed in on the global warming issue, defunding the UN depopulation bill that supported Agenda 21. Trump ordered the EPA to remove several pages from its statement of objectives that supported global warming and climate change. Trump also signed an executive order making US energy independent rather than supporting green energy, calling global warming a hoax.[265]

Analysis of the Four Sections of Agenda 21

Agenda 21 is a three-hundred-page document divided into forty chapters that have been grouped into four sections. What follows is an analysis of each section.

Section I: "Social and Economic Dimensions" is directed toward combating poverty, especially in developing countries; changing consumption patterns; promoting health; achieving a more sustainable population; and sustainable settlement in decision making.

Historically, any attempt at combating poverty, such as President Lyndon Johnson's "war on poverty," whereby a government agency allocates massive resources and tax dollars toward improving the lives of those in poverty, has been an unmitigated failure. Similarly, there have been social programs targeted toward a war on cancer, a war on drugs, and a war on crime, all sounding noble and with the best interests of those affected in mind, yet not even one has produced tangible results. The reason is that these programs were designed to enslave vast numbers of people by inciting them to seek an easier way to sustain their lives rather than empowering them to step out from their enslavement and earn their way into the middle class. The government appears to be philanthropic, while at the core is the motive of achieving a permanent voting block that can essentially suck the wealth out of its coffers while continuing the mantra of class warfare. In all cultures, the poor have ways of getting assistance from churches and organizations set up to assist. Many social programs fail to fund and promote job train as an incentive to become more self-sufficient. This is where compassion begins. "Give a man a fish and he will not go hungry; teach a man to fish and he can feed himself for life."

Sustainable population means government-controlled population, along with the removal of personal wealth and the ability to use one's freedoms and talents to sustain their own life. All of this happens under the guise of protecting the poor or sharing the wealth.

Social programs are riddled with euphemisms for the purpose of keeping the undereducated from learning the truth. Sustainable development relies on the cooperation of the population, accomplished in part by Common Core educational programs for the young.

Section II: "Conservation and Management of Resources for Development" addresses atmospheric protection, combating deforestation, protecting fragile environments, conservation of biological diversity, control of pollution, and the management of biotechnology and radioactive wastes.

Conservation and management of resources began officially in the US in 1970, as the responsibility of the Environmental Protection Agency (EPA). This is an agency of the US federal government created for the purpose of protecting human health and the environment by writing and enforcing regulations based on laws passed by Congress. The EPA was proposed and created via executive order by President Richard Nixon. Once it was signed into law, Congress was directed to construct and enact laws that would effectively change the way business and pleasure would be overseen from then on.

On the surface, it was a promising program. Who would oppose laws that protect our environment and health? The EPA came at the heels of the sixties' revolution and at the height of the hippie/flower child culture, during the time when all eyes were focused on the Vietnam war, with images of napalm and deforestation by Agent Orange burned into the minds of the youth in America. Fueled by the overwhelming support of the younger voters, the time was right for the social revolution to move into high gear with token programs like those that protected endangered species, while at the same time introducing programs that essentially had less to do with protecting health or the environment than with stripping Americans of their freedoms.

Rachel Carson's 1962 release of Silent Spring set the stage for social change. The book sold in twenty-four countries and represented a blueprint for public awareness of and concern for living organisms and public health for the modern environmental movement; this book was basically the inspiration for the first Earth Day in 1970.[266]

Who could have known that the creation of the EPA would eventually lead to a plethora of government regulations that could and would stifle any attempt at another industrial revolution or ways of creating cheaper sources of energy or natural resources? One such case took place in New York and New Jersey in 1989, where a new watershed was proposed and engineered that would ensure less expensive water purification methods, desalinization procedures for sea water, and future safeguards against natural drought conditions. At that time New York and New Jersey were coming off a major water supply crisis that threatened huge areas of the population.[267]

The project came to a halt after the EPA studied the environmental impact on the area. It was found that an indigenous species of small fish called snail darters would be irreparably harmed by the project, thus halting its implementation. Numerous other examples abound in which species of birds like the scrub jay, indigenous to certain areas of Florida, are listed as one of the ten thousand plus endangered species. For properties that contain scrub habitats or are occupied by Florida scrub jays, consultation is required with the United States Fish and Wildlife Service prior to initiating a clearing project and before the county may issue a mulching permit, building permit, or tree removal and protection permit.[268] To date almost all permitting has been denied.

The EPA gained a hostile reputation shortly after the hippie generation became the entrepreneurs of today's world. The US government had to once again provide a distraction to keep the socialist agenda moving forward. Agenda 21 and the birth of sustainable development provided the necessary distraction with the power of enforcement by an international body (UN); 171 countries, including the US, have signed on.

Section III: "Strengthening the Role of Major Groups" includes the roles of children and youth, men, women, non-governmental organizations, local authorities, businesses, and workers and strengthening the role of indigenous peoples, their communities, and farmers.

The rhetoric contained within Agenda 21 is filled with words, phrases, and concepts that appear to represent the needs and goals of all humanity. However, a more detailed analysis, based on actual data contained within the minutes of the UN's numerous meetings, tells a different story. Strengthening the role of "major groups" affects the roles of just about all citizens. In viewing the Agenda 21 summary YouTube video *Agenda 21 for Dummies,* it becomes plain that "strengthening" is a euphemism for "controlling."[269] The term *major groups* refers to the many independent economic, philanthropic, and financial groups that drive our economy and the people who contribute to its success. Independent control is not permitted in a New World Order. Equality really means mediocrity under the control of a grand central government ensuring that everyone gets their fair share, with the elite in control. Thinking of this kind appeals to those who have come to accept government stipends as a way of life, as well as to the millions of illegal immigrants destined to use the American system of voting as a way of sustaining their lives.

The caveat for mentioning indigenous people and farmers, as part of the Agenda 21 umbrella of coverage under sustainable development, literally encompasses the entirety of the population. No one escapes the reach and scope of an all-powerful centralized government. Class warfare will ensure that the populations are kept busy, vying for better positioning.

In the *Agenda 21 for Dummies* video, it is clearly seen that the ultimate goal of a socialized central government for the United States is to divide the US into zones. The eastern zones are for "stack 'em/pack 'em" living with regard to family units, while the western zones are off limits to the United States population, a place for the "founders" of sustainable development to live in peace, while wielding control of all energy, food, finances, healthcare, education, etc. One must understand the clandestine nature of Agenda 21 and the extent of cooperation the concept is getting from countries around the world. Nothing is as it appears to be.

Section IV: "Means of Implementation" includes science, technology transfer, education, international institutions, and financial mechanisms.

What may not yet be noticed by many is that the Agenda 21 elites are comprised of select, interrelated government agencies. The resulting government agencies are implementing international laws that have taken effect through the executive orders of presidents, agreements, and regulations that most Americans do not even know about. These regulations have completely bypassed Congress and the Constitution.

The implementation of Agenda 21 is a silent coup, typical of all socialist takeovers of existing governments. The truly sad part is that, barring a precious few constitutionalist, our elected officials (members of Congress) have allowed this to occur to preserve their positions in government. An example of this is the exclusion of Congress from participation in Obamacare and other social programs imposed on the population. These agencies and councils are forming partnerships with members and groups other than the American people. However, our tax dollars pay for their salaries and for the programs.

No part of American society goes untouched. Technology, education, and corporations become so interwoven with government agencies and international finance that private enterprise all but disappears—and along with it the middle class.

An example of such implementation can be seen with BioEco Working Group,[270] which seems to be part of the Department of the Interior's US Geological Survey, since it is listed as creating the website. But the actual charter has National Science and Technology Council in the heading. The National Science and Technology Council includes twenty of the same agencies that are on the new Rural Council, but with some additional agencies, including the CIA. It also includes the vice-president, Cabinet secretaries, heads of agencies, and some White House officials.

If you look at the United Nations' Agenda 21 (Section 1, 7.28, and 7.29), you see why the BioEco Working Group might be mapping land and creating an inventory of biological resources: "All countries should consider, as appropriate, undertaking a comprehensive national inventory of their land resources in order to establish a land information system in which land resources will be classified according to their most appropriate uses and environmentally fragile or disaster-prone areas will be identified for special protection measures."[271]

The resulting loss of national sovereignties, should all of this materialize, will be catastrophic. We all will, by design, become citizens of a World Government, where individual cultures, customs, and laws will be mere footnotes in future ancient history classics. Few have the foresight and comprehension for understanding the permanency of such international actions controlled by the United Nations. But make no mistake: this was the plan from the beginning. Agenda 21 will be but the beginning. Sustainable development has no boundaries by design, similar to the war on terrorism.

It should be known that Agenda 21 is already morphing into Agenda 2030 and Agenda 2050, with the intent to bring globalism into our everyday life—if we are the lucky ones who survive the planned depopulation.[272]

For Further Reading

"Executive Order 13575 "RURAL COUNCILS" Agenda 21 NWO." InvestmentWatch RSS. http://investmentwatch-blog.com/execuctive-order-13575-rural-councils-agenda-21-nwo/#kvl8dlTai6bgbEz9.99 (accessed July 18, 2014).

YouTube. "The men behind the Earth Summit (World Order)-Geoge Hunt-part 4." YouTube. https://www.youtube.com/watch?v=YdzAzwKNabc&feature=relmfu (accessed July 21, 2014).

Chapter 11

Information Overload or Indifference?

It was evident early in the research for this book that there would be no beginning or ending of topics; the work is a snapshot glimpse of our continued political and philosophical destruction as a country. At times it appears as though we are in the studio audience of a bad sitcom. At other times we are faced with the brutal realities of an out-of-control government.

My intent is to present many of the iconic newsworthy topics that often fall within the parameters of political scandals, in a reader-friendly format. How many times are we faced with confusing journalism, filled with emotion yet lacking substance? News is meant to be reported in an unbiased manner, unencumbered by political motivation or agenda-driven rhetoric. Sadly, journalism has become an entertainment-driven ratings game in which the lines of truth are often blurred beyond recognition. The result is information overload in which "we the people" no longer participate. Never before have I seen such indifference to the facts. As a student of history, I continually ask myself, *Is this what really happened?* The answer often cannot be found by web searches as much as by understanding political agendas—it is here that my quest began.

The Cost of Political Business

The American government is abusing its power in ways that would have infuriated the colonists, yet we sit idly by and let the government rain its tyranny on us.[273] Alexander Hamilton noted, "When government obtains the ability to vote themselves power and money, that will be the downfall of this country." Hamilton's statement concerning government's ability to vote themselves power and money has come to fruition over the last decade, when compensation of federal employees has risen faster than compensation of private-sector employees. Therefore, the average federal civilian worker now earns seventy-four percent more in wages and benefits than the average worker in the US private sector.[274]

Hamilton was specific in pointing out that "A fondness for power is implanted, in most men, and it is natural to abuse it, when acquired." After years of public service, Hamilton clearly understood that "you believe the government is there to protect you, yet I would argue that it is now the single biggest threat to your well-being. I worry more about what the government is going to do to thwart my liberty and freedoms." Since Hamilton's era, government has continued to be the biggest threat to individual liberty and freedom.

As the nongovernment worker was clocking in forty to eighty hours a week, President Obama activated a one percent pay raise for all 4.4 million government workers, by way of executive order.[275] In consequence, these federal employees are receiving an across-the-board pay raise, in addition to a two percent increase implemented in January 2010.[276]

Five years in a row, lawmakers voted not to reject their automatic cost-of-living raise that would increase the annual salary of members by $3,400 to a total of $158,103 per year. In an article published on the Fox News website, Dick Morris writes, "Members of Congress worked only 103 days in 2013 and have the only job in the country whose occupants can set their own salary without regard to performance, profit, or economic climate."[277]

"[This] goes to show how out of touch with reality politicians can be. They forget that their salaries are paid by taxpayers. Average American citizens are being forced to tighten their belts, that is, if they even have a job, yet members of Congress will have an extra $3,400 to do with as they please."[278]

The facts are found in the underreported retirement benefits of Congress and their political leaders:

Salary of retired US Presidents: $450,000/year for life
Salary of Speaker of the House: $223,500/year for life

Compare those numbers with the salaries of military personnel; their average salary when deployed is $38,000. A fully commissioned officer with combat experience and full training toward the safety and security of our country receives fifty percent of their salary rate at retirement, or approximately $46,156/year for life.[279]

In 2012, federal workers had an average wage of $81,704, according to data from the US Bureau of Economic Analysis. By comparison, the average wage of the nation's 104 million private-sector workers was $54,995. When benefits such as health care and pensions are included, the compensation differential for federal over private workers is even larger.[280] In 2019, The Parliamentary Budget Office reported that the average number of federal employees increased from 335,000 in 2012 to 369,000 in 2019 and that these workers' average wages and benefits amount to $115,000 annually, with their private sector counterparts averaging only $65,917.[281]

When people become indifferent to the news and even lose interest in their constitutional responsibilities, the loss of freedom is inevitable. Historically, as I have mentioned repeatedly, democracies do not often exceed a lifespan of two hundred years; the reason is that a democracy is a form of government founded on the principle of either elected individuals representing the people (as with the government of the United States) or of a direct democracy, in which the people themselves are responsible for making all decisions.[282] The success of a democracy is dependent on the willingness of the people to remain involved and accountable for their decisions.

Our country was founded on constitutional principles to ensure freedom from a controlling centralized government. The US Constitution is a limitation on government through the separation of powers via independent branches of government, all designed to protect American citizens from tyranny. Fifteen years after the signing of the US Constitution, it was deemed necessary to further delineate rights that were "unalienable"—rights given to us by our Creator rather than by government.[283] Through the efforts of Thomas Jefferson and James Madison, a constitutional convention of states was formed to add a Bill of Rights to the Constitution.

On December 15, 1791, the first ten amendments to the Constitution, known as the Bill of Rights, were ratified by Congress. The Constitution's first three words, "We the People," emphasize rule by the people—not a king or a dictator and not the president, Supreme Court justices, members of Congress, or state legislators. Foremost in the minds of our founding fathers was the First Amendment to the United States Constitution: Congress shall make no law respecting an establishment of religion or prohibiting the free exercise thereof; or abridging the freedom of speech, or of the press; or the right of the people peaceably to assemble, and to petition the Government for a redress of grievances.[284]

So important is the ability of the citizens to remain above reproach by a controlling government that freedom of speech, the press, and peaceful assembly were uniquely specified by our founding fathers.[285] Little did they know that our freedom of speech would someday be censored by the very people it was designed to protect. Facebook, Google, and other social media platforms are nongovernmental agencies made up of private corporate entities that "we the people" have allowed to dictate what speech is acceptable and what is not. This is an example of why democracies do not last: over time people become too complacent, too willing to trade convenience and pleasure for diligence. There is nothing *free about freedom;* it must be earned. Freedom cannot be bought or sold, but it can be lost to the relentless default system of government called socialism.

FDR's New Deal and LBJ's Great Society were experiments in "social engineering," attempting to reshape the behavior of the poor and the lower class, moving them from being recipients of welfare rolls to membership in a grand middle class. The attitude was that "we are all in this together" and that as such we should partake equally in its successes and failures. The ultimate failure of both of these progressive centralized governmental experiments was that they were experimentally driven engineering projects that had never sought the support or even the acquiescence of popular majorities. In fact, the most notable outcome of progressive ideologies is the expansion of entitlement programs to artificially support what their political theories have failed to produce.[286]

Under the presidency of Woodrow Wilson, the progressive political movement took hold. In 1913, Wilson ran on a platform of social reform, arguing that a strong centralized government was necessary to fight for anti-trust legislation and labor rights with his "New Freedom" initiative.[287] However, his policies became nothing more than regulated monopolies, co-opted by special business interests leading to the passage of the Sixteenth Amendment of the US Constitution, which allowed Congress to levy an income tax without the approval of individual states. This income tax was instituted to support ever-increasing centralized federal government programs.

Soon after the ratification of the Sixteenth Amendment, Congress levied a one percent tax on personal incomes greater than $3,000 and a six percent tax on incomes above $500,000. These taxes affected only a very small proportion of the population. Later in 1913, in the case of *Stratton's Independence v. Howbert,* the Supreme Court redefined income under the tax law as the "gain derived from capital, from labor, or from both combined." Few realize that the original intent of the tax code was to levy taxes on earnings from income and not on the income itself.[288] Changing the tax code was an attempt to drain the wealth of the nation under the guise that it was necessary to finance the costs of World War I. The conclusion of World War I did not reinstate the original intent of the tax code but only served as a progressive ploy to control the wealth of the American population legally.

The Fraud of the Sixteenth Amendment
The intrigue and deception regarding the Sixteenth Amendment continued but were never publicly reported by the press. The outgoing Secretary of State for the Taft administration and probable incoming advisor to the Wilson administration, Philander Knox, committed fraud when he declared the Sixteenth Amendment to have been officially ratified.[289] "There were forty-eight states at that time, and three-fourths, or thirty-six, of them were required to give their approval for the amendment to be ratified. The process took almost the whole term of the Taft administration, from 1909 to 1913.

Knox had received responses from only forty-two states when he declared the amendment ratified on February 25, 1913, under pressure from the Wilson administration to have his signature bill (the Sixteenth Amendment tax code) ratified. Knox acknowledged that four of those states (Utah, Connecticut, Rhode Island, and New Hampshire) had rejected it, bringing the count to thirty-eight, while Kentucky and Oklahoma had not responded, reducing the count to thirty-six. The state constitution of Tennessee prohibited its state legislature from acting on any proposed amendment to the US Constitution sent by Congress until after the next election of state legislators, which dropped the count to thirty-five, one less than the number necessary at the time Wilson announced its ratification. By the final count less than twenty of the required thirty-six states had ratified the amendment. Many attempts have been made to repeal it under grounds that it did not adhere to constitutional law, but all have failed. Those who allow selective dismissal of the law must be held accountable.

President Wilson knew that in order for the progressive movement to fundamentally change the rule of law under the Constitution, he must convince the citizens of the US that the Bill of Rights, and especially the First Amendment, could become a detriment to national security. While the progressives differed in their assessment of the problems and how to resolve them, they believed that government at every level must be actively involved in these reforms. The existing constitutional system was outdated and needed to be made into a dynamic, evolving instrument of social change, aided by scientific knowledge and shared journalistic reviews. In short, constitutional law is to be enforced on the citizens but not on its elected officials.

President Wilson set his sights on breaking the First Amendment, especially in terms of the freedom of the press. He did so by cozying up to the independent media by having dinners at the White House, inviting key journalists and newspaper owners under the guise of cooperation and transparency, when, in fact, the motive was to gain influence into what was being reported to the world.

Four decades later came another landmark progressive case, *New York Times Co. v. United States* (1971), in which the administration of President Richard Nixon sought to ban the publication of the Pentagon Papers (classified government documents about the Vietnam War secretly copied and reported by the *New York Times* analyst Daniel Ellsberg). These documents revealed that the US had secretly enlarged the scale of the Vietnam War with the bombings of nearby Cambodia and Laos, along with the extermination of the North Vietnam village of My Lai, where military intelligence failed to confirm the presence of the Viet Cong, resulting in the slaughter of hundreds of innocent men, women and children. None of this was reported in the mainstream media. Daniel Ellsberg was charged with conspiracy, espionage, and theft of government property, but the charges were later dropped after prosecutors investigating the Watergate Scandal discovered that the Nixon Administration had ordered the so-called White House plumbers to engage in unlawful efforts to discredit Ellsberg.[290]

First Amendment rights were put to the test once again in 2013 with the case of Edward Snowden and the National Security Council (NSA). Snowden will go down in history as one of America's most consequential whistleblowers, alongside Daniel Ellsberg. He is responsible for handing over material from one of the world's most secretive government organizations, the NSA. In a note accompanying the first set of documents Snowden provided, he wrote, "I understand that I will be made to suffer for my actions," but "I will be satisfied if the federation of secret law, unequal pardon and irresistible executive powers that rule the world that I love are revealed even for an instant."

Despite Snowden's determination to be publicly unveiled, he repeatedly insisted that he wanted to avoid the media spotlight: "I don't want public attention because I don't want the story to be about me. I want it to be about what the US government is doing." He also stated, "I have no intention of hiding who I am because I know I have done nothing wrong" and "I know the government will demonize me."

It was then, he said, that he "watched as Obama advanced the very policies that [he] thought would be reined in," and as a result, he "got hardened." He learned just how all-consuming the NSA's surveillance activities were, claiming that "they are intent on making every conversation and every form of behavior in the world known to them." Once Snowden reached the conclusion that the NSA's surveillance net would soon be irrevocable, he revealed that it was just a matter of time before he chose to act: "What they're doing poses an existential threat to democracy." For Snowden, it was a matter of principle: "The government has granted itself power it is not entitled to; there is no public oversight." He stated further, "I carefully evaluated every single document I disclosed to ensure that each was legitimately in the public interest. There are all sorts of documents that would have made a big impact that I didn't turn over, because harming people isn't my goal. Transparency is."[291]

The above information is included here only to disclose the slow, insidious infiltration of the progressive movement onto the dismantling of our constitutional Bill of Rights. Freedom of the press gave unprecedented uniqueness to the transparency of the United States. However, in 2014, under the Obama administration, the US had fallen to forty-sixth in the world in terms of freedom of the press, according to The World for Press Freedom.[292]

Will the citizens of the US view the acts of Ellsberg and Snowden as treason against the United States, or will they see them as heroes for attempting to uphold the very constitutional laws elected and appointed US government officials have chosen to ignore? It is important to realize that freedom, without diligent review, is nothing more than an illusion.

Politics is essentially a game of chess, where one must plan several moves ahead in order to achieve victory. Confusion leads to a lack of planning and an eventual lack of interest in what is happening. So it is with the pace of recent political scandals where progressive ideologies often go unrecognized, leading to the eventual loss of constitutional respect.

Every president since Ronald Reagan has moved this country deeper into the abyss of political chaos and financial disaster. Political parties, as I have pointed out so often, have become nothing more than one party posing as two, keeping us as amused as in a shell game in which we continually guess under which shell the prize is located. The idea of a balanced budget has become a "racist" ideology because of its implication of favoring the people who keep this country prosperous, as opposed to those depending on entitlements. It appears that our entire culture is turning upside down.

President Trump took on the progressives much as Snowden took on the government, knowing full well that it would be at his own peril. The progressive Democratic party, intent on destroying Trump, took our political system to new lows. Under progressive ideology, no longer does the will of the people carry until the next election cycle. Instead of abiding by the rules of constitutional law, the progressives prefer Saul Alinsky's "Rules for Radicals," among which are Rule 5 ("Ridicule is man's most potent weapon. There is no defense. It is irrational. It is infuriating. It also works as a key pressure point to force the enemy into concessions") and Rule 8

("Keep the pressure on. Never let up. Keep trying new things to keep the opposition off balance. As the opposition masters one approach, hit them from the flank with something new").[293]

As of this writing, there were twenty-nine investigations related to Trump, which included ten federal criminal investigations, eight state and local investigations, and eleven congressional Investigations, all designed to find reason for impeachment.[294] The Mueller Report became the progressives' best tool to keep Trump on the defense, but the report failed to prove Russian collusion or interference in the 2016 presidential election.[295] Meanwhile, the public endured actual mishandling of justice within the progressive movement, that had yet to activate any investigations into Hillary Clinton's illegal email server, the phony Steele Dossier and FISA warrant, Comey, Strzok, Page, Clapper, Brennan, etc. Equal justice under the law requires equal treatment under existing laws. Trump was an enigma to the progressives in Congress. Alinsky's rules work if the target reacts as expected. No matter one's political stripe, none can deny that Trump demonstrated that our democratic form of government does not equate to a "social democracy" and can continue to thrive despite progressive pressure.

My mission is not only to make some of our most recent political and physical occurrences understandable but also to offer real solutions that the average American can easily participate in. Keep in mind that for Americans to have a constitution that guarantees limited centralized government in favor of control by individual states and personal rights that ensure our precious freedoms come with a hefty price—participation in the system. Every citizen has the duty to be involved to keep that freedom. Freedom cannot be taken from us unless we give it away.

History is an ever-evolving part of life, with its facts and traditions passed from generation to generation, guaranteeing one thing that cannot be taught: wisdom. Yet those with the desire to alter reality can easily do so by altering the facts of history or, worse, by omitting them entirely. The progressive movement in this country is attempting to alter the facts of our history through Common Core education, allowing interpretation of historical facts to suit the needs of a progressive agenda. A strong centralized government with far-reaching political and economic mandates can easily force publishers of school texts to print what is socially and politically acceptable to its agenda of transforming the American Constitution and the freedoms inherent in its Bill of Rights. Pre-World War II Germany attempted to alter history by ordering the burning of all historical books in favor of the tyrannical teaching of the emerging ideologically motivated racist and white supremacist doctrines of Nazism.[296]

It is the responsibility of every American to never allow the contents of our Constitution to be altered in favor of political expediency or ideological utopia. In 1828, Arthur Stansbury wrote the *Elementary Catechism on the Constitution of the United States.*[297] During the first century of our country's existence, great care was taken to ensure that our schools educated our children about the most enlightened system of government ever created. Stansbury's text consisted of 322 questions and answers on the Constitution and functioning of our federal government in a concise guide for use in public schools.

Following are specific questions and answers from Elementary Catechism on the Constitution of the United States that were included in the text of Miracles and Massacres by Glenn Beck.[298] A few of the key questions and answers are reproduced here exactly as presented, to highlight the need for diligence in the upcoming battle over Common Core education. They are pertinent to this discussion and to the administrative policies affecting education today. It is my experience as a former high school educator in the NYC school system in the 1970s and early 1980s that, once a school board is monetarily or politically influenced by progressive ideology, history is lost.

Q 181: Who executes the laws which Congress have made, that is, who takes care that everybody shall obey the laws?
A. The President of the United States

Q 182: Can he make the law?
A. Not at all. These two powers of making law, and executing law, are kept by the Constitution, entirely separate; the power that makes the law cannot execute it, and the power that executes the law cannot make it. (One of these powers is called the Legislative, and the other is called the Executive power.)

Q 266: Why are not Judges elected from time to time, like Members of the House of Representatives and Senators? And why may they not be removed from their offices unless they are proved to be guilty of great offences?
A. If Judges held their places at the mere good pleasure of the people, they would be greatly tempted to act in a partial and improper manner in order to please those who chose them to office, and to keep their favor; but when they know that no man or number of men can turn them out of office so long as they do their duty, they administer justice without fear and with an equal regard to all who ask it.

Q 267: Why then should not Legislators hold their office in the same way?
A. Because they make the laws, while Judges only explain and apply them. It would be very dangerous to liberty to give our law makers power for life; they require restraint lest they should become our tyrants; therefore, their time of office is made short, so that if the people thought them unwise or unfaithful, they may refuse to give them the office again.

Q 296: The majority of the people of any State may certainly alter its laws, provided they do not violate the Constitution: but may the Constitution itself be altered?
A. Yes. The constitution being nothing more than an expression of the will of the people of the United States, is at all times within their own power, and they may change it as they like, but it ought not to be changed till it is very clearly shown to be the wish of the people.

Q 300: What security have we that the Constitution will be observed?
A. The President, Members of Congress, the Members of all the State Legislatures, and all public officers of the United States, and of each one of the States, take an oath, when they enter upon their several offices, to obey the Constitution. But the great security for its observance lies in the wisdom and excellence of the Constitution itself, and the conviction of the whole people of the United States, that it is for their true interest to observe it inviolate. It has been tried for fifty years, and has done more

to render this nation peaceable, powerful and happy than any form of government that ever existed among men.

Q 308: What do you understand by these expressions?
A. In a free country like ours, every citizen has a right to express his opinion of the character and conduct of our rulers, and of the laws they make for our government; to forbid this, or punish it, would be highly dangerous to our liberty. If those chosen by their fellow citizens to rule the State, rule in a foolish or wicked manner, it ought to be known, that they may be speedily turned out of office, but if nobody might find fault with them without danger of punishment, their bad conduct would never be exposed, and they might continue in power to the great injury of us all. The right to speak our opinions is the freedom of speech; and the right to print them, that they may be read by others, is the freedom of the press.

It would be wise to understand and make public our founding principles; failure to do so is an open invitation for the progressive takeover of this country. Take heed that it is no accident that our country, the innovator of a free press, now ranks forty-sixth in the world in freedom of the press. I fear that it is public ignorance and not stupidity that is driving the forces of the progressive movement. Words have meaning—allowing euphemistic phrases to replace standard constitutional language affecting the future of this country is unacceptable and can be stopped only by an informed citizenry.

Let's Talk Indifference
History is an ever-evolving part of life with its facts and traditions passed from generation to generation, but there is one thing that cannot be taught: wisdom"?

To reiterate a point made earlier, those with the desire to alter the perception of reality can easily do so by altering the facts of history or, worse, omitting them entirely. Events in Charlottesville, Virginia, that took place in September of 2020 typify the movement of progressive socialists in this country to cleanse history of any memory of slavery. The movement is spreading to cities across America, but the simple removal of Confederate statues will not cleanse the history of slavery, nor is this the intent of those orchestrating their removal. The target is the Constitution, not the institution of slavery. Have you noticed that our country seems to be going crazy? Every historical American tradition is under scrutiny. The appearance of new terms like the Alt-right, Antifa, Black Lives Matter, and various groups of violent extremists suddenly showing up at peaceful rallies to instigate violence, on cue when the media cameras begin to roll, is no accident. Doesn't it seem odd that any attempt to bring stability is labeled as racist? To the astute historian, none of this is new. Countries and nations lose control when their citizens become indifferent; confused; or, worse, unaware of what is occurring.

Today, Westerners who willingly capitulate to extremist groups of all stripes, in the name of tolerance, multiculturalism, political correctness, or just plain stupidity, only embolden those hell-bent on the destruction of this country. It has been said that history tends to repeat itself, but few ever seek to know why. Present-day America is experiencing the ugly side of democracy—indifference. The United States is unlike any other country ever formed. It is not a copy of other countries and is the only nation in which the people were given the power and right to run the country. Our Constitution destroys monarchies and dictatorships. It was written as a lasting document, to be changed only by constitutional conventions, not public opinion.

The enemies of our Constitution know that those who benefit from its existence can destroy it, if given the right incentives. Democracies depend on staying ever vigilant to constitutional law. They are destroyed by indifference and accepting radical thinking that plays on emotions rather than intellect. Radicals never address the real issues but instead attack individuals. President Trump was a prime target for activism because he had no ties to the political elite. Enabled by the Federal Communications Commission (FCC) mergers, TV media has become the visual arm of the activists because they are controlled and financed by six major corporations: GE, Newscorp, Disney, Viacom, Time Warner, and CBS. As noted earlier, in 1983 there were fifty diverse companies contributing balanced news to the American people.[299] Most owners of today's mega media corporations have discrete ties to the liberal agenda and want nothing less than control over all advertising and of the way people think. Did you know that the presidents of CBS and ABC have brothers who were top officials in the Obama administration? Is it any wonder that President Obama received none of the harsh treatment or bad press President Trump did?

Keep in mind that the progressive movement was formulated in part by the ultra-liberal writings of Saul Alinsky, the father of community activism and a mentor to Barack Obama. Alinsky's most notable contribution to activism, as already delineated, was his 12 Rules for Radicals, the last of which is a blueprint for today's media: "Pick the target, freeze it, personalize it, and polarize it. Cut off the support network and isolate the target from sympathy. Go after people and not institutions; people hurt faster than institutions."[300]

The destruction of Confederate statues, monuments, and long-held historical traditions stirs hatred against the individuals who represent slavery (Rule 12). What people do not recognize is that this is community organizing at its best. New terms have emerged like the "Alt-right," race-infused extreme conservativism that believes in white supremacy, violence, and the belief that white people are superior to the black race and should therefore dominate society. The term Alt-right is used in the media to focus on the people (Rule 12) as a means of changing principles. The statues being destroyed represent our history, and once they are lost future generations will have no reference, no access to wisdom gained from this aspect of our past. The intent is to convince people that the US was founded on flawed and unjust principles and therefore must be destroyed. By linking slavery to the very names of those who formed our country, progressives can link whatever followed in US ideology as also having been flawed. Remember Obama's campaign slogans "to fundamentally change America" and of "hope and change"? What was never asked was What exactly are we changing?

Obama's roots in community organizations in Chicago was under the mentorship of Saul Alinsky; is there any question now as to what that change was to be? America is silently being taken apart in the name of making it better, without ever describing what "better" means. Our children see only what the media presents—biased reporting. Modern parents are not teaching their children our traditions. Information overload, confusion, and indifference are the tools of the progressive movement. As with all socialist-leaning countries, any questioning of prevailing thought is met with swift condemnation, isolation, and even eventual incarceration for speaking one's mind. How is that free speech working out for you, America? Laws are being pushed through state legislators to criminalize counter thinking. In 2016, the *Washington Times* reported that the California legislature presented a landmark bill that would make it illegal to engage in climate-change dissent.[301]

So, what is next in the progressive playbook? Once the statues are gone, how long will it take for those who seek to destroy our country to focus their attention on our founding fathers? When George Washington was eleven years old, he inherited 10 slaves; by the time of his death, 317 slaves lived at Mount Vernon, including 123 owned by Washington.[302] Thomas Jefferson, the father of the abolitionist movement, worked to gradually end the practice of slavery while himself owning hundreds of African slaves throughout his adult life.[303] Do you have any idea how many monuments, buildings, and cities, let alone currency, bear the names of Washington and Jefferson? Watch out, Washington Times! This is "low hanging fruit" for the activists. The State of New York was one of the original thirteen colonies that formed the United States. New York was named after the seventh-century Duke of York, who himself was a slave owner.[304] (Note: I am a former New Yorker; what will I then call myself?) The recollection and concept of slavery, in the hands of the activists, is an emotional tool used to whip up anxiety, hatred, and the "get even" attitude so necessary for a revolution.

An incredible story by Nikole Hannah Jones appeared in the *New York Times* in May of 2020. She was awarded a Pulitzer Prize for her provocative and personal essay for the groundbreaking 1619 Project. The 1619 Project seeks to place the enslavement of Africans at the center of America's story. The project is the explicit claim that the true history of America did not start in 1776 but in 1619, the year when the first slaves arrived in the colonies. The story is riddled with half-truths and fails to convey that slavery was part of North American culture long before slaves arrived from Africa. Indigenous Indians had slaves, and even wealthy black landowners had black slaves. Slavery was a way of life on most continents, as on the 1619 plantations, and was hardly unique to pre-1776 America.[305]

No one can predict the future, but as a student of history I can attest that every country that collapsed under the relentless pressure of activism; large, centralized governments; the promise of utopia; or tyrants disguised as benevolent servants to the people, all had their middle class destroyed. Most notably, the entitlement programs eventually ended, leaving the economy in shambles and dependent on government for mere survival. Our country may not be perfect, and surely there are parts of our history that are ugly by today's standards, but "we the people" must decide between true freedom and false promises. History is there as a lesson for all to learn. Information overload is leading this country into chaos. Indifference will close the deal.

Chapter 12

What Does It All Mean?

The problem with information is that it can ramble, become dis-jointed, and lose its effectiveness if it is not organized properly. What is happening to our country is a complicated story based on secrecy, deception, and disinformation. So convoluted is the trail of events that the reaction of the average person, when confronted with the truth, is denial and even dismissal.

This reaction by the average American can be described as incredulous and is precisely the reason the events that are disman-tling our country can be hidden in plain sight. I have spent over a decade piecing together the events and inconsistencies in current national and international events, knowing that somewhere there are others doing the same thing. I have been fortunate in travel-ing and meeting people with vital, firsthand information that not only verifies my personal research but lends insights into a deeper world I have yet to discover.

As of this writing, one such source has come to light that has altered my thinking by giving structure, facts, and references nec-essary to put the pieces together with confidence. Foster Gamble, a Princeton University graduate and heir to the Proctor & Gamble Corporation, spent most of his life in the pursuit of energy sources known to world history but never utilized due to corporate and governmental suppression.[306] In his free DVD *Thrive,*[307] documen-tation and solutions are revealed that will instill confidence and insight into what "we the people" can do to stop the progressive takeover and the eventual destruction of our country.

I will devote the rest of this chapter to summarizing the events that have changed our world and the solutions already in play to stop the onslaught; however, this is not a substitute for firsthand recognition and analysis. Although repetition of some events and stories may occur, understand that hearing about these events as they unfold, from different perspectives, only adds em-phasis to their meaning.

The problem we are presently facing is that the creativity of our species has been stifled by controlling forces that have succeeded in altering every aspect of our lives without our consent or knowledge. It can be said that an elite group of people and corporations that controls all our energy, food and water supplies, education and healthcare, in effect controls our lives.

What we are now experiencing in this country began with the 1910 secret meeting on Jekyll Island, where seven of the most important families in banking, corporate, and international commerce met to form a "New World Order." The outcome of that meeting is the basis of all that we are experiencing today. Following, are the areas of civilization most controlled by the New World Order agenda.

Energy

The US can be totally self-sufficient with its vast untapped reserves of coal, oil, and natural gas from fracking, yet we are dependent on foreign energy supplies. The reason is simple: US energy corporations can control prices on imported energy, discouraging venture capital investing in our own natural resources. Numerous other factors exist, creating an illusion of energy shortages, but this is not the forum for such discussion.

Civilizations have long understood the geometric principles of the "Torus" configuration and its relationship to "perfect energy." The Torus shows us how energy moves in its most balanced dynamic flow process. The simplest description of its overall form is that of a donut, where energy flows through a central axis, adapting to environmental challenges.[308] There have been numerous "free" energy developments eventually leading to the discovery of the Torus "free" energy field. The problem was that these discoveries went against the controlling corporate forces reaping in the 200 trillion-dollar oil and nuclear power industries. Profits from oil prices produce enough money to suppress any alternative energy threat to the Rockefeller (Standard Oil) petroleum and agriculture industry.

Energy is the fundamental backbone of society. Ancient civilizations had incredible knowledge of how energy is created and used it to produce projects like the pyramids of Giza in Egypt, Machu Picchu in Peru, and structures that cannot be duplicated with today's advanced technology. John Hutchison, a Canadian inventor who studied the works of engineer Nikola Tesla, developed an anti-gravity device that taps into the "free energy" of the universe.[309] His labs were raided by US government officials and his work destroyed. In 1991, Dr. Eugene Mallove developed a safe cold-fusion energy source available to anyone. He stated and proved with his cold-fusion technology that one gallon of water is equal to three hundred gallons of gasoline. The established scientific research of the day was funded to produce dangerous thermonuclear fusion power. Dr. Mallove was mysteriously murdered, his work disappeared, and his lab was destroyed.[310] Adam Trombly is a scientist with years of experience as an inventor working with game-changing energy and geophysical technologies. He developed a levitation power source.[311] His work was ridiculed by established scientists, and his lab and files were mysteriously burnt to the ground.

Education

The agenda of the Rockefeller, Ford, and Carnegie Foundations is to produce a docile workforce through a mandatory education system designed around reflexive responses, thwarting independent thinking and competition. Independent thinking is not highly regarded. The initial introduction of the new Common Core Curriculum state standards was done to be compliant with government standards and funding. It was not long before the flaws (agenda) in the Common Core Curriculum became apparent. At least twelve states have since introduced legislation to repeal the standards, four or which have totally withdrawn. There are two main reasons for concern: states are losing their constitutional right to determine the educational standards for their particular state, using government funding as the carrot, and the Common Core Curriculum falls short on historical reference while virtually discouraging any opportunity for parental involvement in their child's educational experience.

Medicine

The American Medical Association is a Rockefeller-controlled entity sponsored almost entirely by the corporate-friendly National Dairy Council, Beef.org, American Sugar Alliance, and pharmaceutical and other sponsors. The result is that medical doctors are trained from a pharmaceutical perspective and have only one course in nutrition, with texts that are supplied by the research of corporate sponsors. Deepak Chopra, MD, states that "medical schools are funded by pharmaceutical industry, with the motive to sell drugs, not health." Reality is that pharmaceuticals are designed to treat (as opposed to solve) the problems, thus perpetuating the problems they were intended to eliminate via side effects of the drugs.

Controlling forces suppress true cures in the same way they suppress alternative free-energy experimentation. Dr. Royal Rife developed a Frequency Resonance Generator capable of destroying cancer cells and viruses. His generators were tested on sixteen terminal cancer patients over a three-month period. The result was a one hundred percent cure rate. Shortly thereafter his entire lab was destroyed by fire and his research records lost. While trying to recover, Dr. Rife was forced to defend numerous frivolous and expensive lawsuits by paid-for-hire medical doctors who destroyed him financially. Others, like Dr. Max Gerson and Harry Hoxsey, also had formulations that cured cancer through specific food nutraceuticals (foods that heal), but the AMA vilified them with trumped-up charges and rigged independent testing, showing no significant value to their work.[312], [313] Currently, countries outside the US are using their formulas with incredible success, drawing people with the means to travel out of the country, with the result of nearly complete recoveries.

On a personal note, a terminally ill cancer patient who was predicted to have less than six months to live left the US to treat with the Gerson protocols in Mexico. One year later he returned to my office, completely cured of cancer; he is now helping others outside the US to understand the Gerson protocols. Unless the pharmaceutical industry can patent a product or technology for a cure, that cure will never see the light of day.

What the pharmaceutical industry never anticipated was interference via the executive branch of the federal government, i.e., the president. On May 22, 2018, Congress passed President Trump's "Right to Try Act," fulfilling his promise to expand healthcare options for terminally ill Americans. The bill amends federal law to allow certain FDA-unapproved or experimental drugs to be administered to terminally ill patients who have exhausted all approved treatment options and are unable to participate in clinical drug trials. The Right to Try legislation returns treatment decisions back to patients, giving them the right to make healthcare choices that could save their lives.[314]

Similarly, the pharmaceutical industry and its paid lobbyists have long pushed the narrative that all children must be vaccinated, for their own safety and the safety of society. Vaccines are under great scrutiny by prominent scientists, to ensure safety and efficacy because of the unreported harm caused by nonmedicinal ingredients (see earlier chapter, "Health Care and the Medicine Man"). President Trump has instituted the Department for Conscience and Religious Freedom, also giving new hope for parents of those children caught in the medical cabal of having to participate in all vaccine programs or not being able to participate in society due to the Gestapo tactics of HHS, CDC, and FDA, who have effectively silenced the voices of scientists and medical doctors with opposing data. "The chemicals found in vaccines cause autism, period. The only people and organizations that say otherwise are paid to say so. We know the truth and we will not vaccinate our children to death!" stated Dr. Alvin H Moss, MD, Nephrologist, West Virginia University.[315]

The Automobile Industry

Germany designed and perfected the Wankel Rotary Engine and introduced it to the auto industry in 1964. It was a three-sided rotary combustion chamber that could develop extremely high RPMs and offered incredible fuel economy, low cost, and was as close to a perpetual motion machine as possible (in terms of wear and tear). Various auto manufacturers bid on the engine, but it was Mazda who put it into production. GM eventually bought the patent from Mazda, then created controversy over production problems and basically buried the patent (and the engine). Clearly, this was done to stop any challenge to traditional gas-guzzling piston engines. With ever-rising oil and gasoline prices, people looked to foreign auto manufacturers for fuel-efficient, less expensive automobiles. The market shift hurt American auto manufacturers, resulting in government support in the form of massive bailout windfalls to GM and Chrysler, most of which went to the corporate elite who financially supported the progressive Democratic Party as recognition for their continued support. Almost none of the eighty billion dollars to GM and Chrysler was allocated for its intended job-saving use.

The Economy

The Federal Reserve System is comprised of privately owned corporations that answer to no one and have nothing to do with the government or its banking system. David Icke described the Ponzi scheme of the Federal Reserve:

> You get a bank loan. The bank puts a number representing money into your account. You immediately begin to pay interest totaling 3X the loan value on money that never really existed other than a computer entry. This is called "Fractional Banking," meaning that the Federal Reserve can loan 9X the value of your loan to other banks making loans, knowing that the interest will reap huge financial rewards.[316]

Loaning fictitious money is the printing of fiat money (simply put, it is the printing of money from thin air). Banks therefore can loan nine dollars for every one dollar they receive, and they make a whopping ninety percent profit on all loans. Fractional banking was the product of the Jekyll Island meeting in 1910 and served as one of the founding principles for the formation of the Federal Reserve System.

Politicians, knowing how this system worked, quickly formed alliances with the supporters of this independent banking cartel called the Federal Reserve. In return, the Federal Reserve, with help from member banks, prints fiat money to be used by politicians for their pet programs, often without congressional approval or the support of the people they represent.

It should be no surprise that the IRS was formally established in 1913, essentially taxing the people on their personal income to pay politicians and the federal debt. To this day there is no accounting for the slush fund created by the IRS, which gives the illusion of the money being used to run the government.

The years 2008–2011 represented the most extreme printing of fiat money in the history of the US, disguised as bailouts to major corporations for the purpose of stimulating jobs. The extreme economic pressure presented by the printing of this historic amount of fiat currency caused the devaluation of the real estate market. The devaluation of property forced people to default on their government-owned loans, some of which were underwritten by the government-owned mortgage companies Freddie Mac and Fanny Mae, making the government the owner of a windfall of devalued property. When the time arrives to give the illusion of economic recovery, the government can resell the property and reap the entire new values of the properties under the same fractional banking system of mortgage loans, thus completing the rape of the private property of citizens. To date, any attempt to expose any unconstitutional government activity is met with swift FBI raids, usually on trumped-up charges that take years to unravel—long enough to bankrupt the offending entity while destroying its credibility in the media.

Just sixteen years after the historic Jekyll Island meeting, the first step in the master global plan to bring all countries into a New World Order was implemented. By 1929, the US was in its biggest boom economy ever. Money was invested in internal growth projects, as well as in the stock market, supporting companies with the technology and manpower to provide wealth and independence to the people. However, much of the stock market was supported by the continual influx of money from the banking cartels, often providing money to companies simply to prop the stock market. On that fateful day in 1929, these same banking cartels suddenly and without warning pulled their money from the market, causing a catastrophic panic selling of stocks by the middle class and a crash in stock values. The stock market crash of 1929 marked the beginning of the Great Depression and the visual success of the elite in implementing their grand plan.

After many years of stock devaluation, these same banking cartels began to buy back the same stocks at pennies on the dollar, only this time as partners in these corporations and not just investors. The grand government scheme was to first cause a problem and then to become the solution to the problem. To the astute observer, this same scenario has played out many times over the years, the last taking place in the real estate crash of 2008. To summarize how this scheme works:

1. The member Federal Reserve banks put out loans at low interest rates, creating the illusion of a boom economy.
2. The Federal Reserve raises the interest rates to the point that people become overextended and upside down on their loans.

3. Companies go out of business, and wages and jobs drop drastically.
4. Bankruptcy and short sales take over property at highly devalued amounts.
5. Banks put money back into the economy, giving the illusion of a recovery, and the process repeats itself.

The diversion tactic used is to keep the people busy by creating a continued source of class warfare, immigration, racial tension, terrorism, threatening the disappearance of entitlements, and even the diversion of court activity, as seen in the Zimmerman/Trayvon Martin fiasco. It is the old carnival shell game of misguided distraction. Make no mistake: world domination culminating in a New World Order is the agenda, which requires total control and domination of the essentials of any civilization. There are six major areas of society targeted by the elite controlling class:

- *Money:* The central banks, such as the Federal Reserve System, International Monetary Fund, and the World Bank, are all controlled by the banking cartel families of the world.
- *Energy:* Complete control over oil, natural gas, coal, and nuclear energy. The development of "free" or "natural energy" sources is totally forbidden and intentionally undermined, even when it would seem otherwise to the public. The government bailout of Solyndra, a solar energy company, is a perfect example. Huge sums of money were funneled into Solyndra by the Federal Reserve, similar to the Freddie Mac mortgage scheme. The government also made sure Solyndra received no contracts, therefore ensuring its demise and furthering the myth that viable alternative energy sources are not practicable.
- *Food and Water:* The World Trade Organization is buying up world water sources under the guise of standardizing the purity of drinking water. Under Codex Alimentarius (international food laws), world governments would have the authority to make water a pharmaceutical-grade entity, thus requiring scripts.
- *Healthcare:* The pharmaceutical industry funds most of our medical schools' costs. They also fund the textbook selec-

tion and the curriculum, ensuring that only "drugs" will be taught. The AMA is not at arm's length from the pharmaceutical industry—it's joined at the hip. Medical students receive only one cursory course in nutrition and learn nothing about alternative healthcare.

- *Information:* The elite class ensures a standard, compulsory education entirely centered around "reflexive" learning, where learning is on a "need to know" basis. The media receives most of its operating money and licenses to broadcast, provided that they project the story lines that the elite agenda wants people to see and believe. Progressives within the NWO are working hard to find ways to control the presently uncontrolled internet, under the guise of public safety or military need.
- *Control Descent:* The Patriot Act is working, even as it is supported by trading our freedoms for security. Terrorism is the means to circumvent constitutional laws. The executive branch of government is granting itself the power to stop and search without warrant if there is suspicion of terrorist activity. The person can even be held in prison indefinitely without due process. Surveillance cameras track our every move, under the silly notion of traffic control.

Seven families and their corporations seem to have control over every aspect of our civilization. They are the Rothschilds, Rockefellers, Morgans, Schiffs, Warburgs, Carnegies, and Harrimans. Their goal is not about money but about power and control over the world. To them, freedom is dangerous in the hands of the common man; therefore, they need to control people for their own good. Their divide-and-conquer tactics are put into play by instigating eternal infighting between the races, Republicans and Democrats, and the haves and the have-nots. They believe that the only source of supreme power is a military dictatorship run by a world power like the UN. Our nation has witnessed this as recently as the Iraq war, in which our military generals at times answered to a United Nations peacekeeping force.

Discovering the truth about the world domination agenda is written off as conspiracy theory. Making a public spectacle or court action against such individuals discourages others from doing the same. The whistle-blower Edward Snowden is in the throes of such government activity. Whether his actions were good or evil, he discovered the truth after he had been trained to do otherwise. Are his actions those of a traitor or an unsung hero? Only time will tell.

World domination does not come easily once the game is revealed. The special forces of the elite class are the Illuminati and the FBI. These highly secret organizations dictate what the societal norms will be. If you live according to their norms, then you are normal. If you step out of their box, you are a radical, racist, conspirator, or traitor and must be stopped. The result is that people choose to comply rather than confront.

To further implement the agenda of world domination, the New World Order has broken down the globe into manageable unions. To date, there are the European Union; African Union; Pacific Union; and, as soon as the US falls in line, the American Union. These unions are totally dominated and controlled by the World Trade Organization, World Health Organization, and World Bank.

It was *Confessions of an Economic Hitman* author John Perkins who revealed the method of creating manageable territorial unions. The plan is for the World Government to go into countries and offer huge infrastructure, medical, educational, or social project loans designed to help bring these countries into the modern age. When they agree, vast sums of money are allocated to these countries; however, the money actually goes to American corporations of the elite class (such as Bechtel, Halliburton, GM, GE, and others), who build the projects and reap the profits.[317] The result is that these countries get few benefits from the programs but are responsible for paying back the entire loan with interest. Knowing these countries can never repay these loans, the world powers instead make a deal. If these countries elect presidents favorable to New World Order agendas, the debt is forgiven. If they do not comply, the presidents are ousted, killed, or made into international villains like Osama Bin Laden and Saddam Hussein, both former allies of the Western world who had outlived their usefulness.

After all these years, the real question is how these world dominators keep their agendas a secret. They do so by structuring their hierarchy on a strict "need to know" basis. Power is structured in tiers, such that each tier does not know what its superior tier is doing, until only a precious few at the top tier know the complete truth. This leads to secrecy by implied deniability, where nobody really knows the entire picture.

At this point in the New World Order's evolution, only the US stands in the way. The push is on to bring down the US economically. It must be noted that the plan is working to perfection. On record, the US is presently sixteen trillion dollars in debt, but the actual number may be many times more when factoring in unfunded liabilities like Medicare and Medicaid and government pensions. The US presently borrows more than forty cents of every dollar to pay its debts and prints a good portion of the remainder via the Federal Reserve. This debt is collapsing all six areas of control necessary for takeover. If left to completion, the NWO will have stolen all productivity and wealth of this nation and moved it into its international banking system.

By design, the US is moving closer to an insurmountable debt. The only way to solve the problem is to move into a currency-less monetary system where push-button economics takes over. This allows the NWO banking system to literally remove or steal the wealth of an individual or corporation at the push of a button, as was witnessed recently in Greece.

To do so requires a major distraction from reality. Global disasters provide such stimulus. At the latest G8 summit, the following was discussed: a global tax to combat global warming, a tax on CO2 emissions, and cap-and-trade regulations based on environmental criteria. The talks were to produce a global tax paid to the World Bank, enforced by a World Military Police Force.

To make this happen, the controllers for world domination need a world crisis or the fear of terrorism on US soil. Time and again our country has been faced with occurrences that defy understanding. The occurrence of 9/11 provided such a circumstance. Despite all our intelligence and safeguards, somehow four jetliners slipped through our national defenses, with two achieving direct hits in the middle of New York City. The result was four buildings taken down, 2,996 lives lost, and instituting a Who done it? lasting to this day—which succeeded in bringing on the era of terrorism to the US.[318]

Post-Vietnam, then Secretary of Defense Robert McNamara admitted that the US entered the war under the false pretense that a US ship was torpedoed in the Gulf of Tonka, triggering a swift US military action.[319] The incident never occurred, but the diversion of war deflected attention from the controlling forces.

The Iraq war was entered into under the premise of confirmed weapons of mass destruction hidden by Saddam Hussein in the deserts of Iraq. Weapons of mass destruction were never found, but the war continued long enough to again deflect the true agenda of the NWO. The Afghan war was a mere carryover of the Iraq war, where no clear objective was ever established but resulting in the continuation of a decade of distraction and the draining of vital economic resources, not to mention the loss of life.

Keep in mind that comments made here are not intended to trivialize, disrespect, or compromise any of these events but to point out their usefulness to world-dominating forces. Often these sinister groups instigate warring factions and then financially support both sides of the conflict for the sole purpose of extending its usefulness.

Each of these events was fueled by fictitious stories fed to the media by our government, acting as its personal PR firm. Trial by media ensued, fanning the flames of terrorism and the relentless hunt for Osama and Saddam, both ending in "death to the tyrants" as the storylines came to a close. I personally found the killing of Osama bin Laden lacking the intellectual responsibility for closure. After a decade of hunting, we hear about the killing of bin Laden and the immediate removal of his body to an aircraft carrier for "proper sea burial." Proper sea burial? When has the Navy buried anyone at sea lately, let alone an enemy combatant under the guise of respecting strict Muslim law? Without photographic evidence or identification other than the military's word—without proof of any sort—this event is almost impossible to believe after ten years of anticipation. Such an incident defies logic, would never happen under normal conditions, but is necessary for controlling forces to keep a bewildered population off balance.

Fear is the next criterion that ensures compliance. Create events like the swine flu, bird flu, or the Covid-19 pandemic. Create stories with reasonable believability. Have the media whip the population into frenzy. Have the government provide a solution in the form of a vaccine and force the population to stampede health centers. Once established as a successful campaign, repeat the fear tactic again and again until the population simply stops questioning the events and relies on the creators of the epidemics to provide the solution. The swine flu and bird flu epidemics never occurred but leave the public questioning whether the next epidemic is real. The Covid-19 story was real but riddled with inconsistencies, exaggerations, and outright lies, yet when coupled with the media fearmongering, it matters not whether it was real.

Surveillance is key to a successful world-domination campaign. Unbeknownst to the population, our drivers' licenses and passports are printed with tracking chips to potentially follow our every move.[320], [321] Cameras are everywhere, and GPS technology in our cell phones ensures accurate tracking. Facebook and other social media have opened the door to data collection on a massive, voluntary scale. Even our healthcare records may soon by implanted in our bodies via chips to ensure accurate medical access.

Hundreds of FEMA detention camps have been set up on government-owned lands for times of pandemics or civil unrest. However, the most sinister cornerstone to the global agenda is to lessen the population of the world dramatically via forced sterilization.[322] Much of what took place in 1940s Germany was the byproduct of the Carnegie Institute for Eugenics and the Rockefeller Population Council, which laid the blueprint for deciding who should live or die, based on genetic or social traits.[323] Present-day attempts at eugenics take place under the program of Chem Trails; entire cities are sprayed from the air with unknown agents capable of producing disease and infertility, all in plain sight and never mentioned by an investigative media.

The US has been testing vaccines and toxic substances on the military since WW2 without ever notifying the recipients in any way. The military men and women are chattel property of the government and as such have very little say about what happens to them.

Chapter 13

Creating Solutions to Fight Back

Fortunately, there are a multitude of individuals and organizations that have formed action groups, united in the commitment to take our country back. Using violence to regain our freedom plays into the hands of the police state, yet using violence by radical groups, under the guise of peaceful protests, is ignored.

The film Thrive lays out specific steps and concepts common to all these groups:

1. A healthy, creative society equals freedom and compassion.
2. The NWO agenda is based on secrecy and fear, needing our collusion to make it happen. This is the grounds to fight back.
3. There are presently over one million social organizations and movements around the world committed to stopping this global takeover, outnumbering the elite class 100,000 to 1.
4. Since all elite power centers require our participation, entire countries like Brazil have set up genetically modified free agriculture zones.
5. Protocols have taken place to end the media blackout of vital information.
6. Stopping the bailouts, dismantling the Federal Reserve, and withdrawing support to the International Monetary Fund and World Bank in favor of banking locally in credit union type private banks, where loans are based on real value and moderate shares profitability.
7. Join the movement to "audit" the Federal Reserve and support independent media outlets.
8. Stop any attempt at controlling the flow of free information over the internet.
9. Support the traceable use of paper ballots only in our voting system.
10. Support the use and development of alternative energy sources that have already shown remarkable properties never seen by our population.

There are four strategies that must serve as the basis of economic and social recovery:

1. Bring integrity and responsibility to our economic system.
2. Adhere to conservative views, requiring the shrinking of government and the uniting of common resources, resulting in increased individual freedom, money, and time.
3. No violation of principles affecting creativity and the ability to prosper. "Big Brother" must be removed from acting as a mafia.
4. Accept that we must work with the eternal energy flow of our planet and not try to control it.

Experience is a great teacher. Ignorance is a default mechanism for failure. In 2012, Newsweek gave the US Citizen test to one thousand American citizens; nearly thirty percent failed, and a whopping seventy percent did not know that the US Constitution is the supreme law of the land. I dare say that most of our population who don't know that the Constitution is the supreme law of the land would also have no understanding of socialism, fascism, and communism if it were to kick them in the teeth. How difficult is it, therefore, to understand that losing this nation to the oldest default political mechanism, socialism, is bringing us full circle to what our founding fathers tried to protect against? When democracies fail, the reason is that the past is quickly forgotten, and without the continual diligence of securing and protecting our freedom the forces of tyranny take over by a peaceful surrender.

The necessary element to bond the fabric for the New World Order and secure the mechanism to bring the US to its knees without a military takeover is the concept of terrorism. For Americans, wherever democracy does not exist, terrorism is considered to be a fact of life for countries outside the US. Before 9/11, most Americans had absolutely no understanding of terrorism and its implications. Terrorism is a threat that can be manipulated and shaped in any fashion to create fear (real or perceived), and the public will be none the wiser. The Patriot Act has secured the final pieces for the loss of this country's lasting identity—freedom. The line is rapidly blurring between who are and who are not the terrorists. The strict dictionary definition of terrorism is "the unlawful use or threatened use of force or violence by a person or an organized group against people or property with the intention of intimidating or coercing societies or governments, often for ideological or political reasons."[324] As this country slowly awakens from its slumber of denial, it will recognize that our changing way of life is, by definition, actual internal terrorism by our own government. Once firmly implanted in the minds of the people, terrorism is the eternal boogieman.

In this time of economic and basic philosophical transformation our country is experiencing, the work of Ayn Rand's 1957 book Atlas Shrugged again comes to mind. This truth-filled story portrays what happens when government entities go astray, as well as what happens when people are oppressed by activists who are hell-bent on changing society and the economy to meet their agenda. So similar are the underlying themes in Atlas Shrugged to our present economic and political situation that it appears as though Ayn Rand was writing about present-day society. The lessons of Atlas Shrugged should serve as a blueprint for the recovery of our country. It takes courage to fight in the face of adversity; it also takes a plan.

Time will tell whether the lessons of Atlas Shrugged and the genius of our founding fathers will prevail. Until that time, the clock is ticking!

For Further Reading

"The Global Elite—Jeff Rense and David Icke." The Global Elite—Jeff Rense and David Icke. http://www.bibliotecapleyades.net/biggestsecret/esp_icke02.htm (accessed July 21, 2014).

—

Epilogue

The inspiration to write this book was influenced by the writings of Ayn Rand and her unique insights into American politics. Her metaphors, based on her oppressive upbringing under the Marxist Russian government of the early 1900s, set the stage for an American renaissance some fifty years after her writings. Sadly, the political and educational pendulum is shifting away from the concepts of individual rights and freedoms and back toward the roots of socialism, Marxism, and progressive ideologies. President Obama was the most recent pawn of the socialist movement within this country. His abuse of executive powers, without apparent restraint or resistance by Congress, was a sure indicator that our Constitution has been bastardized. No longer do we have the checks and balances of separation of powers; instead. we have one political party posing as two. Citizens are easily pacified with the illusion of control, making it easier to implement the platform of the total progressive transformation of the American way of life. We even had the US Senator from Vermont, Bernie Sanders, running for president as a Democrat, while publicly exposing socialism.

A glimmer of hope resides in the tenacity of those still able to think outside the restraints of entitlements. They are a small but growing force of young senators and representatives who are publicly putting their careers on the line to resist the progressive movement. The question is do we have enough time and educational expertise to keep the American dream alive? The ultimate litmus test will be whether "we the people" can recognize its inherent constitutional power and not be fooled by the unsubstantiated progressive rhetoric that over-promises and under-delivers.

This country was founded on principles that served as a directive for the Constitution of the United States. The brave souls who dared to challenge the oppressive, established norms of Europe did so with the intent of placing the power and responsibility of self-determination into the hands of the people. Surely there need to be common rules and guidelines to follow to ensure stability and equal opportunity under the laws of the land. In every culture, tribe, or animal species, there is order. That order requires guidelines of enforcement by a leader, chieftain, or alpha male.

The United States is a grouping of individual states encompassing a variety of cultural differences who voluntarily agreed to abide by a constitution.

We talk of founding principles as though they are facts necessary to study for a pop quiz. A closer analysis reveals that these principles were mere statements of common beliefs required for a free society. All rights come from God, not government, meaning that all people are created equal under the Creator. All political power is derived from the people, a reality embodied in the first three words of the constitution: "We the People." A direct democracy can lead to mob rule; therefore, the principle of a limited representative republic protected the people from an oppressive government. A written constitution is a contract among the states, necessary to ensure unity, as well as a guide for security against interpretation by a centralized government. Finally, there had to be private property rights, the hallmark of a free society—not just property but the right itself.

The Constitution of the United States is not a limitation on individual freedoms but a security against a controlling centralized government. There needs to be a leader who acts as the executor of the state, along with representatives from the individual states whose job it is to ensure that the voice of the people is heeded. Together, this representative government is the voice of the people, giving specific direction to the executive, as well as the legislative and judicial branches of government, to carry out the daily administrative tasks of the state.

The reason monarchs are perpetuated is that people lose interest in the actions of the state, relinquishing their rights by default in the hope of benevolence. To move from our founding principles to the present state of executive lawlessness required the one element not anticipated by our founding fathers: the diligence of the people. We must think hard and remain vigilant against the insidious transformation of America, as promised by Obama. President Trump, without the political baggage of the progressive mindset, ran America as a profitable business, not as an entitlement for the masses. You cannot transform America without changing America. The difference between a monarch and a president can be nothing more than "we the people" relinquishing personal freedoms. One thing is for sure: once freedom is lost, it will take another American Revolution to start anew.

Acknowledgments

To the tenacity of my parents, who taught me the ways of the world based on real-life experiences. Theirs was a time of building our great country.

To my wife, who understood my passions and gave me the freedom of expression.

To my children, who understood that Dad wasn't as weird as they thought.

To my many mentors, who encouraged critical thinking, both professionally and privately.

To Edward Griffin and Jon Rappoport, who shared their historical expertise.

To Peter, a man who paid the price to expose truth.

To Vivian Huntington for her editing skills and for holding me accountable.

And to the many significant individuals who, by their example, taught me humility, honor, and trust in the universal intelligence that guides us all.

Endnotes

1   http://quotes.liberty-tree.ca/quote_blog/Josef.Stalin.Quote.CC49

2   http://www.history.com/topics/joseph-stalin

3   https://en.wikipedia.org/wiki/Adolf_Hitler%27s_rise_to_power

4   http://www.examiner.com/article/mussolini-s-rise-to-power

5   http://en.wikipedia.org/wiki/Fascism

6   Reprinted by permission of the author.

7   http://www.washingtonpost.com/wp-dyn/content/article/2010/05/21/AR2010052101854.
html

8   http://www.uft.org/who-we-are/history/albert-shanker

9   http://en.wikipedia.org/wiki/Albert_Shanker

10   https://www.goodreads.com/quotes/34865-there-s-no-way-to-rule-innocent-men-the-only-
power

11   http://www.citylab.com/politics/2014/04/driving-saudi-arabia-woman/8771/

12   http://www.clevelandbanner.com/view/full_story/24686541/article-Women-s-suffrage-cam-
paign-recalled-in-event-at-CSCC

13   http://variety.com/2014/biz/news/mozilla-ceo-steps-down-amid-anti-gay-fu-
ror-1201152360/

14   http://www.slate.com/articles/news_and_politics/politics/2012/05/obama_s_gay_mar-
riage_stance_do_you_believe_he_changed_his_mind_.html

15   http://en.wikipedia.org/wiki/Freedom_of_speech

16   http://freedomoutpost.com/2013/11/historical-parallels-progressivism-nazism-fas-
cism-marxism-accidental/#z47DVe1FqOVgx8Ax.99

17   http://www.history.com/this-day-in-history/us-proclaims-neutrality-in-world-war-i

18   http://www.republicoftheunitedstates.org/what-is-the-republic/history/

19   http://www.prnewswire.com/news-releases/presidential-election-is-rigged-researcher-and-
book-author-dr-kaasem-khaleel-offers-proof-176841591.html

20   https://home.frankspeech.com/tv/video/scientific-proof-internationally-renowned-physi-
cist-absolutely-proves-2020-election-was

21   http://www.zerohedge.com/news/2013-03-06/one-hundred-and-eighteen-million-dollars-
hour

22   http://en.wikipedia.org/wiki/Criticism_of_the_Federal_Reserve#cite_note-29

23   http://www.presidency.ucsb.edu/ws/?pid=29661

24   http://www.oxforddictionaries.com/us/search/american_english/?q=hypocrisy&multi=1

25   https://noqreport.com/2019/04/28/socialism-death-freedom-speech

26   https://www.thoughtco.com/what-is-racism-2834955

27   https://www.americanthinker.com/articles/2020/05/is_trump_a_racist.html

28   http://www.merriam-webster.com/dictionary/social%20democracy

29   http://cnsnews.com/blog/gregory-gwyn-williams-jr/bank-america-freezes-gun-manufactur-
ers-account-company-owner-claims

30   http://newstarget.com/wp-content/uploads/sites/43/2016/05/050416-MedicalErrors.jpg

31   http://www.nbcnews.com/storyline/cia-senate-snooping/snowden-feinstein-hypocrite-blast-
ing-cia-spying-n49881

32   http://en.wikipedia.org/wiki/Health_care

33   http://en.wikipedia.org/wiki/Vital_signs

34   https://www.physiciansweekly.com/pain-5th-vital-sign/

35   https://www.physiciansweekly.com/pain-5th-vital-sign/

36   http://interactive.fusion.net/death-by-fentanyl/intro.html

37   https://seekingalpha.com/article/3977917-revenues-from-opioids-drying-up-for-pharmaceu-
ticals

38   www.reference.com/health/difference-between-drug-medicine-4f273e7f2142b078

39   http://money.cnn.com/2007/07/20/news/companies/purdue/index.htm

40   https://www.castlemedical.com/blog/full/On-Average-How-Many-People

41   http://fortune.com/2011/11/09/oxycontin-purdue-pharmas-painful-medicine/

42   http://chriskresser.com/medical-care-is-the-3rd-leading-cause-of-death-in-the-us

43   http://www.bloomberg.com/news/2012-06-13/health-care-spending-to-reach-20-of-u-s-economy-by-2021.html

44   https://www.citizen.org/documents/Threats_to_Health_Care_Policy.pdf

45   https://www.fda.gov/Drugs/DevelopmentApprovalProcess/HowDrugsareDevelopedandApproved/

46   www.uspharmacist.com/article/record-number-of-fda-new-drug-approvals-in-2015

47   https://www.ncbi.nlm.nih.gov/pmc/articles/PMC3657986/

48   http://www.ratbags.com/rsoles/comment/pasteur.htm

49   http://arizonaenergy.org/BodyEnergy/antoine_bechamp.htm

50   https://principia-scientific.com/smoking-gun-dr-fauci-admits-covid-test-has-fatal-flaw/

51   https://www.who.int/news/item/14-12-2020-who-information-notice-for-ivd-users

52   https://stateofthenation.co/?p=30880

53   https://stateofthenation.co/?p=30925

54   https://www.lewrockwell.com/2021/12/no_author/the-worst-that-could-happen/

55   https://nationalpost.com/news/world/who-chief-scientist-not-confident-vaccines-prevent-transmission

56   https://needtoknow.news/2021/01/the-2020-seasonal-flu-has-dropped-by-98-worldwide-as-it-is-re-labeled-covid-19/?utm_source=rss&utm_medium=rss&utm_campaign=the-2020-seasonal-flu-has-dropped-by-98-worldwide-as-it-is-re-labeled-covid-19

57   https://www.forbes.com/sites/roberthart/2021/10/01/us-covid-death-toll-passes-700000-as-delta-surges-in-some-states/?sh=7321b27d1454

58   https://nypost.com/2020/05/16/why-life-went-on-as-normal-during-the-killer-pandemic-of-1969/

59   http://www.huffingtonpost.com/2013/07/16/jenny-mccarthy-the-view-vaccines-autism_n_3605083.html

60   http://www.wellsphere.com/general-medicine-article/why-herd-immunity-is-moot-in-seasonal-flu-or-swine-flu/810092

61   http://thearrowsoftruth.com/stunning-study-cochrane-collaboration-no-value-in-any-flu-vaccine/

62   https://archpublichealth.biomedcentral.com/articles/10.1186/s13690-017-0182-z https://www.sciencelearn.org.nz/resources/184-virus-strains

63   http://www.wddty.com/aspirin-it-kills-20-000-americans-every-year.html

64   https://www.cdc.gov/vaccines/hcp/conversations/ensuring-safe-vaccines.html

65   http://www.vaccine-side-effects.com/under-reporting-side-effects/

66   https://wellnessandequality.com/2016/06/20/how-much-money-do-pediatricians-really-make-from-vaccines/

67   http://www.wodarg.de/english/3066623.html

68   http://www.hrsa.gov/vaccinecompensation/vaccinetable.html

69   http://www.vaclib.org/sites/debate/web5.html

70   https://nourishingourchildren.org

71   https://www.cdc.gov/mmwr/preview/mmwrhtml/mm4829a1.htm

72   http://articles.mercola.com/sites/articles/archive/2013/04/02/autism-rates.aspx

73   http://www.dailymail.co.uk/health/article-17509/Why-Japan-banned-MMR-vaccine.html

74   https://www.focusforhealth.org/dr-brian-hooker-statement-william-thompson/

75   http://vaxxedthemovie.com

76   http://cancercompassalternateroute.com/doctors-and-clinics/stanislaw-burzynski-and-his-antineoplaston-treatment/

77   http://www.jdnews.com/news/20170329/cost-of-cancer-treatment-battle-all-its-own
78   http://blog.sfgate.com/djsaunders/2012/10/11/nancy-pelosi-says-she-read-obamacare-bill/
79   http://www.forbes.com/sites/theapothecary/2013/05/30/rate-shock-in-califor-nia-obamacare-to-increase-individual-insurance-premiums-by-64-146/
80   http://www.snopes.com/politics/soapbox/trumpobamacare.asp
81   http://www.speaker.gov/video/boehner-if-businesses-get-relief-obamacare-rest-america-should-too
82   http://www.reuters.com/article/2013/08/23/usa-healthcare-republicans-idUSL2N0GN-20M20130823?feedType=RSS&feedName=everything&virtualBrandChannel=11563
83   http://www.bestofbeck.com/wp/activism/saul-alinskys-12-rules-for-radicals
84   http://tenthamendmentcenter.com/2017/10/21/executive-orders-obamacare-and-the-con-stitution/
85   https://www.factcheck.org/2012/06/how-much-is-the-obamacare-tax/
86   https://www.vox.com/policy-and-politics/2018/4/13/17226566/obamacare-penalty-2018-in-dividual-mandate-still-in-effect
87   http://www.newsmax.com/Newsfront/obamacare-lose-health-insurance/2013/11/20/id/537797/
88   http://www.thenewamerican.com/usnews/politics/item/2982-national-healthcare-will-re-quire-national-rfid-chips
89   http://www.abc.net.au/news/2017-03-08/ways-your-technology-is-already-spying-on-you/8334960
90   http://www.newsbusters.org/blogs/culture/alexa-moutevelis-coombs/2017/05/15/conser-vative-new-miss-usa-rejects-feminism-says
91   http://www.washingtontimes.com/news/2012/dec/7/government-borrows-46-cents-every-dollar-it-spends/
92   https://www.cbo.gov/topics/budget
93   https://www.manilatimes.net/2020/09/04/business/foreign-business/us-budget-deficit-to-hit-historic-high-3-3-trillion/763567/
94   http://en.wikipedia.org/wiki/Executive_order_(United_States)
95   http://youtu.be/5eqYdr2iEhM
96   http://www.forbes.com/sites/greatspeculations/2013/04/05/governments-still-heavy-hand-ed-80-years-after-fdrs-gold-confiscation/
97   http://www.independent.org/publications/article.asp?id=1394
98   http://www.wnd.com/2012/03/executive-order-panic-martial-law-in-america/
99   http://www.thepowerhour.com/news/seize_assets.htm
100   http://www.presidency.ucsb.edu/data/orders.php
101   https://www.heritage.org/political-process/heritage-explains/executive-orders
102   https://lawshelf.com/shortvideoscontentview/the-power-of-the-president-the-roles-of-exec-utive-orders-in-american-government/
103   https://people.howstuffworks.com/executive-order.htm
104   http://www.huffingtonpost.com/2013/12/05/syrian-opposition-alleges_n_4393094.html
105   http://www.telegraph.co.uk/news/worldnews/middleeast/syria/10236362/Syrian-rebels-ac-cused-of-sectarian-murders.html
106   http://www.mintpressnews.com/witnesses-of-gas-attack-say-saudis-supplied-rebels-with-chemical-weapons/168135/
107   http://www.npr.org/2013/08/31/217610904/transcript-president-obama-turns-to-congress-on-syria
108   http://en.wikipedia.org/wiki/Quantitative_easing
109   https://www.cnn.com/2021/01/22/politics/joe-biden-executive-orders-first-week/index.html
110   http://www.powerlineblog.com/archives/2013/02/david-horowitz-how-republicans-can-win.php

111 http://flag.blackened.net/revolt/talks/russia.html

112 http://www.snopes.com/crime/statistics/ausguns.asp

113 http://www.washingtontimes.com/news/2014/apr/2/cia-leader-morell-denies-role-benghazi-cover-up/

114 http://pjmedia.com/tatler/2014/04/02/did-cias-mike-morell-lie-under-oath-about-changing-the-benghazi-talking-points/

115 http://www.infoplease.com/spot/campaign2000race.html

116 http://www.washingtonpost.com/politics/transcript-chris-christies-news-conference-on-george-washington-bridge-scandal/2014/01/09/d0f4711c-7944-11e3-8963-b4b654bcc9b2_story.html

117 https://www.rockefellerfoundation.org/about-us/news-media/

118 http://www.usatoday.com/story/news/2015/05/17/taxi-medallion-values-decline-uber-ride-share/27314735/

119 https://www.quora.com/Why-is-are-network-media-personnel-overwhelmingly-liberal

120 http://www.businessinsider.com/this-chart-shows-the-bilderberg-groups-connection-to-everything-in-the-world-2012-6

121 http://www.businessinsider.com/these-6-corporations-control-90-of-the-media-in-america-2012-6

122 https://en.wikipedia.org/wiki/Political_power_in_the_United_States_over_time#Party_Control_of_Congress

123 https://en.wikipedia.org/wiki/Fox_News

124 https://en.wikipedia.org/wiki/Concentration_of_media_ownership

125 http://www.msn.com/en-us/news/us/this-beauty-queen-was-the-face-of-a-fake-news-website-she-says-she-had-no-idea/ar-AAnHZtH?li=BBnb7Kz

126 https://keepthewaterspure.wordpress.com/

127 http://www.huffingtonpost.com/news/james-rosen/

128 https://www.eff.org/deeplinks/2013/06/confirmed-nsa-spying-millions-americans

129 http://www.pbs.org/newshour/rundown/obama-administration-sets-new-record-withholding-foia-requests/

130 http://www.infoplease.com/spot/campaign2000race.html

131 http://www.lifezette.com/polizette/trump-roasts-pelosi-schumer-russian-hypocrisy/

132 http://www.breitbart.com/Big-Government/2013/09/16/PLS-HOLD-FOR-TUESDAY-9-17-AFTER-11AM-ET-Climate-Study-Evidence-Leans-Against-Human-Caused-Global-Warming

133 http://cnsnews.com/news/article/global-warming-temperature-very-close-zero-over-15-years

134 http://www.nationaljournal.com/energy/separating-science-from-spin-on-the-global-warming-pause-20130821

135 http://volcanoes.usgs.gov/hazards/gas/climate.php

136 http://rense.com/general94/nwoplans.htm

137 http://www.nbcnews.com/id/21262661/ns/us_news-environment/t/gore-un-climate-panel-win-nobel-peace-prize/

138 http://leomcneil.net/2014/04/02/adam-weinstein-arrest-climate-change-deniers/

139 http://www.globalistagenda.org/quotes.htm

140 http://blog.heartland.org/2014/03/un-agenda-21-schemes-to-grab-property-rights/

141 http://www.pbs.org/wgbh/pages/frontline/environment/climate-of-doubt/timeline-the-politics-of-climate-change/

142 http://en.wikipedia.org/wiki/Global_warming

143 http://en.wikipedia.org/wiki/United_States_Environmental_Protection_Agency

144 http://www.climatewiki.org/index.php?title=EPA

145 http://www.washingtontimes.com/news/2014/mar/13/report-epa-accused-of-overkill-in-raid-on-alaska-g/

146 http://dailycaller.com/2014/03/28/white-house-looks-to-regulate-cow-flatulence-as-part-of-

climate-agenda/

147 http://ielts-yasi.englishlab.net/political_agenda.htm

148 http://www.globalistagenda.org/quotes.htm

149 http://habitat.igc.org/agenda21/

150 http://www.populartechnology.net/2008/11/carbon-dioxide-co2-is-not-pollution.html

151 http://www.skepticalscience.com/co2-pollutant.htm

152 http://www.skepticalscience.com/global-warming-positives-negatives.htm

153 https://www.telegraph.co.uk/news/picturegalleries/worldnews/10547040/Russian-ship-Ak-ademik-Shokalskiy-trapped-in-ice-in-Antarctica.html

154 http://www.foxnews.com/politics/2013/09/19/new-study-says-threat-global-warming-great-ly-exaggerated/

155 http://clinton2.nara.gov/PCSD/Charter/

156 http://www.theclimategatebook.com/why-al-gore-refuses-to-debate-anyone/

157 http://abcnews.go.com/Politics/GlobalWarming/story?id=2906888

158 http://online.wsj.com/news/articles/SB125383160812639013

159 http://www.cfact.org/2012/09/19/is-oil-a-renewable-resource/

160 http://beforeitsnews.com/alternative/2014/01/imminent-collapse-of-this-global-currency-will-kill-usa-or-launch-www3-the-petro-dollar-2862784.html

161 http://www.huffingtonpost.com/david-sirota/whats-the-difference-betw_b_9140.html

162 https://www.wbap.com/wp-content/uploads/sites/274/2019/11/ALL-THE-WAYS-THE-DEMO-CRATS-HAVE-TRIED-TO-GET-RID-OF-PRESIDENT-TRUMP.pdf

163 http://thefreeandthebrave.blogspot.com/2009/10/can-democracy-last-longer-than-200.html

164 http://en.wikipedia.org/wiki/List_of_U.S._presidential_campaign_slogans#2008

165 http://www.csmonitor.com/USA/Politics/2011/0209/Unemployment-101-Who-pays-for-job-less-benefits-anyway

166 http://budget.house.gov/waronpoverty/

167 http://www.huffingtonpost.com/jeff-faux/nafta-twenty-years-after_b_4528140.html

168 https://www.snopes.com/fact-check/other-peoples-money/

169 https://www.forbes.com/sites/lauraheller/2016/06/28/walmart-made-in-the-usa-products-fact-or-fiction/#23b5ecc23a2b

170 http://www.investopedia.com/ask/answers/042215/what-difference-between-capitalist-sys-tem-and-free-market-system.asp

171 http://www.politifact.com/wisconsin/statements/2013/oct/24/sondy-pope/how-much-fed-eral-government-involved-common-core-s/

172 https://en.wikipedia.org/wiki/Race_to_the_Top

173 https://www.youtube.com/watch?v=hV-05TLiiLU

174 http://www.infowars.com/common-core-nationalizes-and-dumbs-down-public-school-cur-riculum/

175 http://victorygirlsblog.com/common-core-and-the-hitler-youth-can-it-happen-here/

176 http://www.buffalonews.com/city-region/erie-county/obama-trip-to-buffalo-emphasizes-ambitious-plan-to-control-college-costs-20130822

177 http://dailycaller.com/2013/08/22/obama-pushes-for-more-federal-control-over-education/

178 https://en.wikipedia.org/wiki/The_Law_that_Never_Was

179 https://www.youtube.com/watch?v=AW_6XfidxE8

180 https://www.opm.gov/forms/pdf_fill/sf61.pdf

181 http://foavc.org/01page/Articles/18%20U.S.C.%201918.htm

182 https://thehill.com/hilltv/rising/419901-fbi-email-chain-may-provide-most-damning-evi-dence-of-fisa-abuses-yet

183 https://en.wikipedia.org/wiki/Spy_vs._Spy

184 http://www.newyorker.com/online/blogs/newsdesk/2013/05/news-corp-vs-fox-news.html

185 http://www.cnet.com/news/senate-bill-rewrite-lets-feds-read-your-e-mail-without-war-rants/

186 http://www.cnet.com/news/leahy-scuttles-his-warrantless-e-mail-surveillance-bill/
187 https://www.courthousenews.com/secret-fbi-survillance-deemed-unconstiutional/
188 http://www.forbes.com/sites/scottgottlieb/2013/05/15/the-irs-raids-60-million-personal-medical-records/
189 http://abcnews.go.com/Politics/41-secret-service-agents-disciplined-congressmans-person-nel-file/story?id=39411746
190 http://www.examiner.com/article/new-documents-reveal-benghazi-cover-up-emanated-from-white-house
191 https://www.breitbart.com/national-security/2014/04/29/white-house-to-amb-rice-blame-the-video/
192 http://www.scribd.com/doc/110758358/Executive-Summary-Brief-Benghazi
193 http://www.gunsandammo.com/2013/09/27/what-the-united-nations-arms-trade-treaty-means-to-you/
194 http://www.statesman.com/news/news/abbott-warns-arms-treaty-could-spur-texas-to-sue/nZ7K4/
195 http://www.cnn.com/2013/09/22/politics/obama-navy-yard/
196 http://www.frontpagemag.com/2012/dgreenfield/europe-has-same-rate-of-multiple-victim-shootings-as-the-united-state
197 https://www.statista.com/statistics/811487/number-of-mass-shootings-in-the-us/
198 http://newsbusters.org/node/12556
199 https://en.wikipedia.org/wiki/2016_Orlando_nightclub_shooting
200 http://criminal.findlaw.com/criminal-law-basics/self-defense-overview.html
201 http://www.globalresearch.ca/dhs-constitution-free-zones-inside-us-ignored-by-me-dia/5345308
202 https://en.wikipedia.org/wiki/Fourth_Amendment_to_the_United_States_Constitution
203 http://en.wikipedia.org/wiki/United_States_Department_of_Homeland_Security#Structure
204 http://www.storyleak.com/dhs-constitution-free-zones-us/#ixzz2dEUWVXFF
205 http://www.infowars.com/dhs-buys-1-6-billion-bullets/
206 http://beforeitsnews.com/international/2013/04/obama-signs-firearm-and-ammo-kills-witch-2456326.html
207 http://townhall.com/tipsheet/katiepavlich/2013/08/23/homeland-security-employ-ee--has-a-website-dedicated-to-hating-white-people-n1671808
208 http://www.huffingtonpost.com/2013/08/24/ayo-kimathi-paid-leave_n_3809450.html
209 http://www.thirdworldtraveler.com/Fascism/Nazification_GermanyvsAmer.html
210 http://www.bestofbeck.com/wp/activism/saul-alinskys-12-rules-for-radicals
211 http://articles.chicagotribune.com/2013-05-15/news/ct-met-inspector-gener-al-red-light-cameras-0515-20130515_1_red-light-cameras-camera-program-new-speed-cameras
212 http://articles.latimes.com/2012/jun/20/news/la-pn-obama-invokes-executive-privi-lege-over-fast-and-furious-documents-20120620
213 http://www.businessinsider.com/mitch-mcconnell-crush-conservative-insurgents-2014-3
214 https://famguardian.org/Subjects/Politics/Pubs/CongStatistics.htm
215 http://termlimits.com/best.htm
216 http://en.wikipedia.org/wiki/Charles_B._Rangel#2008.E2.80.932010:_Ethics_issues_and_censure
217 https://patch.com/new-york/harlem/election-results-adriano-espaillat-poised-replace-char-lie-rangel-congress
218 https://thenewamerican.com/charles-rangels-fall/
219 http://en.wikipedia.org/wiki/Federal_crime
220 http://www.thefreedictionary.com/socialism
221 http://www.thefreedictionary.com/Marxism
222 http://www.wnd.com/2013/05/obamacares-bigger-plan-destroy-and-rescue/
223 https://en.wikipedia.org/wiki/2008%E2%80%932016_United_States_ammunition_shortage

224 http://townhall.com/columnists/johnhawkins/2012/04/13/12_ways_to_use_saul_alinskys_rules_for_radicals_against_liberals/page/full
225 http://cnsnews.com/news/article/cbo-obamacare-will-leave-30-million-uninsured
226 http://en.wikipedia.org/wiki/Fuel
227 Derived from physical, rather than biological sources.
228 http://rense.com/general67/oils.htm
229 http://www.wnd.com/2008/02/45838/
230 http://rense.com/general63/refil.htm
231 http://www.opec.org/opec_web/en/about_us/24.htm
232 http://www.peakprosperity.com/forum/why-saudis-keep-buying-t-bills/26276
233 https://www.thebalance.com/opec-oil-embargo-causes-and-effects-of-the-crisis-3305806
234 https://www.forbes.com/sites/forbesbooksauthors/2020/03/20/why-oil-prices-will-be-65-per-barrel-by-the-end-of-2020/#25a9579ed70d
235 http://www.eea.europa.eu/about-us/governance/scientific-committee/sc-opinions/opin-ions-on-scientific-issues/sc-opinion-on-greenhouse-gas
236 https://www.ft.com/content/e780d216-5fd5-11dc-b0fe-0000779fd2ac
237 http://www.fuel-testers.com/gasoline_octane_and_ethanol_E10.html
238 http://zfacts.com/p/436.html
239 http://www.cato.org/publications/commentary/is-ethanol-energy-security-solution
240 http://www.bloomberg.com/apps/news?pid=newsarchive&sid=aVWkvzDDYy3I
241 http://en.wikipedia.org/wiki/Food_vs._fuel
242 http://en.wikipedia.org/wiki/Economic_policy_of_Barack_Obama
243 http://www.virginianewssource.com/editors-messsage/972-a-dea
244 http://www.freedomadvocates.org/?s=obama+complies+with+agenda+21
245 http://www.allaboutpopularissues.org/new-world-order-history-faq.htm
246 http://en.wikipedia.org/wiki/New_World_Order_(conspiracy_theory)
247 http://www.theblaze.com/stories/2011/06/21/does-the-new-white-house-rural-council-uns-agenda-21/
248 http://en.wikipedia.org/wiki/Agenda_21
249 http://www.independentsentinel.com/obamas-seizure-of-the-heartland-executive-order-13575-laying-the-groundwork-for-agenda-21/
250 https://humansarefree.com/2018/10/list-of-32-elites-that-support-and-promote-depopula-tion.html
251 http://www.un.org/esa/agenda21/natlinfo/countr/usa/natur.htm
252 https://www.jewishvirtuallibrary.org/jsource/Holocaust/children.html
253 http://www.thenewamerican.com/usnews/politics/item/12675-gop-platform-rejects-un-agenda-21-as-threat-to-sovereignty
254 http://www.nytimes.com/2012/02/04/us/activists-fight-green-projects-seeing-un-plot.html?pagewanted=all&_r=0
255 http://www.citylab.com/politics/2012/08/anti-environmentalist-roots-agenda-21-conspira-cy-theory/3091/
256 http://njcmr.njit.edu/distils/lab/Air_html/man-made.htm
257 http://americanfreepress.net/?p=13240
258 http://www.care2.com/causes/10-most-horrifying-facts-about-the-gulf-oill-spill.html
259 http://finance.yahoo.com/news/discover-11-hot-college-majors-134425722.html
260 http://www.teapartytribune.com/2011/07/02/agenda-21-conspiracy-theory-or-real-threat/
261 https://rightwingnews.com/democrats/agenda-21-conspiracy-theory-or-real-threat/
262 http://www.geocraft.com/WVFossils/greenhouse_data.html
263 http://www.foxnews.com/science/2013/09/17/is-global-warming-actually-far-low-er-than-scientists-predicted/
264 http://www.whitehouse.gov/the-press-office/2011/06/09/executive-order-establish-ment-white-house-rural-council

265 https://www.youtube.com/watch?v=RzKEzzczg7c

266 http://www.earthday.org/earth-day-history-movement

267 http://www.nytimes.com/1989/03/16/nyregion/new-york-facing-major-water-shortage.html

268 http://www.charlottecountyfl.com/CommunityServices/NaturalResources/ScrubJays/

269 http://youtu.be/TzEEgtOFFlM

270 http://www.bioeco.gov/

271 http://ppjg.me/2011/07/18/the-quiet-coup-the-implementation-of-agenda-21/

272 https://www.technocracy.news/globalism-u-n-s-agenda-21-agenda-2030-vision-2050/

273 http://ibankcoin.com/americantyranny/a-day-that-56-men-declared-our-independence-from-tyranny-time-to-do-it-again/

274 http://www.downsizinggovernment.org/overpaid-federal-workers

275 http://www.zerohedge.com/news/2013-12-24/president-obamas-executive-order-raises-government-worker-salaries-1

276 http://www.downsizinggovernment.org/overpaid-federal-workers

277 http://www.foxnews.com/story/2007/06/23/do-nothing-congress-mdash-big-salary-little-work-free-trips/

278 http://usgovinfo.about.com/cs/agencies/a/raise4congress.htm

279 http://usmilitary.about.com/cs/joiningup/a/recruiter5.htm

280 http://www.fedsmith.com/2012/03/25/average-federal-salary-lowest-average-pay/

281 https://tnc.news/2020/09/11/average-federal-employee-costed-taxpayers-115000-in-2019/

282 http://en.wikipedia.org/wiki/Direct_democracy

283 http://www.breitbart.com/Big-Government/2013/09/23/What-Did-Thomas-Jefferson-Mean-By-Unalienable-Rights

284 http://constitutioncenter.org/constitution/preamble/preamble

285 http://en.wikipedia.org/wiki/First_Amendment_to_the_United_States_Constitution

286 http://www.heritage.org/research/reports/2007/07/the-progressive-movement-and-the-transformation-of-american-politics

287 http://www.shmoop.com/progressive-era-politics/woodrow-wilson.html

288 http://www.annenbergclassroom.org/Files/Documents/Books/Our%20Constitution/Sixteenth%20Amendment_Our%20Constitution.pdf

289 http://www.givemeliberty.org/features/taxes/notratified.htm

290 http://en.wikipedia.org/wiki/Pentagon_Papers

291 http://www.theguardian.com/world/2013/jun/09/edward-snowden-nsa-whistleblower-surveillance

292 http://townhall.com/tipsheet/katiepavlich/2014/02/18/united-states-falls-to-46th-in-the-world-for-press-freedom-n1796607

293 http://openculture.com/2017/02/13-rules-for-radicals.html

294 https://www.nytimes.com/interactive/2019/05/13/us/politics/trump-investigations.html

295 https://www.justice.gov/storage/report.pdf

296 http://en.wikipedia.org/wiki/Nazi_book_burnings

297 http://www.constitution.org/cmt/stansbury/elementary_catechism_on_the_constitution.pdf

298 Beck, Glenn, and Kevin Balfe. Miracles and massacres: true and untold stories of the making of America. Threshold Editions, 2013.

299 http://www.businessinsider.com/these-6-corporations-control-90-of-the-media-in-america-2012-6

300 http://www.fbcoverup.com/docs/library/2016-08-27-Saul-Alinsky-12-Rules-for-Radicals-Obama-Hillary-Playbook-posted-Aug-27-2016.pdf

301 http://www.washingtontimes.com/news/2016/jun/2/calif-bill-prosecutes-climate-change-skeptics/

302 https://www.google.com/search?q=how+many+slaves+did+George+Washing+have&o-q=how+many+slaves+did+George+Washing+have&aqs=chrome..69i57.14175j0j8&sourceid=-

chrome&ie=UTF-8

303 https://en.wikipedia.org/wiki/Thomas_Jefferson_and_slavery

304 https://en.wikipedia.org/wiki/New_York_(state)

305 https://www.washingtontimes.com/news/2020/may/24/editorial-1619-project-bad-history-fueled-bad-moti/

306 http://thrivedoucmentaryreview.blogspot.com/2011/11/about-foster-gamble.html

307 http://thrivemovement.com/

308 http://www.cosmometry.net/the-torus---dynamic-flow-process

309 http://rationalwiki.org/wiki/John_Hutchison

310 http://en.wikipedia.org/wiki/Eugene_Mallove

311 http://www.venusproject.org/new-energy/free-energy-device-demonstration-adam-trombly.html

312 http://www.healingcancernaturally.com/medical-history.html

313 http://gersontreatment.com/if-it-is-so-good-why-havent-i/

314 https://www.whitehouse.gov/briefings-statements/president-donald-j-trump-sign-right-try-legislation-fulfilling-promise-made-expand-healthcare-options-terminal-americans/

315 https://www.sorightithurts.com/2019/01/05/trump-signs-order-vaccines-no-longer-required-for-children/

316 https://www.youtube.com/watch?v=R8f826BX6po

317 http://www.bookrags.com/studyguide-confessions-of-an-economic-hit-man/

318 http://www.statisticbrain.com/911-death-statistics/

319 http://www.examiner.com/article/war-under-false-pretenses-and-owning-up-to-the-truth

320 http://www.wanttoknow.info/microchippassport

321 http://www.offthegridnews.com/2013/09/09/drivers-license-chips-soon-will-allow-government-to-track-you/

322 http://www.prisonplanet.com/the-population-reduction-agenda-for-dummies.html

323 http://www.sfgate.com/opinion/article/Eugenics-and-the-Nazis-the-California-2549771.php

324 http://www.thefreedictionary.com/terrorism

Made in United States
Orlando, FL
28 April 2023

32571310R00133